The Manager's Guide to Competitive Intelligence

The Manager's Guide to Competitive Intelligence

John J. McGonagle and Carolyn M. Vella

PRAEGER

Westport, Connecticut
London

Library of Congress Cataloging-in-Publication Data

McGonagle, John J.
  The manager's guide to competitive inelligence / John J. McGonagle and
  Carolyn M. Vella.
    p. cm.
  Includes bibliographical references and index.
  ISBN 1-56720-571-2 (alk. paper)
    1. Business intelligence. 2. Confidential business information. I. Vella,
  Carolyn M. II. Title

HD38.7.M389 2003
658.4'7—dc21   2003045595

British Library Cataloguing in Publication Data is available.

Library of Congress Catalog Card Number: 2003045595
ISBN: 1-56720-571-2

First published in 2003

Praeger Publishers, 88 Post Road West, Westport, CT 06881
An imprint of Greenwood Publishing Group, Inc.
www.greenwood.com

Printed in the United States of America

The paper used in this book complies with the
Permanent Paper Standard issued by the National
Information Standards Organization (Z39.48-1984).

10 9 8 7 6 5 4 3 2 1

Contents

Introduction

Competitive Intelligence (CI) is now becoming a mature profession. With that maturation comes the need to develop and to understand the hows and whys of managing CI, as distinguished from understanding how CI works. To date, almost all the literature on CI has focused on understanding the CI process, explaining and elaborating on the CI cycle (see the Appendix to Chapter 1), developing new analytical tools, and expanding CI's scope to include competitive technical intelligence and defensive activities.

However, very little is as yet available to provide practical, hands-on assistance for the CI professional who is providing CI to a single client, his or her employer. Yet that is the largest single group of CI practitioners in existence. This book is designed to meet that need.[1] Since its focus is on the management of the CI process within a firm, it necessarily deals in general terms with the current state of the art of CI. This book should, we believe, be read in connection with several of our other books on CI, as follows:

- on the current state of CI and its critical elements, *The Internet Age of Competitive Intelligence*[2]
- on understanding how various forms of CI operate and how to assess their impact on the organization, *Bottom Line Competitive Intelligence*[3]
- on understanding how to protect your firm against your competitors, *Protecting Your Company against Competitive Intelligence*[4]

To avoid unnecessary duplication, we have generally avoided repeating any footnotes or even the vast bulk of the citations found in these earlier books when summarizing the topics they cover. So, for those who wish to dig deeper into these topics, we suggest referring to these books for such references. Those who do so will also see that, over time, we have changed the way we see what is happening in CI. That is because CI itself continues to change. We believe that this book is the next logical stage in that process.

Throughout the book you will see references to *Best Practice* or *benchmarking* firms, as well as *experience*.

- The former terms refer to the ongoing series, now up to six, of studies conducted by the International Benchmarking Clearinghouse of the American Productivity & Quality Center, most in conjunction with the Society of Competitive Intelligence Professionals. These are all listed in the Key Resources section. Again, as this is a manager's guide, we have refrained from repeating citations to these documents.
- The latter refers to our direct experience in the CI field over almost twenty years, plus the experiences our clients have related to us.

NOTES

1. We had addressed this subject previously, in our book, *Outsmarting the Competition: Practical Approaches to Finding and Using Competitive Information* (Naperville, Il.: Sourcebooks, 1990), but much has changed in over a decade.

2. John J. McGonagle and Carolyn M. Vella, *The Internet Age of Competitive Intelligence* (Westport, Conn.: Quorum Books, 1999).

3. John J. McGonagle and Carolyn M. Vella, *Bottom Line Competitive Intelligence* (Westport, Conn.: Quorum Books, 2002).

4. John J. McGonagle and Carolyn M. Vella, *Protecting Your Company Against Competitive Intelligence* (Westport, Conn.: Quorum Books, 1998).

The Basics of Competitive Intelligence and What They Mean to a Manager

THE TWO DIVISIONS OF COMPETITIVE INTELLIGENCE

As we noted in our book, *Bottom Line Competitive Intelligence*, competitive intelligence (CI), as it is practiced today, has become divided into two major areas, active and passive.[1]

- *Active CI* is that which we most commonly call CI. It involves the development of intelligence on all aspects of businesses and the competitive environment. Active CI processes are those aimed at collecting raw data and analyzing that data to provide finished intelligence. The active CI may be prepared by a CI unit for use by an internal corporate client, by an external consultant or a research firm as an input to a CI unit's reports, or by the same person who will use it. In each case, the production of the intelligence is conducted following a formal, commonly understood process, known as the CI cycle. It is then to be used as an input to improve decision making. Active CI is, in turn, divided into four different types: strategy-oriented, tactics-oriented, target-oriented and technology-oriented.
- *Defensive CI* is the way we describe the process of protecting your firm against the competitive intelligence efforts of your competitors. Defensive CI processes are heavily dependant on a working knowledge of CI techniques. However, when properly conducted,

defensive CI involves CI professionals in an educational or advisory role only. That is, CI professionals use their skills and experience to help their firm determine what kinds of raw data competitors will probably try to capture, teach all company employees to understand what is competitively sensitive information that they should protect, and to understand how to protect that data.

FOUR TYPES OF ACTIVE CI

Strategy-Oriented Competitive Intelligence

Strategy-oriented competitive intelligence is CI provided in support of strategic-level, as distinguished from tactical, decision making. This means providing the higher levels of management with information on the competitive, economic, legal, and political environment in which your firm and its competitors now operate as well as the environment in which they will operate in the future. In practice, this may include information on products and/or services that differentiate one competitor from another or even an assessment of a criminal environment in which a firm may find itself involuntarily operating.

Strategy-Oriented CI also can involve developing CI on candidates for potential mergers and acquisitions or alliances and partnerships. Most CI, as practiced in the 1980s and early 1990s, including much of what fell within the category of "business intelligence," can be properly considered strategy-oriented CI.

Tactics-Oriented Competitive Intelligence

Tactics-oriented competitive intelligence is CI developed on very current activities and on near-term plans in the marketplace. In a real sense, tactics-oriented competitive intelligence is a child of the computer age's support for the detailed analysis of retail consumer goods sales. It encompasses much of what has previously been called "market" or "sales and marketing" intelligence. However, in spite of that, it can also be a critical component in mergers and acquisitions.

Firms increasingly track what is going on "in the trenches," where competitors face off for customers and consumers, with tactics-oriented CI.[2] In turn, this permits them to fine-tune marketing efforts, including field force support, to respond ever faster. The faster and deeper are the data that are received, the more a firm can, for example:

- find out that a product promotion is less successful than anticipated, and immediately respond to change a promotion that is not working or to intensify one that is working

- determine what other promotions competitors are running against yours, and where and respond appropriately
- "test" product linkages by checking if customers buying your products also buy another product very frequently and then cross-promote your products
- get early warnings of competitor moves and market vulnerabilities
- improve product and/or service development as well as targeting of messages to consumers

Technology-Oriented Competitive Intelligence

Technology-oriented competitive intelligence is CI that permits a firm to respond to threats, as well as to identify and exploit opportunities, resulting from technical and scientific change. Technology-oriented CI, as we use the term, encompasses much of what was, and is, referred to as technology intelligence (TI), or competitive technical intelligence (CTI).

Technology-oriented CI, supporting technology strategies as well as research and development, has become a growth area within CI. Practitioners of technology-oriented CI also provide their own valuable insights on organizational and management issues through technology-oriented CI. In particular, TI is a function that, if executed properly, should result in a saving of from 10 to 100 times the money invested in the effort.

Target-Oriented Competitive Intelligence

Target-oriented CI is intelligence about competitors, their capabilities, current activities, plans, and intentions. It is most often used when CI efforts are best focused on a small number of competitors that a firm faces in several market niches. It encompasses elements of what is sometimes called *business intelligence* or *competitor intelligence*.

Common elements

All of these types of active CI have in common the following:

- They all deal with the same sources for raw data.
- They all make use of a common CI toolbox.
- They all follow the classic CI cycle.

Key Differences

The four types of active CI differ with respect to the following:[3]

- who and what are served
- its primary focus
- its typical time horizon

- the relative balance between raw data and finished analysis
- intelligence-related processes, such as benchmarking and shadow-ing, that they employ

DIFFERENCES BETWEEN ACTIVE AND DEFENSIVE CI AND AMONG TYPES OF ACTIVE CI

The differences between active CI and defensive CI have important implications for CI managers. Above all, managers must keep in mind that active CI is a function that is the primary responsibility of the CI unit (and its end users), whereas defensive CI is a process that involves the CI unit primarily as a catalyst. That is, the CI unit (or its manager) is best deployed in educating and training employees throughout the firm on how each person, unit, and function can best protect the firm's competitive valuable assets.

Within active CI, the critical differences among the four types ulti-mately cause each type of active CI to:

- tend to rely on different sources of raw data
- use varied mixes of options to make the intelligence available to end users
- make the intelligence available at different frequencies
- use different metrics to track their contribution to a firm's bottom line

DECIDING TO SET UP A CI UNIT

During the past two decades, there has been increasing interest and activity among many corporations in creating separate CI units. At first, this was the result of the reported actions and presumed successes of firms which had operated CI-type units for years. As time passed, however, the interest began to reflect a growing appre-ciation of the benefits of CI.

Over these years, we have learned that there are many ways to set up and then run a CI system. However, there are a couple of core steps that are common to them all:

- dealing with customers
- identifying likely targets
- establishing feedback and review processes

When deciding if your firm should have a CI unit, before setting up the unit, you must consider whether you can deal with these steps.

Internal Customers

The first, and most important, step is to establish who could be the "customers" for the CI, and what they would or should use the CI for. Experience shows that there is no point in spending resources to collect "complete" information on every target for everyone in the firm. When a unit does that, it is really running a newsletter, not a CI function.

The key here is to determine what CI will make a difference with which of the firm's, or strategic business unit's (SBU's) key decision makers. What a new CI unit does *not* want is to receive a mission, or even an assignment which says, in essence, "We want to know everything about this target (or targets)." Frankly, given the easy availability of raw data, sometimes in vast quantities, your end users do not want this because they would then spend all their time digesting the data that the CI unit could generate, without ever having the time to act on that small portion of it that is actionable. All this means that, as a part of this effort, one must get to the real decision makers at a firm, the ones we call the *end users*.

Targets

A second, parallel task is to determine which targets your firm could be interested in. Here, the best thing is to determine both which firms are currently in your markets and, of these firms, which are really the critical players in regard to your own firm. Note the word *determine*. In many industries, too many companies really just *assume* who is in a niche, competing with them. Such assumptions are not always correct, however.

For example, we did a study for an insurance company on competition in four product niches. To start, we first summarized the knowledge and findings of the firm's executives, marketers, and so forth. That produced a consensus list of the top ten companies in each niche, *as far as this firm's executives were concerned*. Then we investigated each niche and compared what the client "knew" with what CI disclosed. The results were stunning. The results were approximately the same for each of the four separate niches:

1. Seven of the ten firms on each internally generated list of top competitors were actually among the top ten in that niche.
2. At least two of the three firms identified by the client's personnel were not in the top ten in that niche. In fact, most of the firms misidentified as currently being in that niche had not been in that particular niche for at least two year.
3. Each niche had at least one competitor, always among the top five in that niche, that *no* one in the firm had identified (a *cloaked competitor*[4]).

The lesson here is that setting up a list of targets involves more than merely asking your firm whom to target.[5] It involves checking for the need to include new competitors, and even potential competitors, as well as the need to eliminate those that are no longer in the marketplace.

Now the potential CI unit actually has a matrix, showing both potential targets *and* areas of major CI concern. Experience shows that typically, this level of effort will become further divided into groupings such as these:

- between two and five companies that are head-to-head with your firm at all times in all markets. Here, the areas of interest typically are the broadest, and timeliness of providing that CI is most critical.
- from five to twenty companies that compete in some geographic areas and/or in a few product (or service) lines. Here, your firm's interests are more focused and, usually, less time oriented.
- companies that are on the edges of your markets, in either a geographic or product sense. For them, your firm's interest is in whether they are moving toward (or away from) your core markets. That intelligence is typically provided when it happens rather than on a periodic basis.
- companies that are potential entrants to your markets. Here your firm needs to know of any indications that such firms are getting ready to move.

At this point, a firm will have established the core of its CI reporting pattern, which will drive its research and analysis. Management now knows:

- which kinds of CI it needs
- on which firm it needs CI
- to which internal clients it is to be sent
- when it must be there

Feedback

Finally, the new CI function must develop a review or feedback effort. That means a constant review that seeks answers to questions like these:

- Are the targets still correct?
- Are the areas of interest still correct?
- Should the CI function add or delete targets, areas, internal customers, and so on?

PROBLEM AREAS IN THE CI CYCLE

CI professionals spend excessive effort, in terms of both time and money, on data collection. Over a decade of experience clearly indicates that the optimal distribution of effort (whether measured in terms of time, dollars, or some combination) among these four stages of the CI cycle is approximately as follows:

- needs, 20 percent
- collection, 30 percent
- analysis, 40 percent
- dissemination, 10 percent[6]

Nonetheless, we continue to see a great deal of effort, in fact a dispro-portionate effort, spent on collection instead of analysis. We continually also see that the message of CI does not always get through. However the question is posed, the answer seems to be that many CI profession-als are not providing management with action-oriented CI. The crux of this problem lies in at least two areas.

1. In terms of management's participation, some managers still seems reluctant to share with the CI professional exactly what they need to know and what they know (or think they know) already.
2. The CI professional then compensates for this lack of direction by tending to provide more "data," such as newsletters, and less hard analyses.

The solutions for these problems areas are as follows:

- CI professionals must work much harder on establishing the needs of their internal clients, with or without their assistance. They must continue to collect data on the widest basis possible, but must always understand that their mission is not to collect and report on data. Rather, they must spend more time and effort on analysis. That is where the real value of CI lies.
- They must learn to communicate their completed message prop-erly. That means learning to say things in a clear and convincing style while also availing themselves of new, passive means of dissemination, such as technology like that provided by Lotus software.

APPENDIX: THE CI CYCLE

As shown in Figure 1.1, the CI process is most commonly divided into five basic phases or stages, each linked to all of the others by a feedback loop.[7] These phases, which make up what is known as the CI cycle, are:

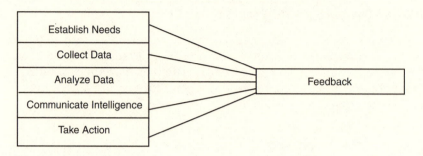

Figure 1.1 The CI process.

1. *Establishing your CI needs:* This means that you both recognize the need for CI and define what kind of CI you (or your end user if you are providing the CI for someone else) need. It also means considering what type of issue (strategic, tactical, marketing, etc.) is motivating the assignment, what questions you want to answer with the CI, who else may be using the CI, and how, by whom, and when the CI will ultimately be used.

2. *Collecting the raw data you need:* First you must translate your end user's needs into an action plan. In the case of the internal CI professional, that is his or her internal client. We prefer the term *end user* because not all CI is used by those who ask for it. However, regardless of terminology, this process involves, either formally or informally, identifying what questions need to be answered and then where it is likely that you can collect the data needed to answer them. You may also have to decide who should be collecting the raw data that will be turned into intelligence through the CI process. This can be one or more of the following: the end user, another internal CI professional, other employees (e.g., sales personnel), or an external CI firm, You should, by this point, have a realistic understanding of any significant constraints you face in carrying out this assignment, such as time, financial, organizational, informational, and legal, that may prevent you from developing the specific CI you are seeking. Thus, you can now identify the data sources that are most likely to produce reliable, useful data and proceed to acquire it.

3. *Evaluating and analyzing the raw data:* In this phase, the data you have collected is evaluated and analyzed, and thus is transformed into CI. This might involve comparing the data you found with data from other sources, integrating your conclusions from the data with other CI, or measuring the results of your CI against

predetermined benchmarks. It can involve the application of experience or the use of sophisticated CI.

4. *Analytical tools and models*: It should be kept in mind that there are two distinct ways in which analysis is applied to the data collected in the CI cycle. The first is the use of analysis to make a selection, such as deciding which of a dozen news articles is important. The second is the use of analysis to add value to one or more pieces of data. That would mean, for example, adding a statement to an article indicating both *why* and *how* its contents are important to the end user. Although CI analysts provide both types of analysis, end users properly regard only the latter process as analysis.

5. *Communicating the finished intelligence*: This phase involves preparing and then presenting the results to the end user in a usable format and in a timely manner. In some cases, the CI may have to be distributed to those who asked for it and, occasionally, to others who might also profit from having it. In other contexts, the CI is simply made available to potential users. In any case, the final form of the CI, as well as its timeliness and security, are important considerations.

6. *Taking action*: This involves using the CI in decision making. The CI may be used as an input to decision making, or it may be the first of several steps in an overall assessment of, for example, a new market. If the end user also does the analysis, then this is just a part of the previous stage.

The feature that runs through, and directly links, all the phases of the CI cycle is the need to monitor, on a continuous basis, what you have done and how well you have done it. The goal is to provide feedback from each phase to the other four phases of the CI cycle. By doing this, you will improve both the product of an individual assignment and the entire CI process even as you are using it.

Feedback to and from each phase of CI to all others is essential. That feedback generates a constant review that seeks to raise and then answer questions like these:

- Are the CI targets still correct?
- Are the areas of interest still of interest?
- Should the CI unit add or delete targets, areas of interest, internal customers, and so on?

"Despite their importance, individual facts and data do not usually provide an effective basis for actions or setting priorities. Actions depend on an understanding of relationships, derived from analysis of facts and data."[8]

However, the feedback process must go further. Here are some examples.

1. A change in the job description of the end-user to whom you are providing the CI could mean that you will have to change the kind of data you are collecting, the type of CI you are providing, or the way in which you are presenting your CI. For example, if your end users in a marketing department are now requiring their managers to track competitive programs, and create and maintain a library of competitive promotional media and tactics,[9] that could translate into a change in your own efforts. You may no longer need to collect this data, but rather to help develop an underlying understanding of what they mean, or, conversely, you may be called on to begin accumulating these materials when you had not been doing so in the past.

2. Similarly, difficulty in collecting important data, if identified in time, may mean that you have to reconsider the type of data you are seeking or even reconsider the specific target, despite the fact you may be in the middle of an assignment.

3. If you find out that regular updates of a CI report you are now preparing might be needed in the future, you should think about changing the way you are collecting the underlying data *now*. The change is that, given a choice, you should leave open, rather than close, routes to potential data sources for the future work. This may mean making sure you identify and capture sources that might have key data in the future, even if they do not now have anything you can use.

As shown in Table 1.1, there appears to be an optimal balance among the four stages of CI with which the typical CI unit is involved: needs, collection, analysis, and communication. This allocation includes the feedback within each phase.

TABLE 1.1   Optimal Balance of CI Stages

Phase	Percentage of Overall Effort
Needs	15–20
Collection	25–30
Analysis	40–45
Communication	10–15
Total	100

THE CI CYCLE: A CHECKLIST FOR THE INTERNAL CI PROFESSIONAL

Phase I: Establishing Your CI Needs

- Identify targets for your end user and yourself.
- Determine what specific CI you or your end users need.
- Establish who will get and use the finished CI.
- If there are several assignments, decide which is most important and must be done first. Also identify those that will not be done by the CI unit, whether because of personnel and financial constraints, because of ethical issues, and so forth.
- Decide when you or your end user needs the CI for it to be useful.
- Review your firm's CI needs in light of the results of the other phases, as well as in light of changes in your firm and its competitive environment.

Phase II: Collecting the Raw Data You Need

- Identify the most likely sources for that raw data.
- Develop research strategies and techniques.
- Assign responsibilities, internally and externally, and deadlines for obtaining needed raw data.
- Arrange to get the needed raw data, either on a regular or a one time basis.
- Conduct supplemental data collection efforts, if necessary.
- Review your data collection efforts in light of results of the other phases, as well as in light of changes in your firm and its competitive environment.

Phase III: Evaluating and Analyzing the Raw Data

- Establish the reliability of the sources for the raw data you obtained.
- Estimate the accuracy of the raw data you have.
- Make sure the data is relevant to your CI needs.
- Analyze the raw data. Draw conclusions, such as anticipating how your competitor thinks, based on what it has done.
- Review and analyze results of supplemental data collection efforts, if necessary.
- Review your final analysis in light of results of the other phases, as well as in light of changes in your firm and its competitive environment.

Phase IV: Preparing, and Presenting Your Resulting CI

- Format the results so the CI is readable, understandable, and useful.
- Deliver the results, in the right manner and in a timely fashion, to the right end users.
- Make sure sensitive data sources are protected from disclosure.
- Review the way you prepare and distribute the CI in light of results of the other phases, as well as in light of changes in your firm and its competitive environment.

Phase V: Using the CI

- Integrate the CI into your firm's business decision-making.
- Keep the CI secure.
- Review the impact that the CI has had on your firm.
- Review the way you use the CI in light of results of the other phases, as well as in light of changes in your firm and its competitive environment.

NOTES

1. John J. McGonagle and Carolyn M. Vella, *Bottom Line Competitive Intelligence* (Westport, Conn.: Quorum Books, 2002), 31–60

2. This has been called "customer intelligence." Annette Rich, "Sales Intelligence: The Marriage of Competitive and Customer Intelligence," *Competitive Intelligence Magazine* 5, no. 3 (May–June 2003), 17–20.

3. See McGonagle and Vella, *Bottom Line Competitive Intelligence*, 40–52.

4. See, e.g., John J. McGonagle and Carolyn M. Vella, *Protecting Your Company against Competitive Intelligence* (Westport, Conn.: Quorum Books, 1998).

5. We believe that this is the result of the common syndrome of making all knowledge current. For example, when asked about a firm where an employee formerly worked, that employee will typically speak in the present, that is "They are doing . . ." So, too, do executives speak of current conditions or participants in the market, when they really should be saying, "The last time I affirmatively refreshed my knowledge, which was seven months/years ago, the following was true . . ."

6. Needs and analysis can be seen as linked, in terms of skills, just as collection and dissemination can be. In our experience and that of our clients, the less effort that needs and analysis command, the poorer will be the outcome of any project or performance of any CI unit.

7. Different analysts use different numbers of stages or steps, but the overall model is the same.

8. Baldrige National Quality Program, *2003 Criteria for Performance Excellence* (Milwaukee, Wisc.: American Society for Quality, 2002), 31.

9. This work description is taken from an actual advertisement for a "promotion assistant" by ConAgra Grocery Products Group, in January 2003. http://www.careerlink.org/0/0/6/5/fm/000436.htm, January 29, 2003.

2

Just How Good Are You?

It is always difficult to look at something you are doing and to see where it can, and must, be improved. We all tend to compare what we are doing with what we were doing previously as well as what we see others doing. In the process, however, we may forfeit the ability, or more properly, the perspective, to understand where we should be improving, as distinguished from what we can do.

To help bridge that gap, we have developed a self-assessment test (Tables 2.1 through 2.4) to help you understand what you are doing and where you can improve yourself, applying some of the principles and experiences outlined in this book. You will quickly note that some of the questions seem to be similar. They are, but they differ in subtle ways. It is our goal to have you think about your own program, not about what is the "right" or "wrong" answer. Also, we are showing you that all elements of a CI program and its proper management are closely linked.

At the end of this short test, you can score yourself and see in what broad areas you, and your staff, need to focus to better manage a CI unit and create a better CI unit to manage. We have also provided a cross-reference table (Table 2.5) taking each question and linking it to a particular section of this book. When do you use which area? The overall scoring is designed to let you rate your current program in three broad areas:

- training and networking
- determining and meeting end user needs
- CI team management and development

Within each area, your overall score will let you assess if your program (a) is a potential world-class program, (b) has some real strength, (c) is in need of improvement, or is (d) very weak. As you read this book, keep in mind those broad areas in terms of the kinds of improvement you need.

You should also look at the individual links. Even if you have a very high score in one area, you should also identify those questions to which your responses scored the lowest. Use the chart to take you directly to the various chapters of this book to help you immediately get to work to begin improvement in the narrower areas highlighted by that test's results. Finally, once you have completed the book, retake this test six months after you finish and then one year afterwards. How much have you really improved? Where should you focus your management efforts now?

SELF-EXAMINATION: COMPETITIVE INTELLIGENCE PRACTICES

Please answer the questions in Table 2.1, about your CI team's current CI efforts, using the following scale: 1 = rarely or no; 2 = sometimes; 3 = regularly or yes

TABLE 2.1   Assessment of CI Efforts

1	2	3	
			1. Our company provides regular education on CI ethical and legal issues to all employees involved in intelligence activities.
			2. Our CI team focuses its intelligence efforts on competitors and products or technologies that management has identified as important.
			3. Our company's management is actively involved in CI activities and ensures that CI is adequately funded.
			4. Our company ensures that CI practitioners are provided professional education in the areas for which they are primarily responsible such as collection, analysis.
			5. Our CI program has its own budget.
			6. Our users of CI have received training on what CI can and cannot provide as well as on legal and ethical issues involved in collecting CI.
			7. Our CI team changes the CI products and services it provides on a regular basis.

			8. Our CI team reports directly to the most important end users of CI at our company.
			9. Our CI program is run by a small group of people who are professionally trained to produce CI for the management team's varying needs, including business planning and decision making.
			10. Our CI team interviews our management team regularly to understand their intelligence requirements and uses those requirements to focus CI efforts and allocate resources.
			11. Our business managers *require* CI inputs for key program reviews.
			12. Our CI team distributes CI findings throughout the company, to those who need them.
			13. Our company recognizes CI as a legitimate and necessary activity for business organizations in today's marketplace.
			14. Our CI program meets its users' needs on an ongoing basis, as determined by a defined process and predetermined objectives.
			15. Our CI unit has established, and uses, an internal network, including employees throughout the company, to collect data.
			16. Our company's legal department regularly reviews the company's CI activities to ensure that they are being conducted legally and ethically.
			17. Our CI unit has a succession plan in place covering the replacement of its current manager.
			18. Our CI team manager has regular, direct contact with our most important CI users.
			19. Our CI team ensures those employees involved in CI activities are given basic intelligence training.
			20. Our CI team has a systematic process for identifying and defining its intelligence needs.
			21. Our CI team regularly meets with the ultimate users of the CI.
			22. Our CI program meets its predetermined objectives and the results are measured in terms of their impact on the organization's business performance.
			23. Our company provides regular training to all employees on the basics of CI.
			24. Our company has a formal set of legal and ethical guidelines designed specifically for CI.
			25. Our CI team affirmatively promotes CI at all levels of the company.

			26. Our CI team has formal plans for ongoing development of the CI process in the company.
			27. Company managers, at all levels, support intelligence activities and use CI effectively in business planning and decision making.
			28. Our CI team has a network that includes CI practitioners outside of the company.
			29. Our CI program has grown over the past three years.
			30. In addition to professional CI training, our organization provides advanced training for CI teams and individuals, including training in managing the CI operation.
			31. Our CI activities have a set of clearly defined objectives, with one or more consciously identified user groups.

1 = rarely or no; 2 = sometimes; 3 = regularly or yes.

Scoring Your Results

Transfer your scores where indicated in Tables 2.2 through 2.4.

TABLE 2.2 Training and Networking	TABLE 2.3 Determining and Meeting End User Needs	TABLE 2.4 CI Team Management and Development
#1		
#4	#2	#3
#6	#9	#5
#15	#10	#7
#16	#13	#8
#19	#14	#11
#23	#18	#12
#24	#20	#17
#28	#21	#22
#30	#27	#25
Total	#31	#26
	Total	#29
		Total

Scoring Your Performance

27+ points: potential world-class
23–26 points: some real strength
15–22 points: needs improvement
14 or less: very weak

TABLE 2.5 Links from the Self-Scoring Questions to Chapters in this Book

Question Number	General Topic	Chapters
1	Training	7
2	Roles of CEOs and senior management	4, 9, 14
3	Roles of CEOs and senior management; financial institutionalization	4, 9, 14, 16
4	Skills CI professionals need; training	3, 7
5	Financial institutionalization	4, 14
6	Relationship with Law Department; training	7, 8
7	Key elements in planning for development; intelligence output	12, 14
8	Physical location	4
9	Intelligence output; Roles of CEOs and senior management; training	4, 7, 9, 12, 14
10	Implementation; feedback	9, 16
11	Roles of CEOs and senior management	4, 9, 14
12	Expanding dissemination and utilization; role of networks	6, 13, 14
13	Roles of CEOs and senior management	4, 9, 14
14	Intelligence output; feedback	11, 13, 16
15	Role of networks	6
16	Intelligence gathering and production; relationship with Law Department	7, 8, 9, 10, 11, 12
17	Key elements in planning for development	14
18	Physical location	4
19	Needs determination	9
20	Feedback	13, 16
21	Implementation; roles of CEOs and senior management	4, 9, 14
22	Feedback	13, 16
23	Training	7
24	Intelligence gathering and production; relationship with Law Department	7, 8, 9, 10, 11, 12
25	Development paths and patterns; key elements in planning for development	6, 14
26	Key elements in planning for development; intelligence output	11, 12, 13, 14
27	Educating management on development	7, 14
28	Role of networks	6
29	Development paths and patterns	14

Table 2.5 continued

Question Number	General Topic	Chapters
30	Educating management on development; key elements in planning for development; roles of CEOs and senior management; training	4, 7, 9, 14
31	Educating management on development	7, 14

3

Staff

SIZE

There does not seem to be any critical mass, that is minimum size, for a CI unit. In fact, most CI units appear to be relatively small. That is not to say that firms do not have many people doing CI; in many firms, there are multiple CI units.

A survey conducted in 2000 indicates that the most common CI unit has only 1 full-time CI professional in it, and that only about 1 unit in 6 has 5 or more full-time professionals. Thus, at present, the typical CI unit has a few full-time professionals and a limited number of full-time supporting staff.[1]

SKILLS

Whether a CI unit has one part-time professional or a dozen full-time professionals, to succeed, each professional, as well as the entire unit, must possess the right skills. Motorola, Inc., has provided its view, based on that firm's experience, of the skills and attitudes that a CI professional should, and should not, possess to succeed there:

To Make a Difference, BI Pros Should be "Sufficiently Annoying"

- Never accept a task without knowing the end goal
- Ask, "What decision are you trying to make?"

- Represent the external view
- Constantly look over the horizon
- Be nosy
- Be persistent
- Know where decisions are being made, and show up
- Continually develop source networks
- Serve as a human router
- Teach others to fetch for themselves
- Challenge the status quo[2]

Best Practice benchmarking studies have shown that a new CI unit needs a different set of skills from an experienced, established unit.

Necessary Skills

First, what skills should a CI professional possess (regardless of how or when they are acquired)? A 1995 study sheds some light on that question. That study first generated a list of skills needed to undertake CI through interviews with experienced CI professionals, academics, and others. This list was then divided into skills that could be acquired from one of four sources: inherent traits, coursework or teaching, professional experience and expertise, and mentoring.[3]

Of particular interest to those establishing or managing a CI unit are skills in the first and fourth groups, that is, those that must already be present or can best be acquired from others in a mentoring relationship. The inherent traits identified include:

- curiosity, flexibility, diplomacy, and persistence
- the ability to withstand pressures toward unethical behavior and to withstand criticism
- the ability to examine both the big picture and small details
- creativity and open-mindedness
- communications and independent learning skills
- analytical ability and business "savvy"
- the ability to be self-critical
- the ability to deal with ambiguity and change with comfort
- networking capabilities

The important skills that can be acquired through mentoring include:

- creativity
- persistence
- strategic thinking
- research skills

Selecting Staff with the Right Skills

Best Practice studies show that having the right staff with the right skills is critical to the *start up of any CI unit*. But what skills does the CI staff need at the start up of a CI unit? These same studies indicate that there are two sets of "must have" skills for a CI unit at the beginning:

- strategic/analytical thinking, such as inductive reasoning
- communication/interpersonal abilities[4]

The need for strategic and analytical thinking skills is probably a surrogate for education and formal training in CI. That is because there are not enough graduate level programs offering a major in CI or even merely emphasizing CI to staff business CI units. As time passes and that changes, the need for strong strategic and analytical thinking skills will be replaced by a need for specific training in CI analysis or other strategic and analytical skills.

The need for communication and interpersonal skills is due to the fact that world-class CI units have found that regular, intensive *face-to-face* communication with their own internal customers throughout CI projects is vital to effective operation of the CI process. As continuous, and two-way, feedback is a vital part of the job, the CI staff must have the associated communication and interpersonal skills to manage such contacts.

But merely possessing specific skills is not all that a new CI unit staff needs. The staff, whether made up of one person or a dozen, also needs certain attitudes. Again, Best Practice studies show that the CI staff at startup must be both risk-takers and committed to the CI profession.

The need for a risk-accepting attitude is due to the fact that, in successful CI units, CI managers *and* end users must allow for, and, in fact, even support, differences of opinion among the staff. In addition, as professionals, the CI staff must be able to openly identify CI failures so they can then learn from them. The commitment to the CI profession, both, inside and outside the firm, enables the CI professional staff to have the opportunity to improve its CI skills to meet the growing demands and needs of the current and future internal clients.

What is interesting is that these same studies that show us what skills are vital have also shown that a common belief held by non-CI experienced managers is not correct. That belief, which is expressed in many ways, is that a new CI staff member must "know the business" or "have prior experience with the company." In fact, that is not true. Studies of the best CI units show that, *in start-up CI units, knowledge of the company, or even of the industry, is not a critical qualification.* Rather it is only "moderately important." Even in the arena of technology-oriented CI, Best Practice firms have similarly found that "While an understanding of technology is important, an STI [science and technology intelligence] professional needs to develop generalist skills."[5] The reason for this is relatively simple: knowledge of the company and of the industry in which it competes is easier to learn than are the necessary analytical skills. In addition, it can be argued that a new CI professional coming to a firm without significant industry or company experience will be able to operate more effectively, as he or she is not burdened with ingrained assumptions, undisclosed biases, or flat-out incorrect information.

DEALING WITH EMPLOYEES

Talented Employees

How will you deal with those who are really good at CI? Here, consider one problem that is not recognized as much as it should be. People who are good at CI tend to be retentive, in a psychological sense. That is, they seek out and retain everything they can, on the basis that "some day" it might be of use. The problem may start as one of too much data solicitation or of excessive data retention, but it ultimately becomes a problem of processing and storage.

The person who seeks data for the sake of collecting it is a kind of mental "pack rat." For example, one member of a CI unit may suggest that the personnel department inform him of the last place of employment of staff who are newly hired and of the place of next employment of all those leaving the corporation. This sort of data may be useful for monitoring a particular competitor's recruitment efforts to determine changes in research and development activities. If the data is not being collected for a particular end, however, you may not want to collect it at all.

Collection versus Analysis and Evaluation Responsibilities

One issue not often considered in setting up a CI unit, but a potentially important one, is determining who will evaluate the accuracy and reliability of the raw data you and others collect. Specifically, do those who collect the data also analyze and evaluate it, or do you separate the collectors from the analysts? As with so many other elements of the CI process, there is no clear-cut answer. What is important is that you recognize the issue and deal with it.

There appears to be an optimal balance among the four stages of CI: needs, collection, analysis, and dissemination. We have found that the

TABLE 3.1 Four Stages Allocated Between Two People

Stage	Percentage of of Overall Efforts	First Person	Second Person	Approximate Ratio
Needs	20%	7%	13%	1:2
Collection	30%	27%	3%	9:1
Analysis	40%	7%	33%	1:5
Dissemination	10%	9%	1%	9:1
Totals	100%	50%	50%	

skills most useful in needs tend to be those most useful in analysis as well. Conversely, the skills most useful in collection tend to be similar to those needed for dissemination. These observations lead to some potential guidelines for assembling and managing a CI team or unit. One way to visualize this is to look at these four stages and see how they might be allocated between, for example, two people (see Table 3.1).

As you can see, this shows the need for two relatively complementary persons. That is because of the difference in skills, and even personalities, required in an ideal staffing situation.

There is now ample evidence that purposeful staffing to acquire people with this radical a divergence in skills, attitudes, and perspectives can provide important contributions, which are not possible from more traditional models of staffing. To obtain the kind of finished intelligence product needed by management today requires managers to understand and work with these skills in newer, nontraditional ways.

Exit Paths for Staff

Where do you go in your own firm to recruit people to staff your CI unit? As noted, you need people with a flair for analysis and good communications and interpersonal skills. These people are typically the ones most often seen as candidates for rapid promotion and long-term development in other areas within the firm. To attract them and keep them in the CI unit, you must avoid creating dead-end positions. As a result, a promotion line must be established from the CI unit upward and a decision must be made about where the unit is located and to whom it is administratively responsible. Moreover, this must be done *before* the unit is created, if possible. If good employees see no way out of a new unit, they will not volunteer to join it. Even if they are transferred in, they will make their own way out, usually to competitors.

JOB DESCRIPTIONS

Overall Tasks

The core of the mission for any CI unit should be to provide needed intelligence, in a timely manner to key decision makers, which will then serve as an element in the firm's decision making and related actions (for more on mission statements, see Chapter 5). That means that those providing the CI must avoid having any preconceived position either for or against any specific policy or outcome that can be affected by their work.

In many cases, firms have found that they are comfortable drawing a bright line between providing intelligence and recommending policy. There are two principal reasons for doing so: to keep CI unbiased and to keep it free from the appearance of being biased. For example, if CI provided by your marketing unit stresses the need for additional distribution channels, that conclusion, even if valid, may be disregarded by non-marketing departments as special pleading.

However, you must not let the need to separate CI from policy making impede effective planning and policy making. For instance, it may be entirely appropriate for a CI analyst to examine the probable effects of alternative corporate policies, particularly when they entail responses of a particular competitor to your initiatives. *The division between policy and CI must never be so rigid that the CI unit is precluded from assessing fairly the impacts of prior policy decisions.*

Conversely, as the goal of CI is to provide the needed intelligence that will serve as a key element in decision making, an internal CI unit must avoid having a preconceived position on any specific corporate policy that may bear on, or be affected by, the CI research it is conducting.

CI Unit

What should job descriptions for those working in CI units contain? Each firm has its own "style" of job descriptions. However, a review of existing job descriptions for CI analysts, the core of the entire process, has shown several common deficiencies:

- Many of these descriptions were developed, and admittedly so, simply by editing existing descriptions for positions such as market researcher. In some cases, no visible effort was made to adapt them completely.
- Some clearly fail to relate to the entire competitive intelligence cycle, in that they omit or cover too poorly issues such as who identifies the CI needs, what function the CI unit supports, and from what internal units the CI unit gets raw data.

- The important issue of how CI findings are communicated is dealt with much too lightly in many situations. At best, some of these descriptions deal only with the need for communication skills, rather than outlining the variety of communication skills needed, including the ability to deliver bad news.
- Some job descriptions properly recognize that analytical skills are critical, but few detail what kinds of skills are needed in each position. For example, financial analytical skills may differ significantly from those skills needed to analyze telephone interviews or prepare patent maps.[6]

It is strongly suggested that people developing job descriptions start with the development of a description for the analyst position. From there, once having developed such a description, it is easier to draft related descriptions, such as researcher, manager, and the like.

Other Units

Remember to consider related, supportive changes. When involved in the process of developing or updating job descriptions, you should seek to modify the job descriptions of personnel in other units, such as purchasing, sales, and employee relations, to require that people holding key positions must, as a part of their anticipated duties, provide raw data to the CI unit on an ongoing basis. For example, in a recent advertisement of an entry-level marketing position, the job description included the following requirements:

Major Duties, Responsibilities and Principal Accountabilities:

- Reviews the deliverables in the Marketing calendar, and helps to create a schedule for creative and program review by the Integrated Marketing department. Functions include promotion, web, media, packaging, research, and advertising . . .
- Tracks competitive programs and keeps library of information . . .[7]

Salaries

How much should your CI professionals be paid? As with many other management decisions, that depends on your firm, its size, and the marketplace for CI professionals and individual education. However, there have been some surveys conducted on this. The most recent, published in 2001, compared its data with a similar survey taken five years earlier.

As expected, salary ranges varied by geographic location, area of work, and professional experience. Some intriguing extracts are found in Tables 3.2 and 3.3.

TABLE 3.2   Basic Salary by Professional Experience

Years of Professional Experience	2001 Mean Salary	1997 Mean Salary[8]
1–5	$47,145	$44,812
6–10	$58,803	$58,091
11–15	$66,065	$63,476
16–20	$73,668	$72,840
21–25	$82,468	$81,149
26–30	$88,324	$85,050
31+	$87,446	$86,238

TABLE 3.3   Basic Salary by Area of Work

Area of Work	2001 Mean Salary	1997 Mean Salary[9]
CI or Analysis	$66,137	$66,363
Market Planning, Research, or Analysis	$66,386	$65,154
Strategic Planning	$71,270	$85,036
Information Center or Services	$60,729	$55,789
Business Development/Product Planning/Research and Development	$73,819	$77,376
Financial Planning/ Counterintelligence	$55,161	$73,918

NOTES

1. Society of Competitive Intelligence Professionals, *2000/'01 Competitive Intelligence Professionals Salary Survey Report and Reference Guide on Analyst Job Descriptions* (Alexandria, Va.: Society of Competitive Intelligence Professionals, 2001), 50–51.

2. Joe Goldberg, "Case Study: Assessing the Fundamental Qualities of a BI Professional—Career Management at Motorola" (presentation, April 2002), 10.

3. Jerry Miller, "Competencies for Intelligence Professionals," *Newsletter of the Society of Competitive Intelligence Professionals*, November 1995, 1–2.

4. These have been described later as confidence, tact, timeliness, dependability, integrity, and sincerity. American Productivity & Quality Center, International Benchmarking Clearinghouse, *User-Driven Competitive Intelligence: Crafting the Value Proposition* (Houston: American Productivity & Quality Center, 2003), 27.

5. American Productivity & Quality Center, International Benchmarking Clearinghouse, *Using Science and Technology Intelligence to Drive Business Results*. (Houston: American Productivity & Quality Center, 2002), 9.

6. John J. McGonagle, "Reference Guide on Analyst Job Descriptions," in Society of Competitive Intelligence Professionals, *2000/'01 Competitive Intelligence Professionals Salary Survey Report*, 59–103

7. "Promotion Assistant [ConAgra Grocery Products Company]," http://www.careerlink.org/0/0/6/5/fm/000436.htm, January 29, 2003.

8. From Society of Competitive Intelligence Professionals, *2000/'01 Competitive Intelligence Professionals Salary Survey Report*, 15.

9. From ibid.

4

Structure

FOUNDATIONS OF CI UNITS

From an historical perspective, it can be said that there are two basic
models for the creation of CI units: the constructed and the evolutionary. In the constructed model, the CI unit owes its existence to the
decision of one person (or, at most, a handful). Someone says, "Let it
happen," and it does. At that point, the CI unit must begin to operate
and justify the decision to create it. In the evolutionary model, the CI
unit owes its existence to a perceived need by the firm, or a part of the
firm, for its services. It gradually comes into existence to meet a particular need, and then must seek out additional tasks and missions to
justify its continued existence.

The way in which each particular unit was established will tend to
influence its growth, manner of operation, and ultimate survival, as
suggested by the following two lists.

Constructed Unit

- The unit hits the deck running.
- The unit has a corporate sponsor, usually called a *champion*, from
  the beginning.
- Survival in its first years is often highly dependent on the career
  of the champion.
- Internal cooperation with other units is easily mandated and en-
  forced.

- The unit is staffed up quickly, so the career path (or lack of one) from the unit quickly becomes evident.
- At the beginning, a positive record of successes is not a factor in its acceptance, so it may have time to mature.
- The initial audience for its services is usually clear and centralized, such as a strategic planning officer.
- The use of its output is often mandated at the same time it is created.
- The name given the unit reflects its purpose, such as Marketing Intelligence or Competitor Research.
- Available funds for the unit's operation are directly appropriated or come from another budget source controlled by its sponsor.
- Given that it has a champion, it has substantial protection from problems of accepted/expected failure (see chapter 15).
- The unit is able quickly to cross the line from analysis to policy making.
- The unit may quickly be perceived, whether accurately or not, as strictly neutral, a "special pleader," or the champion's control device.

Evolutionary Unit

- The unit is a slow starter, and may gradually add to its mission.
- It must develop and survive without a powerful sponsor.
- Survival is not generally tied to the career path of a champion but is often highly dependant on quickly becoming demonstrably successful.
- Internal cooperation with other units must be earned, which takes time.
- Staffing up takes time; career paths (or lack there of) are not usually evident at the beginning.
- A positive record of successes is often critical to widespread acceptance, so as a result, the unit may not be given time to mature.
- The future market for the unit's services is often unclear. At the beginning it is usually a part of a unit and not at the center of decision making.
- The new unit usually must "sell" the need for its services to other units within the company.
- The name given the unit often reflects a previous mission, such as Information Support.
- Funding is initially available if this is an expansion of an existing unit's functions. However, the unit must fight for additional and separate funding as it develops.
- Often there is no protection from problems of accepted/expected failure.

- The unit usually does not face an immediate opportunity to be involved in policy making.
- It takes some time for the unit's neutrality (or lack thereof) to be discerned.

FORMS OF CI UNITS

Today, CI units operate in a wide variety of forms. The most common variations are as follows:

- CI is produced by the end user for the end user's sole benefit.
- CI is produced by an end user for the use of that end user as well as others, usually in the same unit or area of operation.
- CI is produced by an analyst, sometimes with clerical and/or research support. The finished intelligence is generated for a small number of end users, usually in the same SBU.
- CI is produced by an analyst, sometimes with clerical and/or research support. The intelligence is generated for a large number of end users, usually spread throughout the organization or firm.
- CI is produced on a onetime basis by outside firms. It is acquired by a manager or analyst for distribution to, and use by, a specific end user.
- CI is derived from outside reports and/or produced by outside firms. It is acquired by a manager or analyst and then repacked, sometimes with additional research, for distribution to a number of end users. Typically this involves a large number of end users or even posting on an Intranet.

These forms of operation are not mutually exclusive. For example, it may be the case that a CI manager does research and provides analysis for a senior officer in, for example, strategic planning and also contracts with outside research firms who provide onetime reports for the marketing department. Alternately, an information center may acquire prepackaged reports from outside vendors for an entire SBU and also conduct current secondary research to be posted on an Intranet.

LOCATION

Where are CI units located from an organizational point of view? There are a number of structural variations. In practice, they boil down to three:

- All CI is produced in one, central location for distribution to designated individuals or throughout the organization. This is a classic centralized model. It is most often managed as a corporate headquarters function and is most effective in situations where the forms of CI most often needed are strategy oriented, target oriented, and/or technology oriented. Of course, there can be a number of such units throughout a firm. One view has it that such a centralized unit tends to be smaller, with strong ties to its end users and capable of generating high levels of trust in them, which is typical of "high value strategic CI units."[1]

- Each unit that has a need for some form of CI has its own CI unit. For example, each product manager or geographic division, may have a separate CI unit, providing CI to that department or division only. This is a decentralized model. It is most often effective in situations where the forms of CI most often needed are tactics oriented, target oriented, and/or technology oriented. A variation of this is the case where individuals throughout the firm are expected to perform their own necessary CI as a part of their jobs.

- A series of decentralized CI units is controlled or coordinated by a central CI manager. That manager assures that critical intelligence is shared among the various units, helps avoid overlaps in research efforts and spending, provides training and oversight, and also usually conducts CI for a small number of headquarters end users. This is the *hub and spoke* model. It is most often effective in situations where the decentralized units provide tactics-oriented and/or technology-oriented CI while the central CI unit provides strategy-oriented and/or target-oriented CI.

Where will your CI unit be located in the organizational hierarchy? A decision must be made about the administrative responsibility for the CI unit. A "special" unit or joint supervision rarely work. These are the hallmarks of a unit with no real future and little, if any, real impact on the long-term or critical decision making within the organization. Usually they mark the creation of a CI unit in an effort to follow what others, often competitors, have done. Once the unit is created in such enterprises, it will usually suffer the fate of other "flavors of the month."

Having excluded those variations, other options remain. Typically, departments such as marketing, business development, and strategic planning can all make a strong case for having the CI function report to them. A chief information officer (CIO) may also be a logical candidate to supervise and direct a CI unit because of the CI unit's heavy reliance on information gathering and management and its need to provide reliable support to a wide number of corporate functions, all of which may dovetail with the charter of a CIO. However, in actuality that has rarely happened. The probable reasons are as follows:

- Most CIOs manage knowledge or data management systems (KMS) that are essentially quantitative in focus, whereas CI, as a discipline, is most often qualitative in focus.[2]
- CI professionals need to be able to access the *people* who provided the data as well as the data. Most KMS are keyed to storing and manipulating data.
- Most KMS are not set up to capture data on anything that does not involve the company. Yet company personnel, from the CEO down, interface daily with customers, from whom information on competitors can be developed, as well as suppliers, distributors, and the like.
- The sales force, potentially the most powerful source of data in support of CI, is rarely involved with KMS and related efforts. Yet CI units that can tap into the sales force have found significant benefits for both sides of the transaction.
- Few, if any, KMS provide current information on employees. However, knowing which employees are members of what professional association, or where they worked before and what they did there is something desired by many CI professionals.

In what types of units are CI units now located? According to a recent study, CI professionals characterize their managers' areas of work as shown in Table 4.1. [3]

What is interesting about the data on a CI unit's location is how the situation changed over a period of almost a decade. In a 1993 survey, the rank order of areas of work was reported as follows: [4]

- strategic planning
- market research
- corporate information
- marketing
- competitor intelligence unit

TABLE 4.1   Managers' Areas of Work: Percentages

Manager's Area of Work	Percentage
Market planning, research or analysis	20.2%
General corporate	15.6%
Strategic planning	13.6%
Business development	9.0%
Competitive intelligence or analysis	8.7%
Research and development	5.9%
Product or financial planning/operations	5.8%
Information center or services	5.6%
Other or unclassified	15.6%

The changes in organizational location reflect the maturation and growth of technology- and tactics-oriented CI during that period.

The last element of location is the relationship between the CI unit and one or more end users. Research on reporting relationships has tended to focus on how many levels of bureaucracy are between the CI unit and the firm's board of directors.[5] Although the findings are interesting, especially in that they show that almost 50 percent of the units are within two levels of the board of directors, the question is deceptive. That is because it presumes that the appropriate end users are the directors. That is correct if the CI unit provides strategy-oriented or target-oriented CI. However, there are other end users in other locations that are, or should be, receiving one or more forms of CI.

The most appropriate location for the CI unit, experience shows, is to report directly to the end user. If there is more than one end user, the CI unit ideally should be within one level of its best or most important end user. The reason for such a relationship is that the CI unit (see Chapter 9) must be able to work with the end user on an ongoing basis, not only to ascertain his or her CI needs, but also to have access to him or her during the conduct of any CI assignment. The reason for such access is that, contrary to some popular misconceptions, the best CI is not provided when the unit is tasked and sent out to report at the end of the assignment. Rather, it is produced when the end user and the CI staff are in continuing communication during the process of conducting the assignment.

This need for ongoing communications has generated an additional recommendation on "location." In this context, that means answering the question, "Where should the CI unit be physically housed?" The answer is, "as close as is possible to the physical location of the primary or most important end user." The goal is to generate what is sometimes called "hall friction," that is, frequent one-on-one unscheduled contact between the CI end user and those producing the intelligence. If the CI unit cannot be located in close proximity to this end user, then it is better for the unit's manager to be close to the end user than it is to be close to the CI unit's staff.

Requiring the Use of CI

In some firms, the most effective way to put CI to use immediately is to require that every operating business unit (whether it is a small sales department or a large multinational subsidiary) include with its annual plan (whether capital, marketing, or strategy) an appraisal both of current competition and the current marketplace as it impacts its decisions. Experience shows that this formal directive is very often needed in addition to a general admonition that the planning process must take into account competitors and competition.

Put in another way, if management cannot see the competitive information set forth separately, it may have no guarantee that those preparing the plan have actually taken it into account or that they have even looked into it. Also, by seeing the CI that the unit has developed, management can evaluate its appropriateness and adequacy and suggest additional sources.

A second step would be to require that the individual plan not only indicate the current competitive environment but also show how the unit perceives the future environment. From there, management can insist that the specific unit indicate *how* it intends to respond to changes in its competitive environment.

CI can be successfully injected in a similar manner at many stages other than the planning processes. When you consider fundamental corporate decisions, such as an acquisition, divestiture, major capital investment, or introduction of a new product, management can require that those involved, both in considering and in advocating the transaction, prepare a competitive analysis. The analysis should indicate how the planned action will assist your firm to respond to its competitors and how the affected competitors may be expected to respond.

Relationship between CI and Market Research

As indicated, a significant percentage (over 20 percent) of CI professionals polled indicated that their manager's area of work was market planning, research, or analysis. That raises the question of whether CI should, as a general rule, be considered as a part of market research and therefore located in that department.

At present, the differences between CI and market research are more profound than are the similarities (see Table 4.2, page 36).

The result of these differences is that CI is often a poor fit in a market research department, and conversely, market research is also a poor fit within a CI unit. This conclusion is supported by a recent benchmarking survey which found that "When CI personnel had both market intelligence and marketing research responsibilities, the marketing research responsibilities took precedence (90%) and the intelligence shifted to a secondary function."[6] The one exception may be tactics-oriented CI, where the process typically supports marketing efforts. In such cases, so long as managers recognize the critical differences in approach and attitude between typical market research and typical CI, they can work within the same unit.

However, that does not mean that CI and market research should be operating   independently   of   each   other.   Experience   clearly

TABLE 4.2   Difference between CI and Market Research

	Competitive Intelligence	Market Research
Typical Focus	External	External
Typical Orientation	Strategy-, tactics-, technology-, and/or target-oriented	Tactics-oriented
Typical Tools	Qualitative and quantitative	Largely quantitative
Source of Tools	Adapted from market research, planning, benchmarking, and so on.	Largely developed first for market research
Relative Perspectives	Macro- and micro-level	Largely micro-level
Time Horizons	Historical, current, and long-term future	Historical and current; occasionally near term future
Targeting	Constantly redefined by end users	Relatively stable

demonstrates otherwise. For example, in the CI unit at PacBell, the market research and information research (internal information brokers) functions now all have established mechanisms for transferring critical information through networking.

> One example where the synergy between [these three] groups was valuable was when [PacBell] was trying to determine what its level of involvement in the cable TV market should be. One of the pieces that affected the decision whether or not to create a cable TV subsidiary was put in place when market research determined that customers would switch cable companies if they had an option. From a competitive perspective that was the basis of entry into a new marketplace.[7]

BUDGETS AND FINANCING

What is, or will be, the source of financial support for your CI unit? Will the CI be funded from the same budgets that support such corporate functions as planning and legal? Will it be supported by end users, such as marketing personnel, from their budgets? Will the CI unit charge back other functions for the work it provides? Or will it operate under some type of combination arrangement?

Funding through charging back might seem to be an ideal way to operate a CI unit but is a delicate issue in practice. There were estimates ten years ago that over 50 percent of CI units charged back to some degree.[8] Anecdotal data indicates that this number has fallen considerably, probably reflecting the fact that those units that needed such services have created their own CI units. If you charge back other departments for CI your unit provides them, they may be reluctant to use it, thus clouding its future.

Paying for a CI unit from an overhead or unit budget will make it more attractive for other units to use it. Without charging back to these other units, however, you have created what is a "free" resource. But experience shows that in a short time, "free" resources are overused, without regard to cost-effectiveness, simply because they have no direct cost to the user. The other difficulty with creating free resources is that they tend to be the first units that are cut back in a financial downturn. Because you need your CI unit more than ever when you are experiencing a downturn, cutting back on it at that time can be disastrous.

For the CI unit, particularly one seeking to establish itself and grow, this means that it must find some balance between these options. One solution is to start a CI unit without using any charge-back, in order to develop a "market" for the services. However, the unit should have the authority to make such charge backs as it matures. Then, over time, the unit should gradually initiate and manage some interdepartmental fee structure, whether direct or indirect. That is, it can charge back its out-of-pocket costs, it can charge for its time, serving as an internal consultant, or both. At that point, it should be able to demonstrate its value.

Looking at the other side of the budget issue, the question arises: how do CI units spend their budgets? The most recent data available indicates that about 50 percent of any such budget is spent on salaries. Then, in descending order, the budget is spent on travel, purchased research, databases (for secondary research), and training.[9]

NOTES

1. Ted Howard-Jones and Fiona Walker-Davis, "Delivering and Maintaining Tactical Intelligence," in Society of Competitive Intelligence Professionals, *Fifth Annual European Conference and Exhibit: Conference Proceedings* (Alexandria, Va.: Society of Competitive Intelligence Professionals, 2000), 93, 101.

2. See Walle, Alf H., III, *Qualitative Research in Intelligence and Marketing: The New Strategic Convergence* (Westport, Conn.: Quorum Books, 2001).

3. Society of Competitive Intelligence Professionals, *2000/'01 Competitive Intelligence Professionals Salary Survey Report and Reference Guide on Analyst Job Descriptions* (Alexandria, Va.: Society of Competitive Intelligence Professionals), 55.

4. Ruth Stanat, "A Survey of Global CI Practices," *Competitive Intelligence Review* 4, no. 2/3 (Summer/Fall 1993), 20–24.

5. For example, Society of Competitive Intelligence Professionals, *2000/'01 Salary Survey Report*, 53.

6. Conway L. Lackman, Kenneth Saban, and John M. Lanasa, "Organizing the Competitive Intelligence Function: A Benchmarking Study," *Competitive Intelligence Review* 11, no. 1 (1st quarter 2000), 17, 21.

7. Donald Baul, "Super synergy in CI: competitive analysis + market research + library science," *SCIP.online* 1, no. 4 (March 5, 2002).

8. A full 54% of SCIP members charge back for services; 24% charge back fully. See Lera Chitwood, "The View—A Survey of SCIP VIPs," *Competitive Intelligence Review* 4, no. 1 (Spring 1993), 33–37.

9. Stanat, *Global CI Practices*, 1993.

5

Missions and Images

MISSION STATEMENT

A mission statement for a CI unit actually should serve several purposes:

- First, it should identify why the CI unit exists and what the firm expects from it.
- Second, it can be seen as an opportunity for the CI unit (particularly if it is new) to affirmatively sell the concept of CI and its benefits to a wide audience, which should include more parties than only its immediate clients.
- Third, it can be used to deal with potential image problems, related to the concept of "corporate spies" in an affirmative, aggressive basis.

As with the preparation of job descriptions, a mission statement for a CI unit should encompass needs determination, research, analysis, and communication of results. If the CI unit has a role in a defensive program, that role should be explicit, not assumed. Most mission statements tend to omit one or more of these concepts. Take, for example, the following adaptation of a mission statement written around 1990:

The mission of the CI unit is to:
- Maintain general competitive intelligence awareness;

- Provide an input into planning; and
- Conduct special [one-time] assignments.

This statement fails to describe what CI is and does not deal with the critical issue of needs assessment.

Take another example, which was adapted from a later statement:

> The CI unit's mission is to develop and to communicate an in-depth and current understanding of the following to senior management on a regular and as-needed basis:
>
> - Current and future products/services of major competitors.
> - Current technologies underlying the activities of major competitors.
> - Current market activities or major competitors.
> - Current and future business strategies employed by major competitors.
> - Identity of potential new competitors.
>
> This competitive information will be used by officers and managers of the corporation in setting overall business strategies and making decisions on marketing, manufacturing, and distribution tactics.

This statement is far superior in that it identifies, in broad terms, the needs of the end users, the end users themselves, and the obligation to communicate to the end users. However, it could be more focused as to the ultimate end users. It also includes the statement that the end users "will" use it. That is a powerful, and important addition. Regardless, however, you should make sure that you consider related, supportive changes in the mission statements of other units, such as marketing, new business development, and strategic planning. Their mission statement should indicate that they are expected to use CI in their work.

What the statement omits is a brief, self-serving description of what CI is and an indication that the CI unit is expected to be engaged in training efforts (see Chapter 7).

Consider using a variation of this statement to define CI:

> Competitive Intelligence (CI) involves the use of public sources to develop data on competition, competitors, and the market environment. It then transforms, by analysis, that data into information. Public, in CI, means all information you can legally and ethically identify, locate, and then access.[1]

As for language on training, consider beginning with this statement: "The CI unit is responsible for the design and execution of programs to train all employees about CI, including legal and ethical limits on the collection of data."

INTERNAL IMAGE ISSUES

Visibility

How visible should your CI unit be, both within your firm and to outsiders? Put another way, should you call the unit the Competitive Intelligence Section or another name that accurately reflects what it does? Alternately, should you give it a more neutral (but less accurate) title, such as Information Support or Marketing Reference Services?

Ten to fifteen years ago, the most common approach was the most conservative. Many CI units bore other, less precise names. As CI has become recognized as a vital, legal, and ethical support for a variety of corporate functions ranging from planning to marketing and from mergers and acquisitions to technology development, businesses have lost that former reluctance to acknowledge that they in fact conduct CI.

That does not mean that they broadcast the details of their CI operations in terms of unit size, budget, effectiveness, or similar factors. Many do not. In fact, that is the reason why there is so little specific information in the public domain about specific successes and how they were achieved. That kind of data is, itself, seen by many firms as competitively sensitive.

Improving Internal Attitudes toward CI

Merely because management has approved the creation of a CI unit does not mean that the unit or, more properly, the concept of CI will automatically be accepted throughout the enterprise. Anecdotal information unfortunately indicates that today, CI practitioners are more likely to be labeled as "spies" or "spooks" or as being engaged in some form of "espionage" than in the recent past. In fact, it seems that the CI profession has lost some of the ground gained in this area in the past decade.

A Positive Approach. What is important is to learn how to promote CI positively. The word *positively* is important because the most frequent comment that CI professionals make in response to a remark such as, "Oh that means being a corporate spy, doesn't it?" is to rapidly reply, "CI is not spying!"

While that is a response, and technically a correct one, it should never be enough. Negatives never work on their own. Recall statements like "Well, I'm not a crook"[2] or "I did not have sexual relations with that woman, Miss Lewinsky."[3] You remember them because you often associate denials, not with innocence, but rather with attempts to conceal the truth. People tend to believe assertions that are more positive. That means that if someone says, "This is what I did" and then says, "and I did not do that," listeners tend to give the statement more credibility than for a mere denial.

For CI, it means that, when you handle questions and comments about CI, above all, you should say what it is, at least first, before you say what it is not. That means you must learn to say what CI is simply. Exactly what is it? As we noted (on page 40), your mission statement could start with a definition of CI.

While the definition at the bottom page 40 is not a short, easily remembered statement, it does contain all the key elements you must communicate. That is, it tells others that CI is public, not clandestine; legal, not criminal; and ethical, not questionable. So you can also use it to describe CI to those who do not understand it.

Comparisons. In talking about CI, you may—in fact, almost certainly will—be reminded of stories about corporate spies and theft of trade secrets and then asked, "Well isn't *that* CI?" Your short answer should be: "No. CI is legal and ethical. What you described was not." If you can, try to push back, gently, with a longer response, such as this:

> No. CI involves legal and ethical activities. That is no more a fair characterization of CI professionals than it would be to call all doctors Medicare fraud practitioners, all reporters yellow journalists, all accountants tax evaders, and so on.

If you are going to use a comparison like this, try and pick an example with some sensitivity to the critic so you do not provoke a negative response. By doing that, not only are you reinforcing the notion that these "spooks" are a minority, you are also reminding the critic that such (literally) outlaw actions unfairly tar the majority of CI professionals.

When you talk about those outlaws (and that is what some call themselves) you should continually use predicate terms like *outlaw*, *extra-legal*, and *renegade minority*. Language is powerful. Use these terms to continually remind the listener of the difference between what you are doing and what they have done.

Humor. CI professionals hurt their own case when they joke about being "spies" or "spooks," even among coworkers. That means no more jokes, even within the CI unit, about corporate spies or handing out "junior spy kits" at staff meetings. Do not let cuteness come back to haunt you. For example, don't call your internal "flash" intelligence service the "Competitive Intelligence Alert" (with CIA in bold letters). Finally, you must omit the almost mandatory cartoon figure with the spyglass from your presentations.

Terminology. This is an area where you must also exercise a great deal of care. You must avoid leaving even the slightest trace that someone can point to (or rely on) that says you think of what you and your staff as "spies" or of CI as some form of "espionage."

In particular, try to think about the terms you use in discussing what you are doing and work to avoid direct and indirect allusions that damage CI's luster. The most common ways these occur is when you use military or political terms in the context of CI. Examples of this include the following:

- "war room": what about *intelligence* or *operations center*?
- "counterintelligence": why not use the more correct terms, *defensive intelligence* or *defending against competitive intelligence*?
- "surveillance": what about *observation*?

In general, it is best to drop the use of military or warfare analogies entirely and use other analogies. While the use of such analogies can be superficially attractive, they not only carry unnecessary baggage for CI, they are also intellectually flawed. The goal of being competitive is much closer to winning (using a sports analogy) or growing and surviving (an analogy from nature) than it is to "killing people and breaking things" (the underlying purpose of military operations).[4]

Finally, you should eliminate (or at least minimize greatly) use of case studies and stories taken from military or political espionage when advocating the effectiveness of CI. While this may seem to be excessive, it is not. After almost twenty years treating CI as a professional discipline, there are more than enough case studies and examples to call upon without using those from the military or politics.

NOTES

1. See John J. McGonagle and Carolyn M. Vella, *The Internet Age of Competitive Intelligence*, (Westport, Conn.: Quorum Books, 1999), ch. 1.

2. Former President Richard M. Nixon, http://steadfast.tripod.com/nixon.html (May 19, 2003).

3. Former President William J. Clinton, http://www.cnn.com/ALLPOLITICS/1998/01/26/clinton.main (audio accessed June 26, 2003).

4. "War is about killing people and breaking things." Variously attributed to World War II General George S. Patton and talk radio host Rush Limbaugh.

6

Dealing with Other Units

DEALING WITH OTHER CI UNITS

The American Productivity & Quality Center (AP&QC) CI Best Practice Studies support what experience and intuition suggests: there are conflicts that can arise among CI units in the same firm when they possess different orientations, that is strategy, tactics, target, or technology. As we have shown in Chapter 1, each CI orientation tends to differ in terms of:

- internal markets
- time horizons
- balances of raw data with analysis
- cycle times

It is these very differences that immediately impact how CI units with differing orientations, and different end users, work, or fail to work, together. There are differences in the working environments each type of CI unit faces, including in the location and identity of the end users. These differences create natural tensions among the units. Moreover, the experience of the best practice firms shows that this is probably an unavoidable situation. How can it be otherwise when end users are themselves possibly competing within the enterprise, or when senior management seeks to compare the relative value of the outputs of different units, failing to adjust for the inherent differences that exist.[1]

However, while this conflict may be inevitable, that is not the same as saying that it must be a problem, or even destructive. Recall that each of these CI units must have the same skills and that each uses, or at least can select from, the same set of analytical tools. They each face similar issues when it comes to ascertaining the needs of their respective end users, developing data sources, and communicating findings and conclusions. These commonalities can be exploited and developed through affirmative networking within and among these separate groups.

In fact, to achieve CI's true potential, all these types of CI should be coordinated, whether that is formally or informally. Moreover, as the AP&QC CI Best Practice studies show us that coordination must be at the staff level. Coordination at the level of the manager, or even the end user is not sufficient to assure that the commonalities will overcome the natural competition, and even conflicts.

The goal of staff-level coordination is to see that each of these CI units is in a circular relationship with all the others. That is, they each feed, challenge, and reinforce all the others. The experience of the CI Best Practice firms indicates that one pivotal key to this is to advocate and support the ongoing communication of the firm's overall intelligence *needs* among the analysts and researchers to help them coordinate and integrate the firm's intelligence production. This can be accomplished through regular meetings among the various CI units' staff, supplemented by ongoing networking at all levels. There are a wide variety of topics on which theses efforts can focus, all of which will benefit, not only the CI units' staff, but also the quality of the work received by all of their end users.

Consider the following areas as useful subjects of coordination and cooperation:

- intelligence needs
- data collection
- intelligence end products

In terms of cooperating on intelligence needs, an enterprise with several units, whether or not they are officially coordinated through one central manager, CI professionals can, and should, do the following:

- Meet regularly to inform each other of past assignments, current capabilities, and current targeting policies. Thus, for example, a strategy-oriented CI team might note that it is now focusing on a small group of suppliers. Having that knowledge, those providing tactics-oriented CI to a sales force can work better because they do not have to start any new projects dealing with these suppliers from scratch. They can also share with that team bits of data they come across in their own work.

- Create a simple way to avoid having to conduct duplicative research. For example, it is not uncommon for several CI units to be given similar assignments following major internal meetings. That is, the research and development (R&D) team may call from its unit for CI that is similar to that a sales manager asks for from his or her own unit, both coming out of the same meeting dealing with a new acquisition. If they overlap, the units can then take one of several paths, including dividing the research or delegating it to one unit, to serve both groups of end users.

Data collection efforts in CI units with different orientations will tend to be different, but there are areas where coordination can be very profitable and powerful:

- Have the CI units create a way to track all outside, "off the shelf" reports that are purchased or subscribed to. Then, before buying such a document for the unit or an end user, a simple check will show whether a copy already exists in house. Using such a system even a few times can generate significant, easily documented savings to the firm. In addition, it may allow a team to use a resource that it might not be in a position to buy.
- Establish regular networking sessions, perhaps over lunch, to discuss outside contractors. The use of outside firms to conduct CI research and analysis or to provide onetime reports will vary widely from unit to unit and over time. If the CI units know that they can check on how well an outside firm performed, they can quickly eliminate firms with an unsatisfactory track record and put into consideration firms with which they are not familiar but that have performed well for others.
- In the case of overlapping assignments, CI units can divide up some of the data gathering, playing to each unit's strengths. Thus, one might focus on primary research, with telephone interviews of key individuals, while another might take the responsibility for an in-depth literature, or secondary, review. Each unit would do its own analysis and, probably, supplement the work each other has done, but this would still save time and resources in the long run.

The most difficult area to coordinate involves finished intelligence. While it is an easy, and beneficial, matter to allow all CI units to have access to one unit's intelligence intranet, some data or intelligence sharing can be very sensitive. For example, if one unit is given an assignment to profile a potential acquisition candidate, it may not be appropriate, or even possible, to share the final work with other units. However, such restrictions usually fade over time. A workable compromise might be have a CI intranet accessible by all CI unit staff, where members can list what they have done and allow other members to call, rather than post the full results.

INTERNAL AND EXTERNAL NETWORKING

The experience of the Best Practice firms indicates that one of the most valuable processes for CI units to become involved with, on an ongoing, permanent basis, is networking. By networking, we mean both internal and external networking.

Internal Networking

There are several proven benefits to internal networking, that is developing and maintaining a set of contacts on an ongoing basis.[2] They include:

- developing internal data sources
- expanding the universe of individuals who are familiar with CI
- establishing a foundation for running a defensive CI program
- aiding in the long-term development and integration of the CI program

This work should be done by every member of the CI unit because the composition of the unit will change over time. You do not want to have your internal networking run by one person who then leaves the unit for a career change. In addition, different people have different contacts within the firm so they will have different starting sets of contacts.

How do you set up such a network? Calling individuals, explaining what the new (to you) unit is doing is a good start. Also, you may want to offer to help them, even if it is done unofficially. That way, people may feel that they "owe" you a favor. Gratitude is a stronger bond than mere association. One hint is to look, in your ongoing CI research, for small items that might be of interest to someone else in the firm. Then you can e-mail or copy the item and forward it with a note to the effect that you hope that the item will be of interest. Do *not* flood people. A relevant item every few months is more than enough. Then, after a few items have been forwarded, a quick call asking if the items were of any interest is a good step. Follow that with the question, is there anyone else they know who is interested in CI? Finally, keep in touch with a contact as he or she shifts from unit to unit or is promoted.

Since future CI needs are, by definition, unknown, there is no reason not to bring individuals from *every* aspect of the firm into an internal CI network. Not only do you want to have people on whom you can call for assistance, you are also developing a cadre of individuals who can contact your unit. In essence, you have created an early warning system.

Developing Internal Data Sources. One important benefit of an internal network of contacts throughout the firm is that the CI unit can quickly get assistance in developing needed raw data. That assistance may come in the form of direct information from a sales manager, or indirectly, as from the name of a contact at a supplier that is obtained from the purchasing department.

In some situations, you may find that networking is not enough to create a cooperative relationship. In that case, offer incentives to induce critical potential data providers to cooperate with you. For example, your sales force should be make aware of the importance of current, accurate data about both customers and competitors. The sales force should be able to provide important data about loyal, long-standing customers, customers that have recently switched to competitors, new customers, and potential customers. They already have available some or all of the following, which they collect or gather on a regular basis:[3]

- win-loss reports
- customer satisfaction data
- rumors
- competitor materials.

In addition, the sales force should be able to provide at least partial data about potential new product introductions by competitors, which can be gained by listening to customers.[4]

Once you have made the sales force aware of this, you should try to give the salespeople a reason to cooperate. That reason may be recognition at headquarters and by their supervisors, it may come in the form of receiving CI they can use, or it may be financial rewards. Without an appropriate incentive, many salespeople may feel that data gathering is just taking up time they could use to make sales, so they will not cooperate.

Expand the Universe of Individuals Who Are Familiar with CI. As we indicated during the discussion on training, to be successful, a CI unit must make sure that it is known, that the purpose of CI is understood, and that individuals within the firm know who is involved with CI. While training must be a critical part of this process, it is rarely enough. That is why effective CI units also use their internal networks as a way of spreading the word about CI. Just as a few carefully chosen clips disclosing important data may help develop future potential sources of data, the CI unit should carefully use short articles or reports about CI to spread the word about its work. This type of piece is best used following a short telephone call to a potential contact. Select articles that show CI in a positive light and, if possible, find ones that mention what specific companies have done. Then you can use them as a vehicle, both to market CI and to educate individuals about your unit.

Establish a Foundation for Running a Defensive CI Program. Few CI units are involved in setting up and advancing a defensive CI program during their early years. However, it is just those first years when it is often easiest to build up an internal network of contacts to aid in this process at a later date. By the time you are ready to propose a defensive program or are called upon to establish it, you will have a number of individuals who are already sensitive to the process of CI. It is then but a small step to educate them that the kinds of competitively sensitive data they have located for you should be denied to your competitors. They thus become the first groups of individuals to help carry on such a program.[5]

Aid in the Long-Term Development and Integration of the CI Program. Over time, the CI needs of a firm will change.[6] Moreover, as Chapter 14 shows, to be successful, a CI unit must plan for the long-term. In particular, it must plan to change as the firm does. An internal network may be the most effective way to find out about forthcoming changes that can impact future CI needs (and thus, future CI careers). That is, the more the CI staff knows about its own internal environment, the better it can position itself to deliver CI that is of use to its end users.

There may even come a time when management, perhaps the very management that helped create a CI unit, may consider cutting back that effort, or even eliminating it. Frankly, that does not make a lot of sense, but we have seen it happen with respect to particular lines of business that senior management is considering selling or spinning off. The rationale there is that management seeks to cut, for a short time at least, any and all functions that do not directly contribute to the bottom line within a very short period (such as one fiscal quarter or less).

But merely because one SBU no longer wants to conduct CI, for whatever reason, that does not mean that another SBU does not want to start doing it or to expand it. By being realistic, having and utilizing an internal network means that you can, and should, be looking for a place to take a CI program if it loses its "home." In addition, the contacts made through internal networking allow CI professionals to help spread CI throughout an enterprise. Thus units that currently see no need for CI may, after regular contact with a CI unit elsewhere, begin to appreciate its potential value to their operations.

External Networking

There are several proven benefits to external networking, that is developing and maintaining a set of contacts outside the firm on an ongoing basis. They include:

- developing external data sources and leads to such sources
- improving the CI performance of the CI unit's members
- aiding in the long-term development and integration of the CI program

Develop External Data Sources and Leads to Such Sources. Just as with internal benchmarking, creating and maintaining an external network of contacts can be invaluable in conducting certain kinds of research. For example, if you have occasion to talk with a reporter for an industry publication about a story he or she wrote, you have started down the path of developing such a network. What you can do is offer to help the reporter, as long as it is appropriate, at some time in the future. Then you can both exchange the information you seek and he or she has, and any data that you have that might interest the reporter.

Now, the reporter has a source, which you can be certain will be used. You also have a contact. But do not look at this as a just a place for information about articles from that publication. View it in a broader context. Consider how this contact could be used to lead to another contact. For example, you could now call this reporter and ask "do you know anyone I could talk to about supply chain software?" Then, take that name and call, leaving the message, for example, that "Brent Williams of Industry Publications gave me you name and said you would be a good person to talk to about supply chain software. Could you call me back?" Isn't that more likely to get a return call and cooperation than a cold call?

Improve the CI Performance of the CI Unit's Members. Networking with other CI professionals can be a fast and relatively inexpensive way to learn new techniques or even to develop better skills. Here we are talking about CI professionals who are not working for competitors. While CI professionals are uniquely sensitive to the problems of defending against the competitive intelligence efforts of others, they are human, nonetheless. That means that they may fall into too close a relationship with the CI professional at a competitor firm because they "both face the same problems," forgetting that even the questions they ask or complaints they make may, inadvertently, give a competitor a glimpse of competitively sensitive issues.

For that reason, professional networking should be largely limited to dealing with CI professionals at noncompeting firms or consultancies. In that case, as long as you are willing to share your experiences and hints, they can be a powerful way to access the experiences and skills of others.

Aid in the Long-Term Development and Integration of the CI Program. External networking can provide some indirect assistance toward the development and integration of your CI program. One of its primary benefits is that it provides a source for outside CI professionals to visit your firm and explain how and why CI is successful in their firms. These "road shows" have proven, time and again, to be extraordinarily powerful tools for marketing CI internally.

NOTES

1. For more on this situation, see John J. McGonagle and Carolyn M. Vella, *Bottom Line Competitive Intelligence* (Westport, Conn.: Quorum Books, 2002).

2. For a look at some of the issues observed in building an internal CI network in the early and mid-1990s, see Neil J. Simon and Albert B. Blixit, *Navigating in a Sea of Change* (Alexandria, Va.: Society of Competitive Intelligence Professionals, 1996), Appendix C.

3. Ellen Naylor and Stephen Schulz, "Capturing CI through Your Sales Force," in Society of Competitive Intelligence Professionals, *Conference Proceedings* (Alexandria, Va.: Society of Competitive Intelligence Professionals, 1999), 117, 123.

4. For more on using the sales force in the CI process, see Stephen Schulz, "Capturing CI through Your Sales Force," *Competitive Intelligence Magazine* 5, no. 1 (January–February 2002), 20–23; Pia Helna Oremerod, "How Ericssion Turned Its Workforce into Intelligence Gatherers," *Competitive Intelligence Magazine* 5, no. 1 (January–February 2002), 27–29; and William J. West, "Switch-Pitch Drill Produces Intelligence from Sales Force" *Competitive Intelligence Magazine* 5, no. 5 (September–October 2003), 14–16.

5. For more on creating and managing such a program, see John J. McGonagle and Carolyn M. Vella, *Protecting Your Company against Competitive Intelligence* (Westport, Conn.: Quorum Books, 1999), 53–108.

6. For more on how to determining what kinds of CI a firm should develop, see McGonagle and Vella, *Bottom Line Competitive Intelligence*, 61–88.

7

Training

The experience of the Best Practice CI units shows that an ongoing training program, developed with an eye toward their particular situation, is absolutely vital to success and growth. And their experience shows that this is training which is not limited to the CI professionals; there must also be training for the end users of CI and for all other employees within the firm.

TRAINING FOR CI PROFESSIONALS

The areas in which CI professionals can benefit from training are significant. Looking back at a study of CI professionals and skills, we see that it identified the following as "teachable skills,"and thus appropriate for inclusion in training for all CI professionals:

- strategic thinking
- business terminology
- market research and presentation skills
- knowledge of primary information sources and research methods
- enhancement of: journalistic interviewing and communication skills
- analytical ability
- a familiarity with scientific methodology[1]

Again, looking at the experience of the Best Practice CI units, we find that, for the CI professional, an ongoing training process should concentrate on several key areas:

- analytical techniques
- legal and ethical issues
- communications and management

The scope of available analytical techniques is so broad that it has been suggested that CI staff actually undergo at least three separate courses in CI analysis:

- The first would be a basic introduction to analytical techniques and methodologies in CI.
- The second would cover the details of critical skills in use at the firm, such as financial analysis, as well as presentation techniques.
- The third would be offered only after completion of the first two parts. This would focus on providing CI staff with "thinking" skills, and would serve to encourage them to use new ideas in managing, providing, and using CI. [2]

Training in legal and ethical issues deals primarily with restrictions on the way in which the data to be used to generate CI is collected. This subject is deal with in Chapter 7. Training on communications management and skills is vital to assure that the message of the CI unit gets out, and continues to get out, to the appropriate end users. Since the way in which the Best Practice CI units develop requires that they continually review, refine, add to, and delete communications tools (see Chapter 12), this training should be done on a regular basis.

TRAINING FOR CI END USERS

For the end users of CI, the training process must not only be ongoing, but it should actually broaden over time. For these end users, experience shows that the key areas to be covered by such training are CI techniques and ethical and legal issues.

Here, the explicit goal is to use both these subject areas to make these end users of CI into *better* customers. Thus, the goals of this regular training are to control, and eventually eliminate, unreasonable client expectations. Such training is also a significant aid in preventing improper (i.e., unethical or even illegal), intelligence requests from these end users.

One proposal is that, at a minimum, such a course provide a basic understanding of the entire CI process as well as an "awareness of the analytical capabilities of the [CI] under their control."[3] There are several reasons why this should be an ongoing, and not just a onetime, process:

- Over time, the identity of the end users of CI will change.
- The intelligence needs of existing end users will gradually develop as they benefit from the previous work of the CI unit (see Chapter 9).
- The identity of competitors, and even the nature of competition, will change over time.
- Information sources will vanish and appear, changing the nature of the data that can be collected for analysis.
- Legal and ethical considerations governing the collection of the raw data may change.

> "[T]he more a company pays for information, the smaller the number of people who have access to it."[4]

TRAINING FOR ALL OTHER EMPLOYEES

For all other employees, the Best Practice companies offer training in CI basics as well as in the firm's CI needs. One analyst from the law enforcement community suggested that all new employees in a firm, as a part of their "initial training," be presented with an overview of the CI process and how it applies in that particular firm. The objective is to provide both an awareness of the CI process as well and how data, suitable for the firm's CI process, can be collected *and reported.* He suggested that the course should also contain a general review of the CI cycle and a basic understanding of CI analysis.[5]

The goal is to enable all employees to help in collecting CI. This is accomplished by educating employees on what CI can do—and what it cannot do. Again, as with training for the end user, this should never be a onetime effort: it should be offered on a regular basis, for similar reasons.

PURPOSES OF TRAINING

The explicit goal of all training is to make individuals providing CI more effective and efficient, make existing and potential end users of CI into better customers, control unreasonable expectations and prevent improper requests by existing end users, and attune the entire enterprise to the existence of CI efforts so that data collection efforts can become more efficient and widespread over time.

The experience of the Best Practice CI firms shows that such ongoing training also has several key implicit goals, which are intimately linked to the process of institutionalizing CI (covered in Chapter 14). They are:

- Generate and support organizationwide knowledge of, and participation in, CI.
- Link end user successes with CI activity through training connections.

In other words, in the context of CI, training is not merely training, it is also an affirmative form of marketing as well. In fact, a recent study made three specific recommendations for "marketing" competitive intelligence activity inside a firm:

- First, demonstrate the value-adding nature of CI activity, that is, show end users, management, and all employees that there is a bottom-line impact to an effective CI effort. While the importance of any CI should be intuitively obvious, experience shows that CI units are often asked to provide proof that CI is beneficial to the company. For more on that, see Chapter 16.
- Second, conduct extensive promotion efforts to create awareness of and acceptance of CI and, ultimately, assistance for current and future CI efforts.
- Third, lower the costs of participating in CI activities, that is, make sure the benefits of providing data to the CI staff exceed the cost to the individual employee helping the CI effort.

NOTES

1. Jerry Miller, "Competencies for Intelligence Professionals," *Newsletter of the Society of Competitive Intelligence Professionals*, November 1995, 1–2.

2. Raymond Ellis (Cortel Concepts), "Intelligence Analysis in the Business Sector," AIC Conferences, Competitive Intelligence Forum '94, Sydney, Australia, 1994, 6.

3. Ibid.

4. Henry T. Cochran, "Strategic Business Intelligence," *Competitive Intelligence Review* 2, no. 1 (Spring 1991), 20.

5. Ellis, "Intelligence Analysis in the Business Sector," 5.

8

Legal and Ethical Issues

OVERVIEW

CI professionals have to be very careful to avoid crossing either legal or ethical boundaries when collecting data for any intelligence program. In spite of the print media's frequent failure to see this, *there is a distinct and critical difference between competitive intelligence and industrial espionage.* Industrial espionage involves violating criminal or civil law to collect data; CI does not. For example, stealing samples at a trade show and illegally accessing (or hacking) computer files both constitute industrial espionage. In some instances, a gray area exists between industrial espionage and legitimate intelligence collection efforts; in these instances, you may face a decision about taking actions that are not illegal, but that still violate your company's policies or ethical standards or even your own.

Always remember that you should never break the law or engage in unethical practices to develop effective CI. One school of thought puts the relative availability and benefit of so-called "open source information," which is data available to everyone (and which is primarily secondary data) as follows:

- open source information: 80 percent of what is needed to make decisions.
- open proprietary: legally obtained through concentrated efforts, 5 percent more of what is needed.

- closed proprietary: information obtained through so-called gray activities, which are legal but of dubious ethical stature, as well as some that are clearly black, such as industrial espionage, 5 percent more of what is needed.
- classified: closely held, extremely valuable information, such as trade secrets, virtually all black operations, 5 percent of what is needed.[1]

In other words, more than 80 percent of all of the data you would need to develop CI on a target can be accessed without either ethical or legal violations.

WHAT LAWS REALLY IMPACT THE COLLECTION OF CI?

When we say there are legal limits on CI, what we usually mean is that there are legal limitations on the way in which data can be collected as well as on the type of data which can be collected and utilized. In some cases, as indicated later in this chapter, there are a few legal issues that can be considered to deal with how CI is actually used.

The key legal areas that may have an impact on the collection of data for use in CI are the following:

- federal and state laws dealing with trade secrets
- national laws dealing with privacy concerns
- protections of certain property rights in intellectual property
- civil laws enforcing contracts

Federal and State Laws Dealing with Trade Secrets

There are two basic legal schemes that now may indirectly impact the collection of any intelligence, one already in place when CI began to emerge and the other passed in 1996.[2] They are, respectively the Uniform Trade Secrets Act (UTSA) and the U.S. Economic Espionage Act of 1996 (EEA). They both may have an impact on the collection of data for use in developing CI for one, simple reason: they limit what those collecting any economic and competitive information can do vis-à-vis *trade secrets*.

It is critical to be aware of these laws because they apply to everyone in the U.S. marketplace and affect the way in which all must operate with respect to trade secrets. If you violate them, then you or your employer, or both, may face civil, or even criminal, liability. However, to trigger those legal protections, your competitor must be very careful in the ways in which it identifies, handles, and protects its trade secrets. It must be kept clearly in mind that, if you are not dealing with a trade secret, then these laws do not come into play.

At the state level there are two types of civil protections for trade secrets. Over forty states have already enacted laws, which are all variations of the UTSA (last revised in 1985).[3] In the remaining states, their common law (that is, judge-made law) also protects trade secrets.[4] And in these states, the common law generally utilizes the same principles set forth in the UTSA.[5] An additional level of protection is now provided by a federal *criminal* law, the EEA.[6]

State Civil Law: The Uniform Trade Secrets Act. Under state law, a business can bring a civil suit for damages that were caused by "misappropriation" of a "trade secret." Under UTSA, and similarly under the common law of states that have not adopted the UTSA, each of these concepts is carefully defined. First, under the UTSA, a trade secret is comprehensively defined. It is information of virtually any sort, including a formula, pattern compilation, program, device, method, or process that (1) derives economic value from not "being generally known to, and not being readily ascertainable by proper means by" other people or companies who could gain economic value from getting and using it *and* (2) is subject to "efforts that are reasonable under the circumstances to maintain its secrecy." It is critical to keep in mind that a trade secret must meet both these criteria to be covered by the UTSA. Thus, a firm that simply stamps every document "confidential" does not provide the documents with trade secret protection. The document must also contain something of economic value that meets the legal test described previously.

"Misappropriation" of a trade secret requires the existence of *one of two* critical steps: (1) somewhere along the line, the trade secret is acquired by someone who knows, or should know, that the trade secret was acquired by improper means; *or* (2) the person who gets the trade secret knows, or should know, that it was a trade secret and that it was acquired by accident or mistake.

That means, in short, a claim of misappropriation of a trade secret under state law arises only when *both* of two key events have happened:

1. Someone obtains, uses or discloses another person's trade secret.
2. The person against whom the claim of misappropriation is made:
   a. acquired the trade secret by improper means
   b. knew or should have known that somewhere along the line the trade secret was acquired by improper means
   c. knew or should have known that the trade secret was acquired by accident or mistake

    d. knew or should have known that somewhere along the line the trade secret was disclosed in violation of a confidentiality provision

If there is a violation of the UTSA, then the injured company or individual has a variety of options open to it, all available through legal actions that it can bring in state court.

- It can seek an injunction to stop an actual, or even a threatened, misappropriation of a trade secret. In some cases, the injunction may even allow the company or person to collect "royalties" as damages.
- An injured company or person can also seek a court order to compel someone to affirmatively protect a trade secret that has come into his or her hands.
- The company or individual can recover damages for an actual misappropriation. Those damages can cover both any actual loss caused by the misappropriation and damages for the unjust enrichment caused by the misappropriation.
- An injured company may also be able to collect exemplary damages and its attorney fees.

Federal Criminal Law: The Economic Espionage Act of 1996. The EEA is very similar, in some ways, to the UTSA.[7] However, the two key differentiations to keep in mind are that EEA is a criminal law and that it operates at the federal level. That means that violators face jail sentences and/or fines. It also means the EEA applies in every state, whether or not the state has already adopted the UTSA.

Under the EEA, a trade secret is virtually any type of information, in any form, (1) whose owner has taken "reasonable measures to keep such information secret," *and* (2) that derives independent economic value "from not being generally known to, and not being readily ascertainable through proper means by, the public." This federal criminal law then goes on to penalize the theft and unauthorized duplication of a trade secret, as well as the receipt and transfer of a trade secret.

Following the passage of the act, the U.S. Department of Justice adopted written guidelines on how it views the EEA.[8] So far, there have been only a limited number of prosecutions under the EEA.[9] The typical case involves an ex-employee or current employee stealing trade secrets. So, to date, it has not been applied in any context dealing with competitive intelligence professionals or a company's CI program.

Misappropriation of Trade Secrets. While both of these laws appear to be quite sweeping, there are several important concepts embodied in both the UTSA and the EEA that actually mean that their impact on *legitimate* competitive intelligence collection activities is negligible:

- First, the information anyone is trying to protect with either the UTSA and EEA must be specifically identifiable. It is not enough to say, "Everything here is a trade secret." To protect information, someone must first identify it.
- Second, the information involved really must *be* a trade secret. One key to determining if this is the situation is to ask the following question: Has what you are seeking to protect been the subject of reasonable efforts to keep it secret? If the answer is no, it cannot be a trade secret. For example, if it is a document and "Confidential— Trade Secret" is stamped at the bottom of each page, you can be well on the way to protecting it under UTSA and EEA. On the other hand, if the same document is included in promotional materials being given to thousands of customers, it is not a trade secret, no matter how you stamp it.
- And third, under both the EEA and UTSA, is the information you think you are protecting as a trade secret "readily ascertainable by proper means?" That concept, found in both laws, means that the *deduction or reconstruction by proper means of what may, in fact, be a trade secret is not a violation of either law*. This is because deduction or reconstruction is not the same as misappropriation, and the act of misappropriation is also needed to trigger legal protections.[10]

All this means that *trade secret protection can be lost through disclosures, whether accidental or purposeful*, made in any of the following common contexts:

- Information is revealed in published literature, such as trade journal articles or interviews.
- Scholarly articles, containing information sought to be protected, are published by in-house scientists.
- Key data is disseminated to customers in the form of technical bulletins.
- A technical paper containing confidential information is delivered to a trade and professional group.
- Publication of "secret" matter occurs because it is readable in the background of photographs in an annual report.
- Performance data is partially revealed in advertising claims.
- Disclosures of company secrets are made by the company through course instructions to customers.
- Labels on products disclose presumed secret ingredients as well as the relative quantities of ingredients.

- Advertisements in newspapers and trade papers contain significant, previously undisclosed, product details.
- Important technical disclosures are made in the printed operating instructions provided to customers.
- Presumably secret products are displayed at a trade show, where they can be examined by attendees.

Remember that whenever anyone obtains small pieces of intelligence, each of which has been found properly, and then their analysts eventually build a picture of the target's critical intentions, including a trade secret (which it wants to keep secret), they have *not* broken any law. They have just engaged in good, solid CI collection and analysis. For example, the Japan External Trade Organization (JETRO) is regarded by federal intelligence agencies as "the most sophisticated commercial-intelligence-gathering body operated by a foreign government on US soil." However, the same sources concede that "JETRO . . . is almost certainly complying with American law."[11]

National Laws Dealing with Privacy Concerns

The next class of laws that may have an impact on CI data collection are national laws which deal with personal privacy issues. The two major examples of these are the U.S. Fair Credit Reporting Act and the European Community's Directive on Personal Data.

U.S. Fair Credit Reporting Act. First, keep in mind that the federal Fair Credit Reporting Act (FCRA)[12] deals, first and foremost, with reports collected, maintained, sold by, used by consumer reporting agencies, (CRAs). A CRA is very broadly defined as

> any person which, for monetary fees, dues, or on a cooperative nonprofit basis, regularly engages in whole or in part in the practice of assembling or evaluating consumer credit information or other information on consumers for the purpose of furnishing consumer reports to third parties, and which uses any means or facility of interstate commerce for the purpose of preparing or furnishing consumer reports.[13]

This raises the next question: What is a consumer report? A consumer report under this law is more than what individuals commonly refer to as a credit report. It is also broadly defined as

> any written, oral, or other communication of any information by a consumer reporting agency bearing on a consumer's credit worthiness, credit standing, credit capacity, character, general reputation, personal characteristics, or mode of living which is used or expected to be used or collected

in whole or in part for the purpose of serving as a factor in establishing the consumer's eligibility for

(A) credit or insurance to be used primarily for personal, family, or household purposes;

(B) employment purposes; or

(C) any other purpose authorized under section 604.[14]

Over the past few years, the FCRA has been expanded to cover new types of activities, in particular the *investigative consumer report*. The investigative consumer report is defined as

a consumer report or portion thereof in which information on a consumer's character, general reputation, personal characteristics, or mode of living is obtained through personal interviews with neighbors, friends, or associates of the consumer reported on or with others with whom he is acquainted or who may have knowledge concerning any such items of information.[15]

Thus, under the FCRA, an investigative consumer report is just another type of consumer report.

The FCRA requires that an employer must give to an employee (or a potential employee) a specific notice if an investigative consumer report is used as the basis for certain employment-related decisions. The FTC itself suggests how this process is intended to work. It tells employers the following:

Before you can get a consumer report for employment purposes, you must notify the individual in *writing* — in a document consisting solely of this notice — that a report may be used. You also must get the person's *written authorization* before you ask a CRA for the report. . . .

If you rely on a consumer report for an "adverse action"—denying a job application, reassigning or terminating an employee, or denying a promotion—be aware that:

Step 1: Before you take the adverse action, you must give the individual a *pre-adverse action disclosure* that includes a copy of the individual's consumer report and a copy of "A Summary of Your Rights Under the Fair Credit Reporting Act"—a document prescribed by the Federal Trade Commission. The CRA that furnishes the individual's report will give you the summary of consumer rights.

Step 2: After you've taken an adverse action, you must give the individual notice — orally, in writing, or electronically — that the action has been taken in an *adverse action notice*. It must include:

• the name, address, and phone number of the CRA that supplied the report;

- a statement that the CRA that supplied the report did not make the decision to take the adverse action and cannot give specific reasons for it; and
- a notice of the individual's right to dispute the accuracy or completeness of any information the agency furnished, and his or her right to an additional free consumer report from the agency upon request within 60 days. . . .

Before giving you an individual's consumer report, the CRA will require you to certify that you are in compliance with the FCRA and that you will not misuse any information in the report in violation of federal or state equal employment opportunity laws or regulations.[16]

Since CI professionals are not involved in transactions where credit is being offered or where employment decisions are being made, the only possible application might be in situations when CI is being used to develop profiles on top executives at a key competitor. However, a close reading of the FCRA shows that it does not apply in any way in that situation, either. There are at least two reasons:

- There are no employment decisions involved. This is a competitor, not even an acquisition partner.
- The CI firm is not acting as a CRA or using a consumer report from a CRA

There are, however, at least three situations where the FCRA could be applied to CI-like transactions.

The first situation is when data collection efforts are purposefully taken very close to the defined areas of coverage of the FCRA. For example, assume that a CI professional develops a profile on a company for a client and the report includes information from a consumer report or investigative consumer report, properly obtained from a CRA. Then, assume that this profile is, in turn used, at some later time, as a part of an adverse employment decision, which may not be directly covered by the FCRA. How can that happen? For example, suppose a CI firm is hired to profile the chief financial officer (CFO) of a target company. The CI firm legally acquires an investigative consumer report on the CFO. The client at a later time takes over the targeted company and then fires the CFO, based in part on the firm's report, which includes information from a CRA. Unless all the FCRA's notice provisions have been complied with, there are real problems in this situation. However, it seems, but is not clear, that all of this may not technically violate the FCRA because the employee impacted was not working for the client firm (or seeking to work for the client firm) at the time the profile was generated, *and* that the CI firm was unaware of its ultimate use when the profile was generated.

The second is when a CI firm actually places itself under the law. In other words, a CI firm itself may *become* a CRA by its own actions over time. How might that happen? One legal analysis argues it happens this way:

> For example, if an employee in an employer's personnel department calls former employers of job applicants to check on the applicants' work histories and calls various public agencies or courts to check on the applicants' licenses and criminal histories, the FCRA does not apply to the employer's activities. *However, if an employer hires an outside business to similarly investigate and report on job applicants or employees, the FCRA regulates the information gathering and reporting activities of both the employer and the outside business.*[17]

The third situation is that in which a CI professional actually violates the FCRA. Assume here that a CI professional develops a profile for a client, including an internal corporate end user, which includes information from a consumer report or investigative consumer report. And further assume that this was *improperly* obtained from a CRA. A client who is unaware of the source of the report, then acts upon it, firing an employee from a newly acquired firm. That could trigger the entire scope of the FCRA.

The lesson to be taken from a review of the FCRA is that, as with the UTSA and EEA, CI professionals must understand that there are numerous laws that *might* impact them indirectly. However, before you erroneously assume that they *do* directly impact you, it is best to look closely at them rather than rely on casual comments in the press for such guidance.

European Directive on Protection of Personal Data. It is sometimes said that the 1995 European Directive on Protection of Personal Data[18] is the equivalent of the U.S. FCRA. This is not correct, however. First, what CI professionals should be concerned with is not, precisely, the 1995 directive. The Directive is just that, a directive to members of the European Union (EU), telling them to adopt, or to amend, national legislation to guarantee individuals certain rights to protect their privacy and to control the contents of electronic databases that contain personal information.

Second, even though the Directive gave member countries until 1998 to comply, only a few countries have complied completely. The most important one is the United Kingdom which put into place its own Data Protection Act (DPA) implementing the Directive. The Directive itself is a complex document, aimed at bringing together existing national laws and also setting a new, higher, standard. It specifically provides that "This Directive shall apply to the processing of personal data wholly or partly by automatic means, and to the processing otherwise than by automatic means of personal data which form part of a filing system or are intended to form part of a filing system."[19] And the Directive itself defines these key terms:

> (a) "personal data" shall mean any information relating to an identified or identifiable natural person ("data subject"); an identifiable person is one who can be identified, directly or indirectly, in particular by reference to an identification number or to one or more factors specific to his physical, physiological, mental, economic, cultural or social identity;
>
> (b) "processing of personal data"("processing") shall mean any operation or set of operations which is performed upon personal data, whether or not by automatic means, such as collection, recording, organization, storage, adaptation or alteration, retrieval, consultation, use, disclosure by transmission, dissemination or otherwise making available, alignment or combination, blocking, erasure or destruction;
>
> (c) "personal data filing system" ("filing system") shall mean any structured set of personal data which are accessible according to specific criteria, whether centralized, decentralized or dispersed on a functional or geographical basis[20]

Thus, akin to the case in the United States, the triggering event is the operation and maintenance of an ongoing computer (or structured manual) system for collecting and retrieving personal data.[21] As the EU itself characterized it:

> To prevent abuses of personal data and ensure that data subjects are informed of the existence of processing operations, the Directive lays down common rules, to be observed by those who collect, hold or transmit personal data as part of their economic or administrative activities or in the course of the activities of their association. In particular, there is an obligation to collect data only for specified, explicit and legitimate purposes, and to be held only if it is relevant, accurate and up-to-date. . . .

Under the Directive, data subjects are granted a number of important rights including the right of access to that data, the right to know where the data originated (if such information is available), the right to have inaccurate data rectified, a right of recourse in the event of unlawful processing and the right to withhold permission to use their data in certain circumstances (for example, individuals will have the right to opt-out free of charge from being sent direct marketing material, without providing any specific reason).[22]

In general, the focus of the Directive is not on consumer versus personal information, but rather on how and where the data is stored. That is, a triggering event for imposition of the requirements of the Directive is the maintenance of an ongoing computer system (or some other structured system) for collecting and retrieving personal data. While the impact of the Directive and of implementing national legislation is not completely clear, its real impact will probably emerge from the collection/retransmission constraints. That is, to get such data out of the European Community, those sending and receiving it must provide similar protections of personal privacy.

To date, there have been no indications that the Directive and implementing legislation have had any significant impact on the collection of data for CI, at least no more of an impact that the FCRA does. However, on recognizing that the Directive and implementing legislation can have an impact on U.S. firms doing business in Europe, the U.S. Department of Commerce, in consultation with the European Union, developed what is now called a "safe harbor" framework. The framework, which was approved by the EU in 2000, is a way for U.S. companies to avoid experiencing interruptions in their business dealings with the EU or facing prosecution by European authorities under European privacy laws. "Certifying to the safe harbor will assure that EU organizations know that your company provides 'adequate' privacy protection, as defined by the Directive."[23]

To the CI professional conducting legitimate CI operations, there appears to be no need to become involved with a safe harbor certification. However, CI professionals should find out whether their own employer has entered into a safe harbor framework. They should then review that commitment to see if it might, indirectly, impact a U.S.-based CI unit's relationship with its European counterparts in the same firm, as well as with other firms providing CI for it in Europe.

Protections of Certain Property Rights in Intellectual Property

Classic intellectual property programs involve the careful use by businesses of the varied legal protections provided by the patent, trademark, copyright, and associated laws. While the legal protection provided by these laws can be formidable, these legal regimes all have one requirement in common: the materials, ideas, concepts, inventions, designs, or other commodities being protected must all necessarily be disclosed to the public, including to *competitors*, in order to become protected by these laws:

- In the arena of patent law, protection is provided based on filings with the U.S. government. The degree of protection is predicated on what is filed. To put it in an overly simplistic manner, if you do not file it (where it can eventually be reviewed by the public), you cannot protect it. In addition, patent protection itself eventually terminates after a period of time.
- In the arenas of trademarks, service marks, copyrights, and the like, your firm must openly claim a right to use the protected works, designs, and so on. This is accomplished *both* by using them and by marking them with distinctive marks, such as ™, ©, ®, or the equivalent in words. In addition, there may be special filing requirements, again on the public record. These actions then establish your claims to legal protection. However, the entire process occurs in public, not in private.

Thus, it can be seen that these legal regimes do not impede CI data collection efforts. In fact, the use of these protections is actually antithetical to protecting data from CI activities because they all mandate some degree of public disclosure to secure legal protections.

Civil Laws Enforcing Contracts

Confidential materials and information are not the same as trade secrets. While all trade secrets are to be kept in confidence, not all confidential materials are trade secrets. *Confidential* is a much wider concept. If a document is marketed as "confidential," an employee is expected to handle it carefully and to respect that marking. However, if an employee does not know that a particular bit of information is confidential and has not been told that it is confidential, he or she may not be under a legal obligation to keep it a secret. Because of this, employment, consulting, and independent contractor agreements often provide that those signing agree not to reveal or to use any of the business's trade secrets or confidential information.

Contract restrictions dealing with confidential information are growing in popularity for several reasons. Among them are the fact that more businesses are sensitive to the importance of protecting themselves against the leak of confidential information to competitors and that these agreements have historically been relatively easy to enforce.

Classic legal protections for sensitive corporate information usually have been found in the areas of nondisclosure agreements. The goal of the agreements is to create a legal obligation on the part of the employee, even after he or she leaves an employer, to protect the employer's competitive position by protecting certain classes of confidential information from disclosure to competitors. In that way, if a third party, such as a competitor, obtains competitively sensitive data by inducing someone to violate a confidentiality obligation, that party risks a lawsuit for inducing a breach of that obligation. That possibility exists whether the obligation of confidentiality is memorialized in a contract or derived from a common law obligation that the person making the disclosure had to the owner of the confidential information.

However, such agreements do not provide perfect protection. For example, there is a critical distinction between two different situations:

- The first involves "inducing," that is encouraging, or even forcing, someone to breach a confidentiality obligation, which your competitor knows will be breached by the disclosure of the information it is seeking.
- The second occurs when a competitor asks your former employee for information that the former knows the latter has. However, in this case the competitor does not know whether a written confidentiality obligation is in place, or, even if there is an agreement, whether that agreement covers the information it is seeking.

The first situation raises the legal issues described above. The second situation may actually be legally and even ethically fine, *but only so long as* the competitor did not have any reason to know that the information it was seeking was subject to a confidentiality obligation.

There are additional problems with these contract clauses. For example, what is "confidential" or even a trade secret is a very important issue when using these clauses. Courts have ruled that a company cannot sue former employees to stop them from using trade secrets if these were not actually treated as trade secrets by the company seeking to enforce the clause. By analogy, if a company has not treated information as confidential, then it could be precluded from suing an employee for failing to respect an agreement to keep that same information confidential.

Some companies have tried to get around these limitations by asking employees, contractors, and consultants to sign an agreement to bar the "use of any and all information gained" during employment or while a person is under contract. Such broad clauses are usually seen by courts asked to enforce them as unreasonable. For that reason, the courts may not enforce them; to do so could forbid the disclosure of information that is actually common, public knowledge.

Thus we can see that legal, particularly contractual, controls over confidential information are also limited in what they can protect and what they can prevent. While seeking to prevent release by having an employee agree to protect the information, they do have an active aspect. That is that their real value ultimately lies in the ability of the company to go to court to prevent the disclosure or to collect financial damages for the violation of these agreements in a civil lawsuit.

RECORDS RETENTION

Most firms already have a records retention policy. As a manager of a CI unit, you should review it to make sure that your operations conform to those requirements. Typically, the requirements that might apply to the operations of a CI unit are ones such as these:[24]

ITEMS	PERIOD
Correspondence (general)	3
Development Studies	P
Presentations & Proposals	P
Surveys	P
Internal Reports (miscellaneous)	3
Employee Activities, Presentations	P
Market Research and Analysis	P
Market Surveys	5

Key:
"3"—Retain for 3 years
"5"—Retain for 5 years
"P"—Retain Permanently

In addition, when dealing with an outside consultant or contractor, determine, before the beginning of the process, the following:

- Does the consultant keep a copy of the report?
- Is the consultant required to dispose of or to keep notes of interviews and research?
- Is the consultant required to turn over notes and working papers to you, the client?

DO ANY LAWS IMPACT THE USE OF CI?

Most of the concerns expressed about legal limitations on CI actually apply only to the manner in which the CI is collected. However, there are two situations in which there may be some legal issues arising from the way in which CI is used by the client or end user: U.S. anti-trust laws and U.S. securities laws.

U.S. Anti-trust laws

There has been some concern expressed by corporate legal departments that are unfamiliar with CI and its operations that it might somehow violate the restrictions imposed on businesses by the U.S. anti-trust laws. The underlying concern seems to be that gathering information on competitors, particularly data on prices and pricing, is somehow impacted by these laws.

The U.S. anti-trust laws do not apply to the collection of data for CI. Actually, they apply to the purposes for which you use data. If your firm collects data on a competitor's pricing philosophy or cost structure with the aim of fixing prices or dividing up the market in cooperation with that competitor, then those using that CI may have violated the U.S. anti-trust laws. Oh the other hand, if you are collecting the same data with the intent to use it to compete more effectively and aggressively, there should be no anti-trust problem.

U.S. Securities Laws

U.S. laws governing the trading of securities have two aspects of differing importance to CI professionals:

- The first is the requirement that public companies must file a variety of reports with the U.S. Securities and Exchange Commission (SEC) detailing financial and operating information. That is designed to provide those buying and selling the stock with key information so that they can make an informed decision. However, it also means that filing with the SEC can be very valuable to competitors as well.
- The second is the related requirement often called the *ban on insider trading*. It is this requirement that has confused some CI professionals.

The concern that some CI professionals, usually consultants, have had is that U.S. law means that they cannot trade the stock of a public company based on information they have collected on a target. Actually, in practice, the requirement is more properly restated to provide that an employee cannot trade, or give a tip to others to trade, securities on the basis of material inside information if that information is obtained in the course of employment. For the CI professional profiling a competitor, this has no application for two reasons:

1. The CI professional is not an insider vis-à-vis the target.
2. The CI developed by the CI professional is, almost by definition, not "inside" information.

WHAT ARE THE MAJOR ETHICAL ISSUES IN
CI DATA COLLECTION?

There are several different ethical issues involved in dealing with the collection of data for CI, which can be dealt with in any firm's ethical policies. They can be categorized as follows:

- The use of undue influence: Undue influence in data collection can entail actions ranging from bribery to pressuring an interviewee for a job with your firm.
- The use of deception: Deception involves, for example, affirmatively misleading an interviewee as to your identity, such as in the classic ethical violation, posing as a "student doing a paper."
- The use of covert practices: Covert practices are those such as surveillance of a factory from an airplane in the factory's airspace. That should be distinguished from the purchase of commercial satellite photos of the same site, which is legal and ethical, as the owner of the site has no expectation of privacy given the existence of such photographs.
- The handling of unsolicited data: The ways in which any unsolicited data should be handled should be made very clear. An employee who comes into accidental possession of a document marked "trade secret," for example, should know *exactly* what to do, when and how to do it, and what not to do.

From a personal point of view, the best standard to apply to your own conduct is a variation of the simple suggestion, "Avoid doing anything you cannot explain." That means you should never permit yourself or your associates or staff to be influenced by what any of you may think your competitors are doing, or might do, with respect to collecting data on your firm. In fact, one study suggests that people involved in collecting intelligence generally view their competitors very negatively. They believe their competitors will go to much greater lengths and exhibit less ethical behaviors to collect intelligence than they or their own employer would.[25]

DRAFTING AND MANAGING LEGAL AND
ETHICAL POLICIES

The Need for Written Policies

Headlines continue to point to the need to have formal policies governing the operation of a CI unit, as well as of consultants and contractors working for that unit.[26] Of course, CI professionals have to be very careful to avoid crossing either legal *or* ethical boundaries when collecting data for any intelligence program. In fact, it is not necessary to be illegal or unethical to conduct effective CI. As was noted, 80 percent (or more) of what a company needs to know about its competitors is easily available through legal, ethical means. Therefore, any "perceived" need for information that cannot be obtained by legal, ethical means should be very small. When weighed against the potential for damaging business relationships and reputations, the potential benefits of getting such information can *never* outweigh the potential harm.

In spite of the media's frequent failure to accept this, *there is a distinct and critical difference between competitive intelligence and what we commonly call industrial espionage.* Industrial espionage involves violating either criminal or civil laws to collect data. For example, stealing samples from a locked conference room at a trade show constitutes industrial espionage under this standard. On the other hand, accepting samples freely handed out to the general public at the trade show is perfectly legitimate.

In some instances, a gray area may exist between industrial espionage and legitimate intelligence collection efforts. In these instances, we are dealing with taking actions that are not strictly illegal, but that still could violate a reasonable corporate conduct policy or ethical standards. Taking our example one step further, what do you think of someone soliciting samples at a trade show while using a badge that (falsely) labels them as a potential distributor? Does it make a difference if the samples are being given to everyone, anyway? Without a clear directive as to what is in the "gray zone" of unethical behavior, it is all too easy to slide right through into the "black zone" of illegal activity.[27]

There are *positive* benefits to having an ethical policy that applies to how the CI unit operates, whether or not it deals directly with CI by name. Here are a few:

- By developing a statement of ethical standards to complement legal ones, management sends a message to employees that the company expects more from them than the bare minimum of "Don't break the law."
- There is a direct link between the presence of a corporate ethics/business conduct policy and awareness of the limits of legal and ethical behavior on the part of CI practitioners.[28] And while research has shown a direct relationship between a CI professional's *perception* of legal constraints and the success of the CI function, the relationship is not what some CI professionals would have expected. Executives give a *higher* rating to the performance of CI functions, as well as the results to their firm, when the CI professional's perception of legal constraints was higher![29]

- One of the lessons that emerged from the SCIP Team Excellence Awards process during its 1999–2000 test period dealt with efforts to train employees on what such policies mean in the context of CI.
- This training also alerts both legal personnel and corporate CI personnel to the real issues involved in conducting CI, before they can cause problems.
- Looking at the "open source" hierarchy (discussed earlier in this chapter), it is interesting to note the relative "costs" associated with each type of data. If we take open source information (representing 80 percent of the information available on a target) as a baseline of 100 percent, then open proprietary information, which adds 5 percent, does so at a cost equal to 50 percent of what was already spent on open source information. "Closed proprietary," which could also be defined as information obtained through activities of dubious ethical stature as well as some that cross the line, could provide 5 percent, but at a cost equal to what was spent on open source information. The final category, "classified," which is acquired almost exclusively through illegal operations, represents the last 10 percent of the information available on a target but typically costs 2.5 times what was spent on open source information.[30] Therefore, behavior that is unethical (or worse) is not only not proper, it is not even cost-effective.
- Any ethical statement, whether or not it is based on the SCIP Code,[31] also provides an external measuring stick. That is, if your firm is hiring a CI consultant, it should ask that the contractor be bound by the client's own standards. In addition, having your own set of written standard permits you to ask the potential contractor to discuss its own standards with you and compare the fit, or lack of fit, with your own.

In other words, CI involves the legal *and* ethical collection of data. It is more than a practice that is merely "not illegal." And operating both legally and ethically is not only the moral way to conduct business, it is also good business.

Drafting Written Policies

Regardless of content or context, there are several things to keep in mind when drafting written policies governing CI operations:

- They should be drafted in cooperation with the legal department.
- They should be simple and direct.
- They should provide guidance, and not merely tell people to contact someone.
- They should reflect your unique situation and competitive environment.

Draft in cooperation with the Legal Department. As noted, there are no significant legal issues surrounding the normal conduct of CI for a business. In spite of that, those preparing these policies should make sure that the members of the CI unit work closely with members of a legal team in drafting them.

There are several reasons for this. First, the process of drafting the policies and reviewing applicable laws helps overcome any latent prejudice within a legal team that CI is synonymous with, or at least dangerously close to, industrial espionage. Second, by being involved in drafting, the members of the legal team become more educated on how CI actually functions. This better prepares them to respond quickly to any questions or concerns raised by the CI staff once the policies are in place. Third, it can help bring any legal team into the CI unit's internal networking. This can be strengthened by having the legal department become involved in training both CI staff and other employees on the real legal and ethical issues involved with CI.

Simple and Direct. To be most useful, the policy must be understandable. Telling employees that they cannot "misappropriate a trade secret" may be easy to draft, but provides very little guidance. Telling employees that they are "not permitted to try to get trade secrets" and that "if a trade secret comes into your possession, no matter how that happens," they must take specified actions is much more useful.

Provide positive guidance. A corollary to the previous statement is that a policy should not only tell people what not to do, it should also tell them what to do. While there are times when you want a policy to say everyone should "stop and contact" a specified person, always keep in mind that you should be educating employees as to the proper type of conduct they should take, without guidance, in the vast majority of foreseeable cases. If you tell employees to contact someone rather than giving them positive guidance, then do not be surprised if the specified contacts are made again and again.

Reflect your unique situation and competitive environment. Finally, try to develop policies that reflect your own, unique corporate culture and competitive environment. In fact, going through that very process will serve to educate both the CI staff and the legal team on the real problems that will be faced. That, in turn, will improve both the final product and the level of future compliance.

Should You Just Adopt the SCIP Code of Ethics?

The Code of Ethics adopted by the Society of Competitive Intelligence Professionals (SCIP) applies, on a voluntary basis only, to members of SCIP.[32] It is currently as follows:

SCIP Code of Ethics for CI Professionals

- To continually strive to increase the recognition and respect of the profession.
- To comply with all applicable laws, domestic and international.
- To accurately disclose all relevant information, including one's identity and organization, prior to all interviews.
- To fully respect all requests for confidentiality of information.
- To avoid conflicts of interest in fulfilling one's duties.
- To provide honest and realistic recommendations and conclusions in the execution of one's duties.
- To promote this code of ethics within one's company, with third-party contractors and within the entire profession.
- To faithfully adhere to and abide by one's company policies, objectives, and guidelines.

Given the existence of this statement, a number of companies have either adopted it just as written or referred to it in their own written polices. That means they have incorporated it by reference. While this provides a document, it is not enough, for several reasons:

- The very process of adopting and developing a written policy is an educational process.
- Using the SCIP Code produces a circular problem as the code refers to your firm's own policies, even if you have adopted it in place of your own.
- If you have incorporated the code by reference, you are placing changes in your own code in the hands of others.

In addition, the SCIP Code is not as well drafted as it might be. We will deal with just one part, the section dealing with a request for confidentiality. The SCIP Code of Ethics says, in part, that SCIP members agree "To fully respect all requests for confidentiality of information." While that sounds very simple, in the real world it is not so simple.

First, look at the relationship with a client itself and ask what *fully respect* means. Virtually all companies hiring a CI consultant and virtually all CI consultants use some form of confidentiality agreement, often called a nondisclosure agreement (NDA), with respect to a CI assignment. There are firms that work for many sides in the same industry, over time. Just how long between these retentions is enough? The code does not deal with that. One suggestion might be that six months would be appropriate in the case of head-to-head competitors.

What about firms whose primary thrust is other than CI, for example, the global management consulting firms? Many of these firms have, historically, been able to deal with this issue of handling clients who are competitors (or at least in the same industry) by the use of the so-called Chinese wall. That is, they created separate teams that are not "contaminated" with information gained in confidence (or otherwise) from a prior retention.

- From the point of view of expertise, one can wonder how a firm could claim that the wall was effective, yet "sell" that same expertise to other clients. Now, that may actually be a serious issue rather than merely one of passing curiosity.
- What about some of these same firms that now boast that they are using knowledge management (KM) techniques to be able to retain and re-access every "learning" from every participant in every past retention? What does *that* do to the previous requests for confidentiality? If the KM techniques are that good, will they not destroy the Chinese Wall, and with it "full compliance" with a confidentiality request. If they are not that good, then the firms are not being honest. Neither possibility is a comfortable thought.

Take a second look at the standard on confidentiality and note what is missing: *There is no limitation on the source of the request or on the nature of it.* As written then, this admonition certainly is intended to apply to requests from clients (as described previously) and, obviously, to requests from interviewees that their comments be "kept in confidence." But does it apply elsewhere, that is, are there other requests a CI staff member might receive? If so, from whom else might they come? And just what is a "request"?

Samples of Written Policies

Over the past ten years, we have seen a gradual, steady increase in the number of business firms that have adopted policies designed to directly deal with CI. Most of these simply operate to caution employees against violating what are believed to be legal constraints, such as the EEA or UTSA, and against inducing others to violate confidentiality agreements they may have signed with their own employers. In essence they warn employees not to violate criminal or civil laws. Others simply paralleled the SCIP code of ethics (quoted ealier), seeking to put something in writing while struggling with what, if anything else, they wish to say about CI.

A number of firms have in place policies aimed at a wide variety of practices not intending to impact CI, but which may indirectly impact CI activities. Such policies may, for example, preclude any direct contact with competitors. Typically these policies reflect past or present anti-trust concerns. However, they may also serve to limit how a CI program operates. For that reason, individuals drafting a CI policy should review any other company policies that already impact the collection of CI and try to deal with these unintended consequences.

Unfortunately, many firms with well-developed CI policies have declined to release copies of their ethical or legal policies for analysis in the open literature.[33] In some cases, these documents were prepared by another department, typically a legal staff, so CI managers may lack authority to release them. In other cases, CI managers have said, off the record, that their legal departments are concerned about potential liability issues should these documents be released with their names attached.

In spite of that, we have gathered a few typical examples of real policy statements actually in use. The following show a variety of disparate approaches.

- The first is a general statement by a major corporation, dealing with the overall ethical situation posed by CI.
- The second, reflecting the position of a CI research firm, itemizes a series of behavioral standards.
- The third is actually a draft statement by a major corporation designed to cover employees, CI consultants, and outside contractors.
- The fourth outlines a corporation's official view of CI in a presentation format.
- The fifth is a comprehensive approach to the issue from an employee manual.
- The sixth, consisting only of a brief warning, is from the only non-U.S. firm represented.
- The seventh is one used by a society of information professionals.

Following each of these extracts are comments about the positive and negative points of each. To avoid distractions, we have deleted any references to the names of the firms, but the source of each document can be found in the footnotes.

In the course of business, it is not unusual to acquire information about many other organizations, including competitors. Doing so is a normal business activity and is not unethical in itself. In fact, [the company] quite properly gathers this kind of information for such purposes as . . . evaluating suppliers. The company also collects information on competitors from a variety of legitimate sources to evaluate the relative merits of its own products, [etc.] This activity is proper and necessary in a competitive system.

There are, however, limits to the ways that information should be acquired and used, especially information about competitors. No company should use improper means to acquire a competitor?s trade secrets or other confidential information. Illegal practices such as trespassing, [etc.,] are obviously wrong; so is attempting to acquire a competitor's confidential information by hiring the competitor's employees. Improper solicitation of confidential data from a competitor's employees or from [our] customers is wrong. [The company] will not tolerate any form of questionable intelligence gathering.[34]

This statement sets a high moral tone, but it fails to provide any guidance except on clear violations of the law. It also treats CI as if it were, not a positive process, but an afterthought. Moreover, its tone separates the company from its employees.

Competitive intelligence involves the legal and ethical collection and development of data on competition, competitors, and the market environment. It then transforms, by analysis, that data into information. In its competitive intelligence research and analysis assignments, [consultant]:

Collects and disseminates data in full compliance with applicable local and national laws. Specifically, its assignments are always carried out in full compliance with both the Uniform Trade Secrets Act and the U.S. Economic Espionage Act of 1996.

Accurately discloses all relevant information, including the caller's identity and organization, prior to all data collection interviews.

Respects all requests for the confidential handling of information provided to [the consultant] during data collection.

Supplies honest and realistic evaluations of what data and analysis can and cannot be developed for a client before beginning an assignment.

Provides professional, honest and realistic analyses, based on the available data, clearly delineating the difference between fact and opinion, and between what can be confirmed and what cannot be confirmed.

Returns all internal materials provided by a client with respect to an assignment at the conclusion of the assignment. [The consultant] retains no copies of such materials.

Never makes copies of any client materials marked as "confidential" or the equivalent.

Does not disclose to any person, firm or corporation, the identity of any client or any confidential information regarding any client, an assignment, or the business of any client received or developed in connection with an assignment without the client's consent. . . .

Avoids all direct conflicts of interest.

Never employs questionable data collection activities. . . .

Does not engage in undisclosed subcontracting. . . . If a client does authorize a subcontract, [the consultant] requires the subcontractor to abide by these guidelines.

Complies with all applicable client policies and guidelines dealing with the collection of data for competitive intelligence. . . .[35]

This statement is clearly based, in part, on the SCIP Code. Some CI practitioners have properly noted that the SCIP Code cannot be applied to cases where firms have been hired to test corporate security, by posing as potential hackers or otherwise misleading others about their identities. This statement resolves that problem by noting that it applies to data collection. It also takes a positive position with respect to CI as a business process. In terms of content, the statement deals with ethical issues related to the handling of client materials and subcontracting, in addition to ethical issues dealing with CI data gathering. While these are clearly useful for a consultant to discuss, covering these topics, somewhere in some document, should be considered by the firms hiring such consultants as well.

Adhere faithfully to and abide by [Company] policies, objectives, and guidelines. Become familiar with the [Company] policies and guidelines.

Comply with all applicable laws, including laws governing antitrust (unlawful activities in concert with competitors).

Respect requests for confidentiality of individuals and information.

Never misrepresent yourself. (No students doing term papers).

If someone speaks too quickly, politely ask them to slow down. Don't record interviews or conversations. It is unnecessary, and can make people very uncomfortable.

Never *swap* price information with anybody, and avoid situations that could be misinterpreted as involving price information.

Be positive, don't mislead anyone deliberately; be clear and specific enough so that you don't confuse someone, and don't *swap* misinformation.

Be straight forward with your contacts, the information must be given freely. No sending or swapping products or promotional items to a source, and do not accept such items from any contacts. Avoid all chances of leaving the impression of a bribe.

Don't try to pull trade secrets from competitors (or attempt to gain them by hiring competitor's employees away).

Never pump anyone for information that may jeopardize that person's immediate livelihood, or their reputation.[36]

These statements appear to have been derived, at least initially, from the SCIP Code. It is, however, presented in a much more approachable language and deals with additional areas, such as swapping information, not dealt with at all in the SCIP Code. In some cases, but not all, it provides very clear boundaries for what is and is not permitted. However, it does not provide employees with an internal contact point for ethical and legal questions.

Ethics
- Do not break the law
- Do not misrepresent yourself
- Do not lie
- Never steal a secret
- Understand the Economic Espionage Act
- Develop a solid working relationship with your legal staff
- If it feels wrong, it probably is[37]

While this statement of what is expected as ethical behavior seems clear at first, in fact it avoids dealing with any real issues. For example, what does it mean to "misrepresent" yourself? Does that mean you must give an interviewee the name of your firm, your client's firm, the purpose of the call, and a warning that the information will go to a competitor? In addition, it blurs the distinction between ethical and legal obligations. If this is used in training, each of these bullet points should be the subject of detailed discussion and guidance, preferably written.

Competitive Intelligence
Competitive information is a valuable tool that allows us to understand and manage our markets, products and services so we can better meet our customers' needs. However, we must gather and use that information properly.

It is important that we comply with the law in acquiring information, which prohibits theft, blackmail, wiretapping, electronic eavesdropping, bribery, improper inducement, receiving stolen property, threats, and other improper methods.

It is important that we acquire information ethically. We must not misrepresent who we are or who we work for.

We will also respect the confidentiality of our competitors' and suppliers' information. We will not use information another company has marked "proprietary" or "confidential", regardless of how it was obtained, unless the owner gives us the material for a specific purpose or the material has become public information. We should try to make sure that a nondisclosure agreement has been signed by both parties before disclosing or receiving any proprietary information.

Any information we suspect has been obtained improperly or any non-public information contained in a competitor's bid to any government agency should not be used. (See the section on Trading on Inside Information for additional details.)

> *Any material we have reason to think may violate these standards or that may give the appearance of impropriety should be discussed with and turned over to the Legal Department or the Office of Ethics and Compliance.*

A competitor's employees can't be used as improper sources of non-public information, either. New [company] employees should not divulge proprietary information about their former employers, and we shouldn't ask them to.

> *Proprietary information about customers, suppliers, or partners shouldn't be used for inappropriate purposes by the . . . company that received the information. Nor should the information be inappropriately provided to other companies. Make sure consultants and outside contractors are aware of and follow these guidelines. If you have questions about whether the information is proprietary, talk to your supervisor, the Legal Department, or the Intellectual Properties Department.*[38]

While long, this policy happily starts with a positive stand with respect to CI. Again, as with so many such statements, it clearly started with the SCIP Code, but in its development, the company has produced a much more satisfactory set of guidelines. It identifies a contact point for questions, which is a very useful aspect. It also seems to have been drafted with an eye to issues facing this firm in its market, such as how to deal with employees recently hired from competitors. Finally, its overall tone is positive and inclusive. It talks about "us" and "we" in most of the text, rather than taking a more remote tone, as with some of the previous statements.

Competitive Intelligence

The business world is highly competitive and success in it demands an understanding of other . . . industry participants. While collecting data on our potential competitors, we should utilise all legitimate resources, but avoid those actions which are illegal, unethical or which could cause embarrassment to [the firm].[39]

This statement is largely positive with respect to the role of CI, in that it assumes that everyone knows that CI is useful and is being practiced. However, it falls short in terms of assisting its employees because it merely tells them, in essence, to do good and avoid evil. It is of no real value to individuals conducting CI research.

Code of Ethical Business Practice

Uphold the profession's reputation for honesty, competence, and confidentiality.

Give clients the most current and accurate information possible within the budget and time frames provided by the clients.

Help clients understand the sources of information used and the degree of reliability which can be expected from those sources.

Accept only those projects which are legal and are not detrimental to our profession.

Respect client confidentiality.

Recognize intellectual property rights. Respect licensing agreements and other contracts. Explain to clients what their obligations might be with regard to intellectual property rights and licensing agreements.

Maintain a professional relationship with libraries and comply with all their rules of access.

Assume responsibility for employees' compliance with this code.[40]

An analysis of this shows that the primary focus of members of this group is on obtaining information from secondary sources. For that reason, it includes specific requirements that the information professional deal properly with any legal or other restrictions on the retrieval, copying, and transmission of materials that may be subject to copyright or other legal restrictions.

The admonition to help their clients "understand the sources of information used and the degree of reliability which can be expected from those sources" is a standard that can (and should) well be applied to the practice of CI as well.

Applying Policies

Compliance. Good written policies are just that, written policies. To protect your firm, you must have compliance. First, compliance requires knowledge. That, in turn, means that the members of the CI staff should be trained on legal and ethical issues and that training should be renewed on a regular basis. Also, the current and future end users of CI should also be trained on these issues to avoid having them accidentally place a CI staff member in the position of violating legal or ethical concerns.

Second, CI staff members should be encouraged to discuss specific ethical concerns with a supervisor or, if that is not possible or appropriate, with another person outside the reporting relationship chain in which they are located. Specifically, CI staff members should be allowed, or even encouraged, to contact a designated, trained, and educated member of the legal team with any concerns they may have.

Third, CI staff should make sure that contractors, consultants, and other third parties whose services they use have a formal policy dealing with the collection of CI data. That policy should be reviewed before any contract is signed or work begun. Then, the contractor should be made aware of the company's policies and agree, in writing, to be bound by them. If company policies and contractor policies are in conflict, then the best solution is to have the contractor bound by the stricter of the policies.

Fourth, every contractor should also agree that any work it subcontracts will be subject to the same standards. Asking to see any subcontracting agreements is a good way to protect your firm here.

Fifth, if necessary, contractors should be encouraged, or even required, to participate in company-approved training on legal and ethical issues.

Sixth, as with employees, contractors should be able to contact someone out of their reporting chain with any serious concerns about ethical or legal problems. Just as an overzealous end user might pressure a CI staff member into improper activities, it is possible that an overzealous CI staff member's actions could apply the same pressure to an outsider.

Personal Ethical Considerations. Remember, one role for your firm's policy is to help employees resolve whether their actions, or planned actions, violate the law or your firm's formal policies involving legal or legal and ethical considerations. If the actions would be in violation, then they should not be permitted or undertaken. *Only an action that is permitted under all the relevant laws and your own firm's policies can involve a personal ethical question.*

In resolving whether personal ethical issues are raised, consider the following guidance:

- If the action doesn't feel right, don't do it.
- If it could damage a business relationship, don't do it.
- If you or the firm would be embarrassed/ashamed if your conduct was published on the front page of the newspaper, don't do it.
- If there is an alternative way of gathering information that produces equal or greater benefits to the parties affected by the proposed action and does not raise any questions in your mind, you should use the alternative.

NOTES

1. Larry Kahaner, *Competitive Intelligence: From Black Ops to Boardrooms—How Businesses Gather, Analyze and Use Information to Succeed in the Global Marketplace* (New York: Simon & Schuster, 1996), p. 281.
2. For a discussion of other legal regimes that might impact CI, see Craig P. Ehrlich, "A Brief CI Compliance Manual," *Competitive Intelligence Review* 9, no. 1 (January–March 1998), 28–37.
3. For a current list of the states that have adopted the UTSA, check the official Web site of the National Conference of Commissioners on Uniform State Laws, http://www.nccusl.org/nccusl/uniformact_factsheets/uniformacts-fs-utsa.asp.
4. Some of these states may eventually adopt the UTSA as well. At the time this was written, versions of the UTSA were under consideration by two more states.

5. The full text and the official drafting comments can be found in Appendix B of of John J. McGonagle and Carolyn M. Vella, *Protecting Your Firm against Competitive Intelligence* (Westport, Conn.: Quorum Books, 1998), 121–34.

6. The full text of the EEA is set forth in Appendix B of ibid. In spite of the fact that the problems addressed by this law were the subject of hearings for several years, the legislative "history" of what the law, as finally adopted, is intended to do is remarkably slender. For that reason, we complied and reprinted the only official section by section analysis of the almost-final version of the act, together with the few comments in the U.S. Senate and House of Representatives debate that bear on the act in that book.

7. "The definition of the term 'trade secret' [in EEA] is based largely on the definition of that term in the Uniform Trade Secrets Act." U.S. House of Representatives, H. Rep. 104-788, "Economic Espionage Act of 1996," 104th Congress, 2d Session, September 16, 1996, p. 16.

8. This is available on-line at http://www.cybercrime.gov/ipmanual/08ipma.htm (May 30, 2002).

9. For a current list of such cases, see http://www.cybercrime.gov/eeapub.htm (May 30, 2002).

10. A very powerful analysis of this issue noted that the Restatement of Torts supports this position. See Richard Horowitz, "The Economic Espionage Act: The Rules Have Not Changed," *Competitive Intelligence Review* 9, no. 1 (July–September 1998), 30, 33.

11. "With Friends Like These," *U.S. News & World Report*, 16 June 1997, 46–48.

12. 15 U.S.C. § 1681 et seq. All references to the FCRA in this article are to the text version provided by the U.S. Federal Trade Commission (FTC) on its homepage (http://www.ftc.gov/os/statutes/fcra.htm). The FTC is responsible for enforcing the FCRA.

13. FCRA, sec. 603(f).

14. FCRA, sec. 603(d). Section 604 repeats language from the definitions and includes many of the limits on how these reports are handled. It also allows their use for governmental purposes.

15. FCRA sec. 603(e).

16. U.S. Federal Trade Commission, *Using Credit Reports: What Employers Need to Know*, December 1997. Emphasis in the original. Available on-line at http://www.ftc.gov/bcp/conline/pubs/buspubs/credempl.htm

17. Lawrence C. Winger, *Fair Credit Reporting Act Update*, September 15, 1998, http://www.kraftwinger.com/fcra.htm (emphasis added).

18. "Directive 95/46/EC of the European Parliament and of the Council of 24 October 1995 on the protection of individuals with regard to the processing of personal data and on the free movement of such data," Official Journal of the European Communities of 23 November 1995, No L. 281 p. 31 et seq. (Directive). For general information on the Directive, as well as related documents, see http://europa.eu.int/comm/internal_market/en/dataprot/ (accessed May 30, 2002).

19. Directive, Article 3(1).

20. Directive , Article 2(a), (b), and (c).

21. See I. Lloyd, "An Outline of the European Data Protection Directive," *Journal of Information, Law and Technology (JILT)* (1996). Available on-line at http://elj.warwick.ac.uk/elj/jilt/dp/intros/.

22. European Commission Press Release: IP/95/822, Document Date: July 25, 1995, "Council Definitively Adopts Directive on Protection of Personal Data."

23. This is the official website for the US Department of Commerce dealing with this issue, http://www.export.gov/safeharbor/.

24. These are extracted from a series of commonly advertised requirements. See http://www.securityshredders.com/sub/retention.htm and http://www. kentnersellers.com/Record_retain.html. Of course, federal, state, and local laws continue to change and each individual situation is different, so professional guidance is critical.

25. William Cohen and Helena Czepiec, "The Role of Ethics in Gathering Corporate Intelligence," *Journal of Business Ethics* 7 (1988), 199–203.

26. For example, "Kraft sues Schwan's, putting spotlight on corporate spying," *USA Today,* Feb 19, 2001.

27. In fact, one study suggests that people involved in collecting intelligence generally view their competitors very negatively. They believe competitors will go to much greater lengths and exhibit less ethical behaviors to collect intelligence than they or their own employer would. William Cohen and Helena Czepiec, "The Role of Ethics in Gathering Corporate Intelligence," *Journal of Business Ethics* 7 (1988), 199–203.

28. Alfonso Sapia and Robert S. Tancer, "Navigating through the Legal/Ethical Gray Zone," *Competitive Intelligence Magazine* 1, no. 1 (April–June 1998) 22–31.

29. Jokull Johannesson and Patrick Sullivan, "Legal Constraints and Success of the Competitive Intelligence Function," *Competitive Intelligence Review* 6, no. 3 (Fall 1995), 5–11.

30. Kahaner, *Competitive Intelligence*, 281.

31. Disclaimer: one of the coauthors was a member of the SCIP Ethics Committee, which reviewed SCIP's proper role in enforcing such a policy.

32. Available online at http://www.scip.org/ci/ethics.asp (Accessed May 30, 2002).

33. A few that were collected in the late 1990s can be found in Society of Competitive Intelligence Professionals, *Navigating through the Gray Zone: A Collection of Corporate Codes of Conduct and Ethical Guidelines* (Alexandria, Va.: Society of Competitive Intelligence Professionals, 1997).

34. Lynn Behnke and Paul Slayton, "Shaping a Corporate Competitive Intelligence Function at IBM," *Competitive Intelligence Review* 9, no. 2 (April–June 1998), 4, 7.

35. Copyright 2002, the Helicon Group; reprinted with perrmission.

36. Drafted 2001. Identity withheld.

37. Timothy J. Kindler (Director, Corporate Competitive Intelligence, Eastman Kodak Company), "Competitive Intelligence in Today's Corporate Environment," presentation April 2002.

38. BellSouth Corporation, Office of Ethics and Compliance, "Building Relationships: Competitive Intelligence," http://ethics.bellsouth.com/commitmentbooklet_buildingrelationships_competitiveintelligence.html (accessed May 30, 2002).

39. Woolstock [Australia Limited], "Ethics Statement and Code of Conduct," July 2000, page 6, http://www.woolstock.com.au/pdf/ethics-conduct.pdf (accessed May 31, 2002).

40. The Association of Independent Information Professionals, "Code of Ethical Business Practice," http://www.aiip.org/AboutAIIP/aiipethics.html (March 26, 2003). An independent information professional "is an entrepreneur who has demonstrated continuing expertise in the art of finding and organizing information. Each provides information services on a contractual basis to more than one client and serves as an objective intermediary between the client and the information world."

9

Internal Client Management

DEFINING CLIENTS AND OVERALL NEEDS

The first, and most important, step in managing any CI unit is to establish who are the "clients" for the CI and, as a part of that first step, what they would or should use the CI for. This is because experience shows that there is no point in spending CI resources to collect "complete" information on every target for everyone. When a firm does that, it is really running a newsletter, not a CI function.

It does not really matter whether the CI unit has been told who its clients are. That is because, to truly be effective, the CI unit must establish and maintain regular relationships with its end users. There is an important reason we have used the term *end user*: that is because, regardless of corporate organization or statements of mission, to be effective, every CI unit must be focused on the needs of its end users.

What a new or established CI unit does *not* want or need is to receive a mission or even an assignment, that says, in essence, "We want to know everything about this Target (or Targets)." Frankly, given the easy availability of raw data (sometimes in vast quantities), your end users do *not* really want this. That is because they would then spend the vast bulk of their time digesting all the data the CI unit could accumulate, without ever having the time to find, much less act on, that small portion of it that is potentially actionable.[1] All this means that, as a part of this effort, one must get to the real decision-makers at a firm, the ones we call the *end users*.

The key, then, is to assure that what CI the unit provides, and will provide, should make a difference with the firm's key decision makers, the end users of the CI. And who are these key decision makers? They are those the CI unit actually supports, regardless of to whom it reports or where it is located. For example, for strategy-oriented CI, that would be senior management teams, senior staff, and senior executives, as well as strategic planning and business development units.[2]

One proven way to accomplish this form of global needs assessment is through internal interviews. In fact, that is really the best way to do this. A quick way to start this process is to ask the end users questions designed to elicit their real needs, based on their experience. Of course, you should discuss what they see as their CI needs, but take that as only the first step in the process. That is because end users who are not familiar with what CI can and cannot do often frame their replies in terms of what they think the CI unit can provide (find), rather than what they want or need to know.

Keeping that in mind, you can redirect the discussion to bring the focus to needs by asking questions like these:

What has happened in the past one to two years with respect to key competitors that had an impact on our firm? Of those events, which ones do you think that our firm [or your unit or SBU] might have avoided or exploited had it only had some early warning of the events?

By doing this, the interviewer is placing the focus on real decision making, and not on what the end users think the CI unit might be able to provide. Then, those involved with creating or managing the CI function can do some quick retrospective research. That research should be designed to find out if the use of CI, at the relevant point in time, might have been able to provide your firm with the desired early warning. If so, then you have identified one critical area for the CI function. But be very careful: the danger is that this sort of inquiry, if not controlled, can become a blame game.

Those managing a CI function also have to determine *when* their end users will typically need CI, as well as what they need it for. As we discuss later in this chapter, the type of CI you provide, the uses to which the end users apply it, the sources to which you will go for research, the manner in which you deliver it, and the turnaround time are all interconnected.

For example, if your firm has formal planning cycles, are there key dates that you should know about to make sure that strategy-oriented CI is available for that process? It is not helpful to offer profiles of expansion plans to senior management a month after the usual close of the planning cycle. Similarly, if your firm regularly launches new products or services and the CI function has a tactics orientation, and therefore might be directed to check on potential new products hitting the market, when is your own go–no go date with respect to the launch date? Intelligence about a new launch by a competitor provides no benefit if it arrives after your own firm has made an irrevocable decision.

DETERMINING NEEDS

Overview

> "A problem well stated is a problem half solved." Charles Kettering (General Motors).[3]

The process of determining your end user's needs is the first stage of the CI cycle. It is also one of the most important. If your end user has not communicated his or her needs adequately, then the CI unit is left to guess what is really needed.

The process of determining the needs of the end user, even with respect to a single assignment, is not a simple one. The least successful model is for the CI unit to be given an assignment in writing, through an intermediary, which, in essence says: "[The end user] would like to know about [Target] in connection with some emerging issues. Get it to me by June 5, 2004." Deconstructing this statement will help to show why it is a problem and what the better practices are:

- The assignment is in writing. That means that no one representing the CI process had the opportunity to meet, *face-to-face,* with the end user about the assignment. Direct, personal contact is vital to the effective determination of the real needs of the end user.
- The assignment comes *through an intermediary.* As talented as staff may be, in the CI process, every hand-off of an assignment adds what the communications engineers call "noise," making the communication process less effective.
- The assignment is one of "want to know." In CI, there is, and should be, a marked distinction between *want to know and need to know.* To be blunt, *want to know* is a term better applied to curiosity, as in seeking generalized information. It has no immediate, real value. *Need to know* connotes that the information actually is expected to have real, immediate value. CI units should not be in the *want to know* business.
- The request says that the research is to be used "in connection with some emerging issues." In the vast majority of cases, it is critical for the CI unit to know *for what purpose the CI is to be used.* Some-

times the CI sought will not really serve to meet the end user's real needs.

- There is no indication that the CI staff will be able to have any *ongoing contact* with the end user during the development of the requested CI. In fact, the opposite seems to be the clear inference of the memo. Contrary to some opinions, the most effective CI, even of the most technology-oriented type, is rarely provided this way.
- The date given is one possibly set by the intermediary, and may not be *the date by which the end user needs it*. That is due to the normal tendency of many managers to make sure they will have what they need when they need it by setting earlier deadlines.

These concerns apply even when the end user is the very person who helped to create the CI unit, its champion. Experience shows that a new CI unit must work to maintain support among those very executives and end users who were instrumental in creating the demand for the unit.[4] One particular problem in maintaining that support has been described as *information deficit*. That is a situation where end users have unrealistic expectations about the kind of CI that can be provided, or at least that can be provided in the early stages of the unit's development. This is, in turn, usually linked to the failure of the very same end user to help, or let, the CI unit articulate the end user's exact CI needs.[5]

Needs Determination: Face-to-face and Alternatives

CI professionals will always need to focus on determining what it is that the end user really needs. That means before you even start to gather any data, the CI professional *must* ask the right questions, which in turn means he or she must have someone to ask questions of. The answers to these questions will help make CI research, and then analysis, more useful and comprehensive than if the research is started based only on a general request for "some information on. . . ."

There are many techniques that can help the CI professional structure thinking about and developing plans for CI research. Always keep in mind, and plant in the minds of your end users, that CI research that starts without a clear understanding of what is really needed is rarely satisfactory. The results inevitably reflect that lack of direction from the end user.

There are also a variety of techniques available to try to correctly ascertain the real needs of the ultimate end user.

- Experience shows that the first technique, directly interviewing the end user, is always the most effective. However, that is not always an option, particularly when the end user is not accessible or there are multiple end users.

- Given that, the next two techniques, determining your firm's underlying competitive assumptions and surveying overall CI needs, can help to focus on the real needs of the end user by relying on a clear understanding of the firm's overall CI needs. They tend to have their greatest application when used in connection with strategy-oriented and technology-oriented CI projects.
- The fourth, using a checklist, can be useful in understanding exactly what your firm is seeking to learn about a targeted competitor. It tends to be most useful when the CI unit is providing largely target-oriented CI.

While we explore several proven techniques here, there is no one guaranteed correct approach for every case. For example, in past years, CI professionals were encouraged to undertake very extensive internal surveys, called CI audits. The goal was to learn both the CI needs of the firm, and the scope of internal resources and access paths to data present in the firm.[6] While the approach is still a valid option, the small initial staffing of most new CI units, coupled with typical difficulties in getting started and recognized, have made the CI audit less attractive. This is because it is a labor- and time-intensive approach, which may also delay the start of the CI unit's operations.

CI professionals should use whichever techniques they feel comfortable with. Research on Best Practices now indicates that the needs development process is most often driven by "a somewhat informal process initiated by events in the marketplace, unsolicited requests, changes in strategy or tactics, and internally-generated analysis."[7] Experience shows that CI professionals probably should use something more or different than they are doing now and that they should always try to start with the most effective technique: the face-to-face meeting with the end user. As has been said in the governmental context, "[I]ntelligence effectiveness depends to an enormous degree on the system it serves." [8]

Direct Interviewing. In conducting effective CI, it is increasingly clear that the best CI projects are those in which the CI professional conducting the research and analysis have direct access to the end users, particularly before beginning the work. Why is this important? The experience of the Best Practice firms shows this, again and again. But why is that so vital? Perhaps an analogy to medicine can be drawn.

If a patient comes to a doctor and says he needs a particular prescription for an allergy, one he saw advertised on television, some doctors may too quickly accede to the request, following a superficial examination. But if the prescription medicine fails to do what the patient expected, typically he will blame the doctor, the medicine, or both. In fact, the patient should blame himself, as well, if not exclusively. He has, in essence, tried to diagnose his own problem and then decided that a particular compound (not based on its track record and clinical trials, nor taking into account potential side effects) is best. From there, he has given the doctor very little leeway except to accede to his request.

On the other hand, if the same patient comes to a doctor and asks for an allergy medicine, most doctors will properly ask, "Why do you think you need that medicine?" That will, in turn, bring out the patient's complaints about sneezing, stuffiness, and other symptoms. Those complaints might, in turn, lead the doctor to do a further examination or to run a test for allergies, only to find out that the patient's real problem is not an allergy, but rather is a sinus infection. The proper treatment for that is thus not an allergy prescription, but an antibiotic. Now, if the patient's problems continue, at least blaming the doctor or the prescribed drugs will be appropriate.

Unfortunately, too many CI professionals are more often in the position of the first doctor. What they must do is to put themselves into the second position. If the end user cannot be interviewed, the CI professional should at least interview the intermediary from whom an assignment originates.

What kinds of questions should be asked of the end user or intermediary? The interview should move away from what the end user says he or she wants to an articulation, and eventually an understanding by all parties, of what the end user actually needs. While the end user may say that these are identical, they are all too often not the same.

What a client asks a CI professional for is usually influenced by a number of factors, both conscious and unconscious. For example:

- End users may tend to ask for specific intelligence that they believe is easily accessible.
- End users may be influenced in what they ask for by what they believe is actually happening with a competitor.
- End users may subconsciously assume that a competitor is not any different than their own firm, and thus severely limit the CI they ask for or where that CI may be found.
- End users may have an underlying belief or even an unconscious assumption that they already know what is going on. Then the scope of the CI assignment may end up as an effort to validate that belief.

What kinds of questions should be asked? We suggest getting to the core of each of the following broad areas:

- Who is asking for the CI being sought? Is that person or group the real, and ultimate, end user? If not, who *is* the end user? Is the CI being sought *exactly* what that person asked for, or has the request been translated or elaborated upon? One problem you are trying to avoid is having several people asking for similar, but not identical, CI as a result of the same meeting or request from one common end user.
- When does the end user, as distinguished from an intermediary, need the CI? That is not the due date for the assignment. Rather it is the date on which the decision maker will be incorporating the finished CI into the decision-making process. If this is an ongoing process, then the CI professional should be given a sense of that and told how to update the analysis provided. CI is only valid for a relatively short period of time. It should not be "ordered up" ahead of time, as you might purchase firewood in anticipation of a long winter.
- What will this CI be used to do? One way to probe in this area is to ask whether, if the answer to the question or questions were here today, what the company or the end user would then do as a result. If no specific action can be given as a response to the output of the CI project, then perhaps this project is not an efficient use of CI resources. At a minimum, the end user and the CI professional should work to refine or redefine the assignment to make sure that the results that are generated can produce some action by the firm.
- If the CI project does appear to be justified, then why is this specific question being posed? For example, if an end user is asking for CI on a competitor's future product launches, is that because that is the only market change that can impact the firm or does that request reflect an underlying assumption by the end user that no significant product changes, price changes, or product withdrawals are likely? Is the request a verbal shorthand, actually reflecting an underlying, unexpressed need for the CI unit to track any and all forthcoming changes in product offerings? If so, how long in advance should that be done, and at what level of detail?
- How much detail is *really* needed? That is, how much is needed by the end user, at the point a decision will be made? Educate your end users that, in general, the more detail is needed, the more costly is the research and the less likely it is that the final product will generate all the data sought. For example, does the company need to know *exact* market shares of all competitors or is it enough to have a good approximation of the market shares of only those firms that have a greater market share than it does?
- What do the end users already know or, at least, think they know? If they have any raw data, all of that that should be provided to the analyst at the beginning. One reason is that the firm should not

pay, either in dollars or staff time, to have it gathered again. Even if the data is inadequate, the CI analyst may be able to determine more about the end user's needs by seeing what was not responsive to the end user's own research. Also, reviewing these materials may help pop up some underlying misconceptions about what can be found out about the target.

- For past completed projects, what use was made of the CI provided? Seeing how the CI was, or was not, used may help the end user focus more on his or her real needs and help the CI professional provide a better product as well. Consequently, not only will this process help refocus future assignments, but it will also provide needed support for justification for the CI function's very existence.

Determine your firm's competitive assumptions. Motorola Inc. provided us with a good example of this option through the process it originally used to establish its own corporate-wide intelligence system, one we would now label as primarily strategy- and target-oriented. At the beginning, Motorola's director of corporate analytical research ascertained the company's overall CI needs by a means of a direct assault. The process he used is the origin of the now very common key intelligence topics/key intelligence questions (KIT/ KIQ) approach.[9] It is most helpful for a CI unit whose assignments are largely self-directed, that is, it does not deal with one-time, fast turnaround projects.

Motorola's director met with fifteen top vice presidents and general managers who were responsible for the corporation's operational divisions, as well as with those responsible for its staff functions, such as personnel, international, and finance. He asked each one in turn the same question: "What are the five most important things you need to know about the external world?"

The answers [I received] varied a lot, from "I want to know about a particular competitor who's really eating our lunch" and "I want to know who my competitors are going to be in China," to "I need to know more about a new technology that will affect the way we build our microprocessors."

From those discussions, I drew up a list of about 35 key intelligence topics and [then] assigned each a priority. That exercise produced the table of contents for our program, which, in turn, determined the kind of talent we needed on [our] staff and the kind of information to collect.[10]

Another variation in frontal approaches to determining both what you know and what you need to know is to sit down with the key personnel in your business. Have everyone contribute to a list of major assumptions (you can call them beliefs) they all have about the competition. Be very careful to be noncritical in compiling the list, however, to encourage everyone to contribute assumptions freely.

Then have the CI professional organize that list, combining similar assumptions. If possible, reword all of the assumptions so that it is not easy for anyone to identify the source for any assumption. This makes those participating feel more comfortable, since they can speak freely without feeling that they are being criticized or critiquing the beliefs of others. For example, if one officer said that a particular competitor only competed on price and another said that a second competitor never worries about quality, you should combine these statements. The result may be, "Our two largest competitors do not compete on reputation, or innovation." At that point, without ever attributing any single assumption to any particular person or unit, you then have each participant identify those assumptions on your list for which they now see little or even no supporting data that they can *specifically* point to.

You may be surprised how many assumptions fall into this category. However, if it seems that all or virtually all of these assumptions are likely to be pointed to as supportable by the participants, you can just reverse the process. That means you have each person give *one* brief example of a fact he or she believes offers support for each assumption. Then, those assumptions with few or no supporting facts will quickly stand out from the others.

If neither approach works, then try to restate the assumptions, recombining related ones. The goal is to have the group approach the process and sort out erroneous, or at least unsupportable, assumptions that drive the way they do business without feeling threatened by the process.

Now, regardless of which way it was compiled, you will have generated a list of apparently supported key competitive assumptions, as well as a group of partially, or even totally, unsupported competitive assumptions. From the group of partially and unsupported assumptions, you can then isolate those that appear to be the most critical to the way in which your firm operates and you and others in the firm make decisions about your market and your competitors. The latter set of competitive assumptions are the ones that should be reviewed and challenged, so that they are then either supported or supplanted by good CI. The same two processes can be used to identify which competitors you should monitor and to what degree.

Surveying Overall CI Needs. Another approach to pinpointing your real firm's CI needs is to undertake a structured series of questions, in survey form, to elicit answers from your current end users one by one. By responding to the questions and prompts noted here, you can get them to help establish exactly the kinds of CI your firm needs and also help these internal clients put their own needs in perspective.

Start by asking, "What information about your competitor do you think you need?" This will open up the survey. Then ask, "Why do you think you need that specific information?" Finally ask, "How would you or others at the firm will use that information?" If the CI being identified would be used by others who are not present, ask, "Exactly who are they and why would you expect them to use this information?"

Next, restate the first-round CI needs identified by the end user in the form of a few questions that the end user would like to have answered. Then, continue to narrow the broadest questions into a set of specific, detailed questions. For example, refocus a rather general concern, such as, "What are my competitors' current marketing plans?" into a narrower question, such as, "Is [a named competitor] preparing to introduce any new products that compete in the United States with our consumer products in the next three months?"

Then, for each of these questions, try to establish how important or valuable good CI would be to the end user. To do this, make sure you raise the following in the one-on-one interview:

- What does the firm do if you cannot answer these questions?
- What could you do, that you cannot do now, if you knew the answer?
- How much might a lack of good CI on this subject cost the firm?
- How much can you spend, or what portion of our CI efforts should be focused on developing good CI in this area?

The importance and value of the CI, both in terms of opportunities identified and risks averted, should help you decide on the effort and resources that should be allocated to answering these questions for this end user.

For each CI issue raised in the survey, also discuss related needs issues, such as the following:

- How often will you need this data? Will you need it on a regular basis or only once?
- How quickly do you need this CI? The time frame within which you have to operate will dictate the depth of your research and limit the available avenues for that effort.
- What kind of end product will best help you answer your specific questions? For example, do you need direct evidence of your competitor's marketing intentions (say, an announcement that the target has hired a new advertising agency for a particular product)? Will an assessment based on indirect evidence do (such as a

report in local business newspaper of recent promotions that hint
of the development of a new marketing campaign)?

- What type of data do you usually need: macro-level (general),
  micro-level (specific), or both?
- Will the data tend to be current data, historical data, predictions,
  or some combination of these? How far backward and forward will
  such assessments have to go? For capital plans, for example, you
  may need to go forward five years, while marketing positioning
  may only have a three-month horizon.
- What data do you already have internally on this subject? What
  can you now access from internal resources, such as staff or members of trade associations?

Using a Competitor Analysis Checklist. The competitor analysis checklist
can help you define, as well as refine, your efforts to ascertain the CI needs
of your end user by helping to identify both the specific targets and the
relevant CI you may need to seek on each. Almost no reports will (or can)
cover all the topics listed there. This type of extensive checklist, however,
provides one way to make sure you and your end user are not accidentally
omitting anything critical. One effective way to use it is to have it available
when talking to an end user about an assignment. Quickly review it to see
if either of you have omitted to discuss the need for CI on topics that are
proximate to those you have covered. You can use the sample in the
Appendix to develop your own checklist, which can be customized for
your own competitor profiling efforts.[11]

When you use this checklist, you should always also determine
whether your CI assessment will need qualitative data (narrative responses), quantitative data (numbers and statistics), or both. For example, if you are trying to determine how your competitors see you and
your marketing activities, you are probably looking for qualitative,
rather than quantitative, data. Overall, the types of questions you are
trying to answer have a major impact on the types of data you will need
to develop.

Intermediaries

The communication of a CI assignment through an intermediary,
while often justified from an organizational point of view, is not justi-
fiable from the point of view of effectively managing CI. That is because
any intermediary will communicate his or her perception of what the
end user wants, even if merely transmitting, or even transcribing, what
seems like a simple request. For example, the end user may want to
know "what our competitors say when they sell" particular competing
products. The request that is transmitted may suggest that the end user

wants to know what strong points competitors stress in selling their products, when in fact, the end user may really only want to know what the competitors say about each other, and not what they say about themselves.

Without direct contact with the end user at the initiation of the request, the CI professional cannot try to pursue this distinction. The situation becomes even worse when the CI professional tries to get more specification on the scope of the assignment, often called "pushing back." Pushing back should not be done with an intermediary; it requires that the CI professional have direct access to the end user. The memo following this section shows such a process in action.

If done with an intermediary, pushing back will more often fail than succeed. There are two basic ways that can happen:

- The intermediary will not go back to the end user, but rather will communicate what the intermediary thinks the end user needs, couched in terms of a flat assertion.
- The intermediary will go back to the end user and get a response to the CI professional's question. That response will generate yet another valid question. At some point, however, the intermediary will refuse to go back for additional clarification.

Sample Memo on Reshaping a CI Project[12]

November 2, 2000

[The Financial Institution] is seeking to develop common intelligence on up to twelve major national and regional competitors.

Each of these competitors may be facing us in up to four separate market niches. [For the sake of discussion, we will assume they are each in all four niches]. For each competitor and niche, we will be seeking CI on the following areas:

- marketing strategy
- promotional thrust
- advertising expenditures

First, based on our conversations with others on your staff who will be using this CI, I would suggest that the CI project include, in addition to the above, the following considerations:

- a summary of the overall strategic thrust of the parent organization, as that thrust directly impacts or drives the direct competitors' marketing, goals, budgets, and so on

- a separation of what the competitor has done in the past year from what it should or could be expected to do in the next year

Having said this, I should alert you to the fact that a project like this can quickly become so complex as to be unmanageable in any limited period of time. In this case, for example, we might have the following template for each competitor (see Figure 9.1)

A model such as this generates 8 separate cells to be completed for Market Niche D alone, and thus 32 for this single competitor. Taking 12 competitors then produces 384 separate cells of intelligence, with some, but not always much, overlap among them.

As you know, time and cost are trade-offs in CI. Therefore, the more data sets that have to be generated, the higher the cost and usually the longer it will take. And the more cells we create, particularly when it splits a cell into smaller parts (such as by size, date, geography, etc.), the more likely it quickly becomes that we will *not* be able to get all the cells filled.

A project like this can quickly and innocently become unmanageable. Let me show you how. Take an apparently simple request to subdivide present and future advertising expenditures into radio, TV, print, and

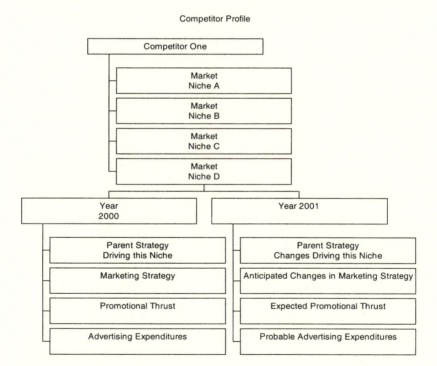

Figure 9.1 Competitor templates.

direct mail expenditures. That one change would immediately add 8 cells (4 for the year 2000 and 4 for the year 2001) to each market niche for each competitor. That alone suddenly doubles the number of niches, to 768 separate intelligence tasks.

For these reasons, we should consider using one or more of several strategies:

- Severely limit the level of detail sought on each of the twelve target competitors;
- Develop significant detail *only* on those niches and below for which the cost and time to produce/acquire it can be justified; and/or
- Select a few, very key competitors and, for each of them, select only a limited set of market niches. Then, develop the targeted intelligence on them. From there, evaluate the utility of such intelligence to us in light of the time and cost. Then we can decide whether expand the research to cover more competitors, more niches, and more subsets in the future.

Need to Know Versus Want to Know

It may sound presumptuous for a CI professional to ask an end user to answer the question "Do you need to know this or do you just *want* to know it?" But it is a critical distinction. If CI unit does not provide CI that supports decision-making, then experience shows that the unit will eventually will cease to exist because it is not providing any value to the firm. Moreover, a CI unit cannot be effective and bring value to the firm if much of its work is not directed to supporting or improving sound decision-making.

Once a CI unit has become a proven commodity by being effective, experience shows that the demand for its services by departments and managers other than the CI unit's originally intended end users will begin and increase, and may do so very rapidly. Operating CI units have quickly discovered that they must limit the number of assignments and even then they must establish priorities among them. The driving constraints are typically cost and time. The CI unit simply cannot afford to do everything it is asked to do.

Thus, it is critical to establish, at the very beginning, exactly who needs what information and how frequently. Moreover, not only must you separate those who need to know from those who just want to know, you must also identify those whose needs you cannot afford to support at all. For that reason, it is vital to get the ability to say "no" to assignments.[13] And the best time to get that is at the very earliest date possible. In addition, you should recognize and deal with a related issue: you may have to refuse to provide CI to certain potential users because of special considerations, such as the need to keep CI sources confidential. If that is a possibility, it is also easier to deal with at the beginning than when the issue actually arises.

Purpose of the CI Assignment

Knowing what the end user says he or she needs is not the same as understanding the underlying CI needs. To provide the best level of service, CI professionals should also know *why* the assignment is being given out. The reason is that, in some cases, the way the assignment has been framed is colored by undisclosed ideas or even preconceptions. Knowing the purpose of the assignment not only helps the CI professional properly frame the research phase, it may actually change the nature and content of the final product.

For example, in one case we were asked by a client to provide intelligence on the investment strategies and related plans of a group of named competitors. We asked the client why this data was being requested. The answer was that the client was planning an overseas expansion and needed to know if the domestic environment would be subject to overinvestment. It felt that possible over investment domestically by competitors could impact its ability to expand overseas quickly. The final report, providing the requested CI, also noted that one competitor that did most of its business overseas was probably for sale. The client later bought that competitor, rather than start from scratch from overseas. Had the client not indicated the real purpose, it might not have gotten the extremely valuable CI when it did.

Ongoing Contact

The experiences of dozens of the world's best practice firms in CI clearly indicates that the best CI emerges when the end user and the CI professional have regular contact, scheduled and unscheduled, during the work on the assignment. That way the end users can be involved at every stage of the CI cycle, to a greater or lesser degree. The result is that the end users will receive a superior intelligence product, particularly when the CI managers realize this and take care to make sure that the end users continue such involvement.

The need for ongoing contact during the assignment, as well as the need to have face-to-face contact at the needs phase, means that the best-performing CI units are closest to their end users, physically and organizationally (see chapters 2 and 13).

Due Dates

CI should be provided when and to whom needed. That is because CI, like many other types of information, often has a relatively short "half-life." *Half-life* refers to the period of time for which the data you have collected and the analysis you have generated retains at least 50 percent of its accuracy and relevance.

In the case of raw data collected for CI, the half-lives can vary widely. Typically the more micro-level and the more future oriented the information is, the shorter is the half-life, while the more macro level and historically oriented the data is , the longer is its half-life. In the case of raw data collected for CI, the half lives are typically like those described in Figure 9.2.

The same concept of half-life also applies to the resulting CI analysis you develop. When the intelligence is important, try to caution your end users to be conscious of its short "shelf life." CI end users should not just store an intelligence estimate and then drag it out a year later, expecting it still to be accurate. The conclusion you draw or the report you present is completely valid *only* as of the date you completed it. Therefore, the less time there is between the dates the research and analysis ended and the date when the CI is needed, the better the outcome will be for all concerned.

In addition, when dealing with an intermediary, the due date a CI professional is given may frequently be one that allows the intermediary time to digest or use the CI, thus making the information even older than it has to be. CI should properly be treated more as an input to a just-in-time process than as an asset that can be warehoused until needed.

There is another facet to due dates. That relates to the habit of some managers to move up previously established deadlines. In the case of CI, this does not mean, for example, if the time for an assignment is cut by 25 percent, then the end user can expect 75 percent of the anticipated product. Such a cut, for example, would mean that the CI professional would probably still be in the data-gathering stage. Any cuts would come from the analysis stage. In other words, by cutting the time for a CI project once it has begun, the end user is removing most, if not all,

| Level of Data | Time Frame | Half-Life | |
		Minimum	*Maximum*
Micro	Historic	2 months	12 months
	Current	1 day	3 months
	Projection	1 day	2 months
Macro	Historic	3 months	24 months
	Current	1 month	6 months
	Projection	1 month	4 months

Figure 9.2 Typical half-lives for CI data.

of that time from the analysis stage. The result is that the end user will get something more like a "data dump" than a finished, usable analysis.

ISSUES ASSOCIATED WITH NEEDS DETERMINATION

CI versus Policy Making

The key mission for a CI unit should be to provide needed information that will serve as a key element in a firm's decision making. That means that those providing the CI must avoid having any preconceived position either for or against any specific policy or outcome that can be affected by their research. In some firms, that has meant that the CI unit must avoid making policy or even suggesting the correct decisions the firm should make.

There are two principal reasons for drawing and maintaining a line between CI and policy making:

- The first is the need to keep CI unbiased. The CI professionals cannot use their position or that of the unit to "take sides" in any internal divisions. To do so even once is to condemn the CI unit to a peripheral position, at best.
- The second is the need to keep CI free from the appearance of special pleading. For example, the tactics-oriented CI provided by your marketing unit may stress the need for additional distribution channels. However, that conclusion, even if valid, may be disregarded by some managers in nonmarketing areas as special pleading. Implicitly, it would their position that only those with the operating responsibility must be the ones to recommend and ultimately carry out policy decisions.

However, there is no essential need to separate CI and policy or decision-making. In fact, the most effective CI is "actionable," that is it provides the end users with, not only intelligence, but also options and possible actions. For instance, it may be entirely appropriate for a strategy-oriented CI report to assess the probable effects of alternative corporate marketing policies, particularly when these policies entail strategic responses of a particular competitor to these very initiatives. The end users themselves must also not take a hard line with respect to such a distinction. The division between CI and operations must not be so rigid that the CI unit is precluded from even assessing the impact of past decisions already made and currently in practice.

Tracking and Feedback

It is critical that CI end users and the CI professionals providing them with intelligence are continually aware of what kinds of projects are underway, status, progress, any problems, and what decisions are needed by the end user. Whatever options are selected, the CI professionals should not merely accept the assignment, go away, and then bring back a finished product. Best Practice firms, involving all types of CI, have shown that the best intelligence is the result of continuing communication with and feedback from the end users during the assignment.

When dealing with projects which are of a prolonged duration, such as three or more months, it is probably necessary only to report every three to four weeks. Those that are shorter can involve more frequent reports. One way to handle this, while keeping track of accomplishments, is to use a simple form of report. This can be hard copy or e-mail. In any case, it should contain the following elements:

- a clear indication of the date of the report, in the top line
- a summary of assignments that have been closed or finished since the last report. Two to three lines of test describing the assignment, plus a separate line noting the status or results is sufficient.
- a list, in due date or priority order, of current assignment. Here the descriptions should be more completed, possibly including the end user's intentions. A separate status section should indicate when the assignment was given, when it is due, and where it stands now. That includes noting interim briefing, critical problems, and the like.
- It may be useful to separate or highlight any questions that have been taken back to the end user, so that the end user has a "gentle" reminder of what is needed to keep the project moving on schedule.

Consider using the following form as a starting template.

CI Tracking—Current Tasks (in priority order) and Status Report as of May 24, 2002

CI Projects Just Closed

ABC Manufacturing

Obtain for Joan Maxwell copy of a presentation to analysts by ABC Manufacturing, delivered March 11, on new product plans.

Status: Company is releasing an executive summary. We have been told this week (5/23) that it will be emailed shortly.

CI Projects Still Open (in order of Priority)

Employee Benefits

Competitors [list deleted]: The key issue deals with [deleted]. [End user number one] wants to know competitors' process for [deleted] and find out just how "common" and "easy" it is. In addition, for each of the competitors, what products can [delete] sell on the web site? Does it automatically link to the backend systems or does it download to paper which is then uploaded to the [deleted] system?

Status: [End user] would like a report by June 19.

Comment: Awaiting telephone briefing from [end user number two] before beginning.

CI Projects On Hold

None.

APPENDIX: COMPETITOR ANALYSIS CHECKLIST

For the Industry and Market

Industry Structure

- ○ number of competitors, their product lines (or range of services), and locations
- ○ market shares, gross sales, and net profitability of all competitors
- ○ expansion potentialities of all competitors
- ○ important differences among all competitors
- ○ industry marketing, distribution, and pricing practices
- ○ rate of technological change in this niche
- ○ need for new technology
- ○ barriers to entry and exit
- ○ regulatory constraints
- ○ potential entrants and future competitors
- ○ indirect competition

For Individual Competitive Target(s)

- □ identity
- □ decision making
- □ products and services
- □ sales and pricing

- marketing
- financial and legal positions
- technology, R&D
- personnel, resources, and facilities
- strategies, objectives, and perception of self
- perceptions about competitors and customers
- CI capabilities

Identity

- full name
- name or acronym commonly used
- ultimate parent
- major shareholders or partners.
- directors and officers, their backgrounds, and other business relationships
- corporate and management organization: formal and informal
- ownership history

Decision Making

- management styles, abilities, and emphases
- depth, capabilities, and weaknesses of management in key functional areas
- new personnel and recent restructuring
- corporate politics

Products and Services

- product lines and services currently offered
- current and future applications of products and services
- depth and breadth of products and services currently offered
- analysis of new products and services, including impact on the market and on competition
- who makes decisions on new products and services and on what basis
- customer service policies and performance
- history of key products and services
- products or services likely to be introduced, changed, or eliminated in the near future
- channels of distribution, including strengths and weaknesses
- possible changes in distribution channels

Sales and Pricing

- commercial, nonprofit, and government sales
- domestic versus foreign sales
- seasonal and cyclical patterns and problems

- pricing strategy: who prices products and services and how
- price levels and flexibility
- credit, discounts, incentives, consignments, and other special pricing policies
- type of sales force: in-house versus independent sales agents
- organization of sales force: by product and service line, by geographic market, or by end user
- training, capability, and compensation of sales force
- number of customers
- distribution and concentration of customers
- analysis of largest and most important customers

Marketing
- market shares by product and service line, by geographic area, and by industry segment
- marketing approaches and their current effectiveness
- samples of advertising, product literature, and other promotional materials
- samples of products and services
- probable future changes in marketing direction and timing
- history of any questionable marketing practices

Financial and Legal Positions
- long-term borrowing capacities and ability to secure equity financing
- short-term borrowing capacities
- sources of financing, including duration and strength of the relationship
- sales margin, return on assets, and return on equity
- profitability of key divisions, products, or services
- projections of financial position, margins and profitability over next two to five years
- comparison of profitability, cash flow, and other key ratios with those of major competitors
- major liabilities
- regulation of company/unit
- major lawsuits, regulatory enforcement, and rule-making actions: probable impacts on unit

Technology, R&D
- current manufacturing methods and processes
- key patents and proprietary technology
- access to, use of, and dependence on outside technology
- need for new technology

- potential changes in manufacturing methods and processes
- size and capabilities of research staff
- usual lead-time between a research and development break-through and the delivery of a product or service to market
- types and levels of research and development, including current and future expenditures

Personnel, Resources, and Facilities

- labor force: cost, availability, turnover, and quality
- union status, contracts
- raw materials: prices, sources, and availability
- quality control programs in place or planned
- level and consistency of quality control
- manufacturing and operating costs
- facilities: locations, current performance, and potential
- planned improvements to existing facilities or new facilities
- facilities closings or divestitures planned
- productivity programs
- joint ventures, minority interests, and other investments or ownership interests
- make or buy policies

Strategies, Objectives, and Perception of Self

- business philosophy and corporate strategy
- how strategy is made and implemented
- targeted markets and market shares
- target growth rates and other financial objectives
- technological trends and objectives
- information technology (IT) strategy
- recent improvement and restructuring initiatives and their results
- supply chain management structure and strategies
- how the company sees itself

Perceptions about Competitors and Customers

- quality of product or service
- pricing
- marketing and service capabilities and reliability
- management and organization
- technological base and capabilities

CI Capabilities

- separate CI (or other intelligence) unit
- number of SCIP members
- outside intelligence consultants used

- level of intelligence efforts
- targets of intelligence efforts
- defensive activities

NOTES

1. An ironic confirmation of this is found in the work of the Joint House-Senate Committee on Intelligence, investigating the intelligence community and its practices before the 9/11 attacks. Reports indicate that the intelligence community provided copies of the data it accumulated, overwhelming the Committee with the volume that the agencies had to deal with. Ken Guggenheim, "Panel Overwhelmed by 9/11 Data," Associated Press, June 5, 2002, http://story.news.yahoo.com/news?tmpl=story&cid=514&ncid=716&e=2&u =/ap/20020605/ap_on_go_co/attacks_intelligence_29 (Accessed June 5, 2002).

2. See, for example, American Productivity & Quality Center, International Benchmarking Clearinghouse, *User-Driven Competitive Intelligence: Crafting the Value Proposition* (Houston: American Productivity & Quality Center, 2003), 11.

3. As quoted in William A. Rusher, *How to Win Arguments* (Garden City, N.Y.: Doubleday, 1981), 28.

4. Rosi Griffin, Strategic Marketing Manager, Siemens Ltd., "Establishing a CI Program: What Is Needed?" AIC Conferences, Competitive Intelligence Forum '94. Sydney, Australia, 1994, p. 7.

5. Ibid, p. 8.

6. See, for example, John J. McGonagle and Carolyn M. Vella, *Outsmarting the Competition: Practical Approaches to Finding and Using Competitive Information* (Naperville, Ill.: Sourcebooks, Inc., 1990), 65–92.

7. American Productivity & Quality Center, International Benchmarking Clearinghouse, *User-Driven Competitive Intelligence,* 11.

8. Douglas Porch, *The French Secret Services* (New York: Farrar, Straus and Giroux, 1995), 112.

9. See John J. McGonagle and Carolyn M. Vella, *Bottom Line Competitive Intelligence* (Westport, Conn.: Quorum Books, 2002), 121–22.

10. Quoted in The Conference Board, Inc., *Competitive Intelligence,* Research Report No. 913 (1988), 12.

11. This same type of document can be used to help assess the relationship between the various orientations of CI and the subjects needed to be assessed. See McGonagle and Vella, *Bottom Line Competitive* Intelligence, 61–88.

12. This is based on an actual memo circulated in 2000.

13. Saying "no" may be done diplomatically. For example, a CI manager may suggest outside resources, including consultants, who can provide the requested information out of the budget of the person making the inquiry.

10

Overview of Managing Data Gathering

Regardless of the methodology used in designing data collection efforts, there are really only two effective ways that CI analysts can visualize potential data sources when designing their CI data gathering:

- You can visualize the raw data you are seeking as a commodity.
- You can start with a list of potential resources for the raw data, and then proceed methodically through them.

COMPETITOR DATA AS A COMMODITY

Instead of looking at data sources at the beginning of your CI research, approach the task by thinking of the data on a competitor that you are seeking as a commodity, a tangible product. When you do that, then ask and answer the following questions:

- Who produces the raw data I want?
- Who collects the raw data I want?
- Where is the raw data that I want transferred, and why?
- Who uses the raw data I want?
- Who accumulates the raw data that I want?
- Who else has an interest in the raw data I want?

By answering these questions, you will quickly begin to narrow down where you can begin to look for the raw data you need to develop the CI for your end users.

Producers of Raw Data

Take, for example, a case where you are seeking company-level or even divisional-level data. That would seem to mean that a targeted competitor actually produces it. But, regardless of that first impression, you should inquire further. Specifically, who at the competitor is most likely to produce this raw data? For example, is marketing strategy determined by the marketing department, dictated by a strategic plan prepared by the planning department, or the result of input from each? If the answer is that the marketing strategy is a blend of marketing and planning department inputs, when you are, for example, interviewing personnel formerly with a target firm, make sure you get people from the appropriate department involved in the process.[1]

Data Collectors

The person or department you identify here may not be the same person or department that actually produced the data. The key concept here is transmission: when data is being transmitted, it is first assembled and sometimes analyzed, but always moved. One key to locating raw data is to determine where the data is moving so you can try to intercept it, in a figurative sense only. That is why the next question also becomes important.

Data Transfers

Assume that, for any number of reasons, your firm wants detailed, but apparently unavailable, data on the performance of the U.S. gambling operations of a casino partially owned or managed by a competitor. Perhaps your end user wants to determine whether the casino is so profitable that your competitor can expand into other lines or thinks that it is losing so much money that the competitor will have to delay expansion plans in the other areas in which it competes head to head with you.

You should at least check with the Casino Control Commissions for the state or states in which the competitor has casinos. This is because, as regulators, these commissions have a number of areas of interest in that same subject, one of which may be the profitability, or at least dollar volume, of the casino. And because these are public agencies, data the commissions require casinos to provide may be considered as non-proprietary and therefore can be made public and available to you.

Data Users

To determine who uses the kind of raw data you want to locate, you seek out individuals, such as securities analysts, who want data from companies to generate company and/or industry forecasts. For you, what the analyst has to offer is, first of all, his or her analysis and conclusions. However, of potentially greater importance may be the raw data—whether numeric or narrative—provided by the target competitor to the analyst. That data may, in turn, be disclosed in the analyst's reports. If not, you may be able to get it by direct contact with the analyst. If not, you may still be able to extract it from the reports by carefully reviewing them.

Data Accumulators

To reach the handiest repository of accumulated data, contact government regulatory bodies and, in the case of publicly traded companies, investment analysts and trade associations. Each of these sources has data of differing types and quality. The type and quality of that data depends on why each collected the data in the first place. For example, investment analysts are often privy to information that differs from that made available to the press, including the financial press.

Organizations such as the Census Bureau and trade associations generally (but not always) work with aggregated data, as opposed to data at the company or lower level. Using disaggregation may enable you to isolate significant data that you and the providers of the data both assume to be masked by the aggregation efforts of those providing the data.

Others with Interests in the Data

To learn what other organizations and people may have already collected some or all of the data you are seeking, your focus will move to a relatively wide range of potential resources. These can range from the advertising departments of trade publications to academic research centers. Trade publications' advertising departments may collect or even generate data similar to what you are seeking in an effort to show that their publication represents the audience an advertiser wants to reach. To do that, the advertising department may choose to collect data or even commission new surveys to educate potential advertisers about the industry and about key participants that can be reached by advertising there.

Academic centers can be a useful resource because their access to data is sometimes much freer and broader than that of trade associations and the like. This may be because those associated with the centers may be able to interview or research your competitors. Moreover, the companies they deal with will sometimes assume that giving academic researchers access to the data is "harmless," in a competitive sense. Of course, some competitors are savvy enough to insist that the academics who are given access to competitively sensitive data do not release any of the data, except in some aggregated form. However, there are often ways around such blocks. For example, if a researcher is operating under such a limit, in interviewing him or her you may be able to discern some of the underlying data by a close discussion of the conclusions he or she has drawn.

STARTING WITH SOURCES OF RAW DATA

The numerous sources listed throughout the balance of this chapter will serve only as starting points for your efforts to design the search for raw data. While potential sources for raw data are almost endless, we have divided the most likely potential sources of raw data into four basic categories:

- governments
- specialized Interests
- private sector
- media

Grouping data sources allows you and your staff to keep track of them, in broad terms. More importantly, data sources within each category have important characteristics in common. Knowing these can be very useful you move to the analytical stage.

Government Data Sources

As a group, government sources generally provide only indirect assistance. That is because the vast bulk of the data that they can access and release is highly aggregated, as with business census reports, or consists of data already collected by another provider, such as information taken from a commercial directory.

Examples of Government Data Sources

U.S. Government
regulatory agencies
trade promotion offices
congressional hearings
winning competitive bids
court cases and records
patents and trademarks
agency and contractor studies: regular and onetime

Foreign Governments
reglatory agencies
trade promotion offices
quasi-government bodies
regular publications
patents
commerical attachés

State Governments
regulatory agencies
court cases and records
winning competitive bids
environmental permits and other regulatory filings
trademarks

Local Governments
zoning and building permits and other filings
court cases and records
winning competitive bids
industrial development authorities
boards of taxation and assessment

However, your competitors also provide governmental units with significant company-level data through other channels. Here, we refer to areas such as licensing, regulation, taxation, and litigation files. Data collected through these channels tends to be very company or subject specific rather than aggregated. And it tends to be relatively easily and inexpensively accessed, although it may take a relatively long time to do so.

Specialized Interest Data Sources

This group is composed of sources that collect data to advance their own specialized interests, hence the name. Those interests may be professional or may reflect what the group's members see as a "public" or "industry" interest.

Examples of Common Specialized Interest Data Sources

Consumer and Other Advocacy Groups
product tests and comparisons
regular publications
onetime studies and position papers

Experts
consultants
expert witnesses
security (stock) analysts

Trade Associations
regular publications
membership directories
special studies and reports
meetings and reprints of speeches
statistical abstracts

Academics and Academic Resources
faculty
regular publications, special and onetime studies
industry research centers and specialized libraries
teaching materials and case studies

The specialized interests all collect and provide data for a reason: to advance what they each see as their own best interests, or the best interests of those that they represent.

Advocacy groups of all types have an "ax to grind." That is typically framed as the advancement of the public good, as that group defines it. In doing this, they may well be spending significant time and funds to collect data, publish reports, bring lawsuits, or test products and services, all of which may be a source of raw data for you.

Experts includes everyone from consultants to expert witnesses and from clinical laboratories to security analysts. Their work reflects a common goal: to advance the individual's career, whether it is by obtaining assignments, helping an employer sell stock, or some other means. But each is providing data for a particular audience, which can color, not only how they say things, but what they say and do not say.

Trade associations exist for the good of their industry. In some industries, trade associations are unwilling, or even unable, to share data with nonassociation members. In other industries, the trade associations are important, but little known, research and resource centers whose data is available to all outsiders.[2]

Academics may seek funding support for research in which they are interested, advancement of their professional careers, or consulting assignments, in addition to their own research interests. In these efforts the professors and researchers may provide you with such useful input as publications, special detailed studies, and access to research centers for collecting important historical data.

Private Sector

The private sector grouping includes people and organizations whose business directly involves producing or selling the kinds of data you may be seeking. For some, providing the data *is* their business.

Others may come across data on your competitor as a part of their own business.

Common Private Sector Data Sources

Your Primary Competitor's Employees
sales
market research
planning
engineering
purchasing
former employees of the target company

Your Primary Competitor
Internet home page
catalogs and price lists
in-house publicaitons
press releases and speeches
advertisements and promotional materials
products
annual reports
regulatory filings
customers and suppliers
retailers, distributors, and agents
advertising and marketing agencies

Other Competitors

Business Information Services
Dun & Bradstreet
Standard & Poor's
credit reporting agencies
proprietary research firms

Chambers of Commerce
domestic
foreign chambers in the United States
U.S. chambers of commerce abroad

The private sector makes up the most eclectic of the four groups. In dealing with these sources, you and other CI professionals must avoid confusing the package with its contents. For example, assume that you have received a proprietary research report on a targeted company and are now reviewing the data it provides you on the firm's size, employees, sales, and so on. To verify the data, you may compare it with data you have obtained from another business information source, such as a business profile report. Suppose the facts appear identical. To an unskilled analyst, this appears to provide confirmation of the first set of data. However, that is not necessarily correct. You see, the report's author could have purchased the data on your competitor. So if it looks the same as data from another business source, that may be because it *is* the same. That does not mean it is correct. It is just a false confirmation.

Media

These varied sources all collect, generate, and process data for a specific audience. To fully understand both the data you may find on your competitor and how to analyze it, you *must* understand from whom the media collects that data, how, and why.

Common Media Data Sources

Business Newspapers and Magazines
advertisements and want ads
articles
reporters

Wire Services
articles
reporters

Directories and Reference Aids

Local and National Newspapers
advertisements and want ads
articles
reporters
obituaries

Technical Journals
articles
authors

Trade Papers and Journals, Financial Periodicals
advertisements and want ads
articles
reporters

marketing studies and media kits
special issues
related publications

Security Analysts' Reports
company reports
industry profiles

The media, in the broadest sense, can be one of the most fruitful resources for obtaining raw data. But always remember that many publications exist to serve a particular industry or market. Thus, they are positioned to help you locate some important data and develop leads for additional data, but may have significant blind spots as well.

Who Creates Data versus Where You Locate It

As you focus on where the raw data you need might be located and accessed, always keep in mind that the place you get data is not necessarily the ultimate source of that data. This distinction is too often overlooked yet can be a critical. This means that you may be able to access the data you want without having to contact the data's original source. It also means that you must ensure that you know whether a source of data actually produces the data or merely transmits it. Confusing the data producer with the data provider can have important, sometimes dangerous, consequences. For example, cross-checking past estimates made by a trade publication that prints market predictions with the industry's actual performance might show that this publication is often incorrect in its predictions. If you find that such information in a particular trade publication is consistently wrong, you may decide you cannot rely on it for accurate information about your competitors' plans.

VISUALIZATION AND RESEARCH PLANNING

Another option for developing a CI research strategy in a case where you are faced only with a general statement of end user needs is to visualize a blank page in front of you. In fact, some CI analysts have had good luck with starting with a blank page in word processing. Then you visualize, filling it with what you think the final report might be in response to the general needs statement given you by an end user. To do this, you ask and then answer, as best you can, the following:

- What points are critical for you to make dealing with the subject matter of the CI inquiry?
- What raw data do you probably need to make a clear statement or draw a conclusion for each of those points?
- How specific and current does that raw data have to be to allow you to draw a conclusion and to answer the CI inquiry?

This approach starts the process at the very end of the project—dealing with the goals you were given—rather than the beginning. This way you can avoid being influenced by any preconceptions about what you may expect to find and where. Instead, you set as your goal the raw data you think need and then work backward to identify exactly what data you need and then go and locate *that* specific data. This entails four basic steps.

Step 1

To develop your research goals, outline the first page of a possible report on your project. Make sure that outline shows a possible recommended course of action, even if your end user has not asked for one. After all, the CI will be used by someone to make a decision. Begin by restating the needs statement as a conclusion and as an action statement. For example, if the question is "How can we catch up with competitor A in terms of costs of production?" you can, for example, restate it as follows:

> Our competitor's most significant cost advantage is in its use of CAD-CAM [computer-assisted design–computer assisted manufacturing] systems in its manufacturing activities. [Remember, this is only hypothetical.] For our firm to catch up, we must change our manufacturing processes to incorporate the newest European CAD-CAM technology.

Step 2

Following the action statement, list the kinds of key findings that might tend to support your recommendation. Following this example, you could write:

> Our competitor has, and will continue to have, substantially lower costs than we do for manufacturing the same products. This is due to its CAD-CAM systems plus lower costs of raw materials.
>
> The experience of manufacturers in other, similar industries indicates that CAD-CAM systems can be successfully adapted to our manufacturing operations within a short period of time, providing important cost savings.

Step 3

Now, again transform these statements into questions. First, convert the conclusion you drew in Step 1 into the following:

Does our competitor have lower costs?

Why are its costs lower?

For the two most important reasons for lower costs, can we duplicate or improve on these?

You are now drawing closer to a statement of the focus for your CI research. *Knowing the research focus is crucial.* It enables you to control and limit the data gathering efforts to those that have the greatest likelihood of responding to the general needs statement from your end user.

Also, once you know the focus of the research for the assignment, you will also be more likely to identify other data of potential interest to you and your end user, or leads to that data, even if it does not go into your final report. For example, here, if your research disclosed that a major consulting firm had just created a CAD-CAM systems consulting practice, you might want to save that information for future reference because you or your internal client might well be seeking such expertise after the CI project is over.

Step 4

Now, repeat the conversion process in Step 3 for all of the draft key findings you developed in Step 2, like this:

Does our competition have substantially lower costs than we do for manufacturing? If they do, will that continue?

Are existing CAD-CAM systems sufficiently developed to be able to support our manufacturing techniques?

What has been the experience of manufacturing firms in other, similar industries with the same CAD-CAM systems? Specifically, can it be successfully adapted to our manufacturing operations within a short period of time and will this provide a cost savings?

If you need to, you can repeat the process until you have created a series of smaller questions on which you can focus your CI research efforts. As you progress, you should find that, if any of your small assumptions are not correct, you can quickly adjust your focus while the research is underway.

Data-gathering constraints

Your CI research and collection strategy must reflect the unique needs of each assignment. Among the critical points to take into account in developing a research and collection strategy are the following:

- time constraints
- financial restrictions
- staffing limitations
- self-imposed constraints

Time constraints

Time is one of the most critical elements in limiting CI research. There are a wide variety of time constraints, some, or even all, of which may be applicable to a particular project. They can be most easily understood by asking, and then answering, the following questions:

- How long will data collection probably take?
- How much time do you have to conduct the project?
- How much of the total time is allocated to data collection?
- How long will it take to collect the raw data that you *really* need, that is, to answer the most important questions, but not all questions?
- Can you start your analysis work with only partial data (if so, when, or else what data do you require)?
- How much time is available for analysis?
- How much of *your own* time is available, and when?

In general, the key factor here is for you to determine when the CI is needed and then work backward. For instance, if you have three weeks to develop data on the market plans for new products of three key competitors, planning to go to a trade show that will be held in four weeks is obviously not a viable option. However, knowing about the trade show may cause you to try to change the assignment, by trying to get a later due date. For example, you might want to spend the time before the trade show researching marketing strategies and then attend the trade show or review the trade press coverage of the show to complete the research.

Financial constraints

Financial restrictions control more CI-gathering decisions than most people are willing to acknowledge. For example, should you hire a CI consultant who plans to interview key executives in person or should he or she do this over the telephone? In-person interviews are likely to produce more useful raw data but will cost considerably more than using the telephone.

Similarly, if you are tracking a competitor over a prolonged period of time, using an article-clipping service may be a cost-effective way to collect background and general interest articles about the firm. However, if the analysis of the same competitor is just a one-time project or has a short time frame, you might do better using on-line commercial databases, even through their costs average $250 an hour. That is because these services provide you the data you need virtually immediately and permit you to go back in time, whereas a clipping service has delays in providing materials and generally only allows you to go forward. That is, you cannot ask the service to go back in time and add another topic to its monitoring.

Overall, you must appreciate (and, in turn, teach your end users) that time and money are always trade-offs in CI research. As a rough rule of thumb, cutting the time available for a project by half can be expected to at least double the costs of acquiring the same raw data. If time constraints are too critical, this can cause costs to escalate significantly. For example, your research strategy may identify four possible avenues of research. If you have sufficient time, you might logically pursue the one with the highest likelihood of success first. Then if that does not provide enough data, you would move to the second, and so on.

However, if you are put under severe time constraints, you might have to engage in parallel activity. That is, instead of proceeding sequentially through research options, you may have to start all four at once. You do not have the time to do otherwise. And the costs will rise accordingly.

Staffing constraints

The amount and timing of CI staff resources that you can put on a project at a particular point in time can be a very important constraint. Other types of staffing constraints include considerations such as how many people are available, what each of them can and cannot do, and when they have time available. Typically—if there is a typical case—a CI assignment requires fewer personnel during the planning and early collection phases than it does in the middle, when the data collection and review work begin to pile up. And at the end, bottlenecks will tend to develop as stacks of unanalyzed data accumulate.

You probably can use a relatively small number of staff to help you analyze the raw data and eventually disseminate it, but the process of analysis may consume most of the time of each of those involved. This means that these people (including you) may not be available to handle the collection of supplementary data critical to the assignment. You may need to plan for quick access to a few people familiar with the earlier stages to help with supplemental research toward the end.

Self-Imposed constraints

Self-imposed constraints can vary widely. You may be comfortable with contacting your competitors directly. However, you may also find that you can no longer do this due to a change in company policy. This may force you to approach future projects from a different angle.

Another constraint may be a legitimate concern about allowing too many of your employees to learn about a CI project. That is, you or your end users may not want other employees, perhaps even other CI staff members, to be involved with the assignment at all. That can and has happened in cases involving a potential acquisition. This constraint can be so severe that you may have the choice of either abandoning all other projects to take this on yourself or turning it over to outside CI firms.

DEVELOPING CI RESEARCH STRATEGIES

The success of your CI efforts depends on how well you recognize the constraints you are subject to, how well you structure the data-gathering process, and how practical your decisions are about the trade-offs among your potential raw data sources.

Basic Guidelines

If there is any rule to follow in conducting your firm's CI research, it is to be realistic but optimistic. If you can determine what you need, the data is almost always somewhere to be found. To locate where the raw data you may need for your CI may be accessible, remember to identify who else has an interest in that data and why they have an interest. Each person and/or organization you identify is a potential source for your raw data, as well as a potential linkage (described later). For example, if you are interested in the sales of in certain departments in chain food stores, using these criteria should lead you to trade associations, corporate annual reports, and trade publications.

Do not limit yourself with, and do not be limited by, indexing or database searches. For example, if you have identified a trade publication of potential interest, check whether that publisher has a special annual issue, or even a separate publication, that covers the areas of particular concern to you.

How Likely Are You to Get What You Need?

Always think about making a preliminary determination of the likelihood that you will get good data from each target source you have identified. Assume that you have concluded that a particular trade association may be a good source for the raw data you need. What is the likelihood that the association will have exactly what you want, that it will provide it to you (if your firm is not a member), and that this can happen within your time and cost limitations? Similarly, if your project involves reviewing the back issues of a local newspaper for want ads placed by a target competitor two and three years ago, is it really likely that you can access a complete set of issues for those years and that you will be able to review them in a cost-effective manner? If not, before you start on such an effort, you should try to identify alternative approaches or sources of data that may satisfy your data needs.

What Do You Need First?

Throughout your CI research, you should maintain a clear idea of the relative importance of the data you and you staff are seeking and of the data sources you are trying to locate. Do not waste time tracking down minor pieces of data to produce a picture-perfect product. CI is not academic research, but rather a commercial activity, one in which the final product ages rapidly. In fact, CI that is not delivered on time may be worthless.

In managing your CI research and data collection needs, you may see that progress depends on collecting certain data first. For example, if you are going to interview key personnel at a competitor's distributors, you must first identify the distributors and then identify the key people at each one before you can start interviews.

Also, some data will arrive more slowly than other data, even when you have located it. To understand the trade-offs involved in timeliness, compare the following potential ways of obtaining the contents of documents filed by a target competitor with the U.S. SEC:

- You can ask the target firm for copies. It is slow, but cheap, if the firm responds. Remember, it does not have to send you these materials.
- You can see if the target firm provides them on its home page, or if they are available through the SEC's EDGAR database system. This is free or virtually free, but not all documents, particularly the annual report to shareholders as well as older filings, will be accessible this way.
- You can get summaries of key documents on-line through a database. That is faster, but will not show photographs in an annual report and a subscription may not be a financial option for all firms.

- You can hire a commercial service to copy the documents directly from the SEC's files and air-express or fax them directly to you. This is more costly but complete.

Tiering CI research

Often, you may not be able to find the exact data you think you need either quickly or easily. This is particularly problematic when your time, money, or personnel resources are limited. If a project looks like it could turn out to be excessively demanding, you should divide your assignment into tiers, or levels, of research. Your research is designed to take you to the next stage, while narrowing the number of targets or scope of the research at each level.

For example, take an assignment in which the task is to determine the capital expansion plans of ten competitors. Tiering might allow the CI research to start by taking all ten firms and determining whether each is planning any significant capital expansions. If three of the ten are not planning any expansions, tiering will permit you to drop these names from the research. Then the work will focus on detailed information on the remaining targets.

That means you attack the most general level first and go after the most easily obtained data, which can then be reviewed quickly. Next, you would analyze that data in terms of what it tells you about what additional, more specific data you need to complete your task, as well as where that data may be located.

Then, you move to the next tier. At that point, you narrow the scope of the research, perhaps by eliminating potential targets or data sets, and then collect more data and analyze the results. If possible, you drop additional targets in the third tier, continuing in this way until you are done. By using this process, you can often save both time and money because you focus your resources on locating the most critical bits of more specific data in the second and following tiers.

Linkages

When you look for raw data, you should never mentally restrict your search. Not only can one source provide several different and important types of data, but multiple sources should be cross-checked to generate data on the same point. They should also be checked for leads to other data sources, including people.

Soft Data

Do not assume that you should only look for hard data (that is quantitative data) for your CI projects. In some cases, you may find that all that is available is "soft," or qualitative, data. In other cases, the best

CI is soft. For example, in discussing the problems of keeping up with Japanese research and development activities, four scientists at the Battelle Pacific Northwest Laboratories observed:

> [W]e have found that scientific and technological advances in Japan are often first communicated by word of mouth within the Japanese scientific community. . . . It is also important to recognize that many significant technical developments in Japan do not appear directly as experimental results or as business news. . . . Thus technical journals and databases are helpful but only supplementary. Closer contact between our countries' specialists is the primary way to supply the necessary details and overall insights.[3]

In many cases, you may be faced with an end user insisting on hard data to be used to compare your firm with the target in some way. You may—more likely will—quickly find that such numbers do not appear to be readily available. There can be two important reasons for that:

- The industry may be very sensitive about the competitive importance of such metrics. One test of such importance would be to see if your own firm permits such data to become public.
- No two companies in this industry use (or even calculate) key metrics the same way. Therefore, seeking hard numbers in such an area may be fruitless. Rather, one must make the internal clients understand that soft data is available and that it can be just as important (if not more so).

To locate substitute, soft data, exploiting linkages is often the best way. The key is to understand that while the targets themselves do not usually disclose all that information, other parties, close to the targets, may be able to provide some supplemental data.

TELEPHONE INTERVIEWS

Telephone interviews can be a powerful way to supplement secondary research. However, effective telephone interviewing can be a difficult process. Before undertaking it or authorizing others to do it for your firm, you should first acquaint yourself with a number of key precepts.

- Preparation
- Interview strategies
- Techniques to keep an interview moving.

Preparation

Have you thought how you will identify yourself? *Never* misrepresent who you are. (Do not say *"I'm a student."*) There are several problems in such misrepresentation.

- Foremost is the ethical issue. This conduct violates the SCIP statement on ethical conduct. (See chapter 8 on legal and ethical issues)
- Allowing such behavior is actually counterproductive. Such conduct feeds a tendency toward a downward spiral in behavior.
- Misrepresentation can result in data contamination. That occurs when the interviewee provides the type of information he or she believes this specific interviewer needs or wants. Thus, someone pretending to be a student may get student-level, assimilated data.

Realistically, you are obligated to say who you work for, but is there an obligation to make excessive disclosures? For example, is this proper? *"I am calling from the Information Center in Harrisburg, Pennsylvania."* Note that the name of the firm was not given. Is this misrepresentation? No, it is not.

Be clear in your own mind what you want to accomplish in the interview. Specifically, what types of data do you expect the interview to contribute? Keep your questions as short as possible. Decide whether you want to ask very focused questions or very broad-ranging ones. The former provide more specific, statistically usable data, but people feel more comfortable dealing with broad, open-ended questions, especially if their answers draw on personal experience.

Consider such mechanical issues as note taking, interviewee's caller ID and getting calls returned:

- Will you use a script?
- How will you take notes? Will the interviewee let you record the conversation? Remember, the recording of a telephone conversation without the consent of the other party is almost always illegal.
- Do you want your interviewee to sense or know that you are taking notes? Can you wait until after an interview and still be able to record everything that is important?
- The impact of caller ID is still unknown; it is just emerging. While not yet widespread, if it is in use, the number displayed may impact whether your call is even taken.
- When trying to get calls returned, consider issues such as whether or not you want to use a toll-free number.

Be frank about any limitations you will face with telephone interviews. For example, do you have to complete them in a very short time? Do you expect the interviewees to be easy to reach and cooperative? You may need to have to give your interviewee some reason to participate. For example, if you are going to interview a newspaper reporter, you may want to offer the reporter *public* information you have already developed on the target company in exchange for the reporter's assistance.

Finally, consider the physical and time constraints involved. Set your own deadline for conducting interviews and stick to it. Unless you do that, you can quickly get enmeshed in an endless round of interviews that provide decreasing amounts of useful data. An interviewer should probably limit the number of interview calls per day for several reasons.

- For one, it's important to pace yourself. It takes time to complete an interview, review the notes, and prepare for the next call.
- By limiting the number of outgoing calls, you can more easily set aside a specific callback time, if needed.
- Finally, if you limit the outgoing calls, you will minimize the likelihood that you will miss a returned call. In fact, if you have a call waiting signal, you might consider disabling (or at least ignoring) it so you do not interrupt an interview in process.

Selecting Interview Strategies

Having determined what you want to get from an interview (or interviews), an interviewer should next establish strategies for:

- identifying, and then dealing with, time constraints
- approaching your targets
- approaching sensitive targets

Time Constraints. In dealing with interviews, make sure that you have a clear understanding of the following:

- How much time do you have available? The answer has at least two different aspects. The first is how much time you have from the beginning of the interviews until they must be completed. Second is how much time the interviewers you select can give to the assignment.
- Given the length of time available, just how available is that time? For example, have you allowed sufficient time for preparation (and practice if needed)? How much time do you allow for the calls themselves? What will you do about returned calls? Will the interviewer be easily available when interviewees may call back? Did you allow time for follow-up calls to complete outstanding interviews? How much time is allotted for completing reports on calls and then analyzing the results of each completed interview?

Experience shows that, for every hour on the telephone, you will need from a half-hour to an hour to identify and make contact with a potential interviewee, and up to an hour to write up the results of that interview.

Planning on Approaches. When planning for your interviews, first plan on how you will approach them. First, what is your opening? (Why are you calling? What are you looking for?) In general, keep your opening short and practice it. Consider how you will talk about what you are interested in and conduct the interview. For example, are there key words or buzzwords that are used by those who are to be interviewed? If so, you should identify them and understand what they mean. This does not, however, mean that you should use them in the interview process.

There are several situations when it is not appropriate to use technical terms:

- You are not fully conversant with them, so you might make a mistake in using them or in translating them in your notes.
- Using such terms gives your interviewee the belief that he or she is dealing with an expert. That could limit the background or context that is given, which may be exactly what you are seeking.

However, you may want to use such terms when you deal with a gatekeeper. That is the case if you do not know who your interview target is, but do know in what area he or she works. Then, having a command of these terms makes it easier for a gatekeeper, such as the switchboard, to connect you to the right person.

Sensitive Targets. There will be situations when you have to approach an interviewee who is sensitive. By sensitive, we mean someone who:

- has a limited amount of time to talk with you
- is difficult to reach
- has a great deal of expertise so is likely to refuse to talk for very long
- may be uncomfortable talking with you (or anyone in your firm)

In these cases, you should do as much work as possible *before* starting the interview to maximize the value of the limited time you may have. For example, if you are dealing with a high-profile expert, exhaust all public sources first. Make sure you know what the person has already said or written so you can seek something new or different.

Also, be prepared for a hand-off, that is, a desire to have you talk to someone else, or at least to get rid of you. In that case, get a name and telephone number, if possible, as soon as you see this happening. Try then to ask your interviewee if there is anything he or she can add to what that source will probably say. In other words, exploit what you have while you have it.

Keep the Interview Moving. There are a wide variety of techniques available to keep an interview moving. All are based on an understanding of the interviewee, a mastery of the subject in question, and patience. What follows are several of those that have most often been overlooked.

Set the Stage. When you start, do not say you are "seeking information" or "doing a survey." This can put off your interviewee and quickly result in him or her seeking to transfer you to someone else or terminating the call. Rather, you should approach the situation more personally, pulling the interviewee into the discussion. Consider opening approaches such as "I'd like to get your opinion on this," or "Do you have any thoughts (experiences) on this that you can share?"

Prepare yourself, perhaps by a rehearsal, to anticipate problems (or objections) and have ready answers for them. For example, be prepared to deal with the following common objections:

I'm too busy now.

I really don't know much about that.

I can't talk about this.

Why are you calling?

You'll have to talk to [name] about that (but he's not in).

What are you going to do with this information?

We do not give out information (like that).

Approach the Interview in an Orderly Manner. Before you start, remember the memory trick for writing newspaper stories: "Who, What, Why, Where, When, and How." For you, this means that your interview notes should cover all these aspects.

When talking with an interviewee, it is usually better to start with the easy subjects first and move to hard ones or to move from the general to the specific. This way, you and the interviewee move naturally through what should be a discussion.

If there are subjects the interviewee may find sensitive or even objectionable, keep them for the end of the interview. That way you will have extracted as much as you can for the interview before your subject decides to terminate the discussion.

Adopt the Right Attitude. When you approach the interviewee, convey the attitude that you are seeking a "chance" to get *some* information. Do not try to get it all at once from only one subject. Often that will result in getting nothing at all.

When covering the points you wish to deal with, speak less rather than more. Silence literally is golden. Experience demonstrates that if an answer you receive is not enough, a careful pause can often result in the subject continuing to elaborate.

When conducting the interview, make sure to listen for what your interviewee knows (and what he or she does not know). Specifically, you should do the following:

- Modify your questions to fit the evidenced level of knowledge of your interviewee.
- Broaden your questions by using his or her answers as a springboard.
- Try using challenging statements instead of questions, for example, "There are reports that profits are down over 15 percent." Such a statement may elicit a quick rebuttal.
- Work at inducing clarification and cooperation. One technique is to repeat what you just heard instead of asking a new question. Another is to avoid making yourself the source of a potentially controversial question. That means you might preface a sensitive topic with, "*Some in the industry feel that . . .*", so your interviewee knows that this is not your opinion.

FINISHING

In planning and executing your research strategy, be thorough, not obsessive. You and your end users should always understand that in CI, you must learn to accept something that is less than perfect but still accomplishes the desired end. In other words, many times you have to say to your end user, "It's close enough."

How do you know when you are done? There is an informal test we have found useful. It is called *tail chasing* or, more elegantly, *closing the loop*. This occurs when new sources of raw data seem continually to give you leads that take you back to previously identified or exploited sources. At that point, you are usually at the end of your basic research.

PLANNING FOR AS-YET UNCOMMISSIONED RESEARCH

If you face the likelihood that you will have to conduct research against any one of an identifiable set of targets, but you do not know when that will happen, it might be useful to develop a summary of the potential target, and, most importantly, where you can locate data on it if and when you need it. Consider using the following form to conduct that sort of advance work.

Target
Ultimate parent company
  Identification information
    Address/Telephone/Product(s):
    Does it make filing with the U.S. Securities and Exchange Commission?
  Target data sources
    SEC filings and related releases: Yes/No
      Comments/suggestions
    Newsletter(s): Yes/No
      Name:
      Frequency:
      Published by:
      Contents:
      Distribution:
      Comments/suggestions:
    Table of organization:
      Commercially available:
    Directory
      Commercially available:
    Advertising agencies
    Public relations
      Internal
        Contact:
        Coverage:
        Comments/suggestions:
      External
        Name:
        Address:
        Contact:
        Coverage:
        Comments/suggestions:
    800/Consumer information number(s):
    Business school cases:
    Other:
  Overall remarks:

This form actually captures some preliminary research efforts. In doing this, you spend a limited amount of time determining *where* information on your target will probably be *when* you eventually need it. You do *not* collect it now. However, if and when you need to start collecting that data, you will already have an idea of where it might be and, just as important, where it is not likely to be

NOTES

1. Such interviews are subject, of course, to the legal and ethical limits set forth in Chapter 8.

2. A trade association can also serve as a means of identifying, or even gaining access to, some of your employees. For instance, purchasing a trade association's membership directory may enable your competitor to find out who at your firm is responsible for the area in which it has a particular interest. Similarly, attending an association's meetings may give your competitor access, not only to products and promotional materials, but also to your own people. Finally, trade association committee meetings can be good places for collecting raw data.

3. "Getting to the Heart of Japanese R&D," *High Technology*, February 1987, 7.

11

Tips on Managing Analysis

TOOLS FOR ANALYSIS

Over the past two decades, CI has begun to develop an impressive body of literature on the tools available to CI analysts. The very best place to start would be with Craig S. Fleisher and Babette E. Bensoussan, *Strategic and Competitive Analysis: Methods and Techniques for Analyzing Business Competition*.[1] Other books that are almost as essential for understanding CI analytical techniques are Liam Fahey, *Competitors: Outwitting, Outmaneuvering, and Outperforming*.[2] Conor Vibert, *Web-Based Analysis for Competitive Intelligence*,[3] and Ben Gilad and Jan P. Herring (eds.), *The Art and Science of Business Intelligence Analysis [Advances in Applied Business Strategy, Supplement 2, 1996]: Part B: Intelligence Analysis and Its Applications*.[4]

Which analytical tool is best for an individual project is a matter of professional training and personal preference, coupled with an understanding of the data available. In practice, most analysts rely on a very few tools. As the art of analysis is difficult, if not impossible, to teach,[5] the best way to improve analytical skills is through training, that is, exposing CI analysts to more and different tools and how the tools work.

THE PROCESS OF ANALYSIS

In preparing a CI report, the analyst faces a mass of data, which has probably been accumulated in no particular order. It is usually incomplete and can contain misinformation and even disinformation. Analysis is the process by which this mass of raw data is handled, so that the CI analyst can produce a finished product. In the context of CI, the process of analysis is made up of separate sub processes:

- gathering
- incorporation
- enlightenment
- incubation
- validation

Gathering All the Relevant Data

Gathering the raw data involves more than the collection of raw data that appears directly related to the problem at hand. It includes getting access to all of the data accumulated, touching on these subjects or targets. That accumulation has taken place both within this particular context and over a lifetime of experiences.

Incorporating the Data

Here the CI analyst carefully reviews all of the raw data. This is not a onetime, quick-pass reading. It requires a slow and careful reading of all materials, usually twice or even more. The best CI analysts will review the materials in different ways each time: once organized by source, another time organized by topic, and a third time in chronological order. The goal is to master all the data, even that which does not, at first seem to be important. Experience shows that it is often those particular bits of raw data that later are found to have an unexpected connection or importance.

Incubation

Now the CI analyst thinks about everything that has been collected. Consciously and unconsciously, the analyst assembles the facts in various ways, so that one or more logical pictures begin to emerge. Incubation almost always overlaps incorporation of the data because:

- Both start as the data begins to come.
- Both involve an evaluation of the validity of the data, as well as the credibility of the source.

Beyond merely incorporating, however, incubation marks the beginning of the real interpretation of the meaning of the raw data.

Enlightenment

After studying the problem presented by the end user and the data bearing on it, the *real* meaning of the data, and thus a solution to the problem, finally become clear. Sometimes this enlightenment can occur in a flash, but more often, it is a gradual process. Enlightenment encompasses the actual analysis of the raw data, in the sense of drawing conclusions, data interpretation, and the formation and testing of hypotheses.

Validation

In this stage the CI analyst seeks to prove, or disprove, the solution that presented itself during enlightenment. This is *not* merely verifying the raw data. It involves drawing specific conclusions and then testing the validity of the conclusions against the observed facts, *before* presenting them to management.

HINTS FOR HANDLING CI DATA

While the process of analyzing the results of data gathering differs for each project, there are several process techniques that a CI analyst should keep in mind in every situation. For convenience, we have divided them between evaluating data, on the one hand, and organizing your analysis, on the other.

Both evaluation and analysis are steps critical to the CI process. In practice, it is somewhat difficult to distinguish exactly where they begin and the process of collecting raw data ends. To try to separate them, use the following division:

- *Evaluation:* studying the raw data, usually as you are collecting it, to determine if and how you can use it
- *Analysis:* Studying raw data, after evaluation, to turn it into CI

Using these steps requires that you test the reliability of the data you obtained from your CI collection program and then eliminate false confirmations from data sources.

Evaluating the Raw Data

Dealing with Accuracy and Reliability. You can never assume that all data is accurate or that all sources are equally as reliable. If you make that assumption, by not probing both accuracy and reliability, you may be generating CI out of a concoction of very good data, marginally correct data, bad data, and even disinformation.

Even if you find that you can draw some sort of conclusion from that mishmash, you risk drawing the wrong conclusion. However, once you have a sense of the relative accuracy of the individual pieces of data, you can then begin to analyze all your data properly.

There are three basic elements in evaluating the accuracy of raw data:

- Identify the actual source of the data so you can evaluate the reliability of the source.
- Estimate the data's accuracy so you can classify the data.
- Eliminate false confirmations.

In CI, *reliability* refers to the believability of the source of your data. You often can estimate how much you can believe any data coming from a particular source, based on that source's past performance. On the other hand, *accuracy* relates to the correctness of the particular piece of data you have. There, you are estimating how correct the data is, based on factors such as whether it is confirmed by data from a reliable source as well as the reliability of the original source of the data.

Reliability of the Source. To evaluate the probable accuracy of any raw data, you must have at least a sense of its ultimate source. That helps you figure out why the data was produced, collected, and even released.

You should assume that all data is produced and released to advance some particular purpose or to be read by a particular audience. You must not ignore the origins of data, either. Data is only as good as its source. Keep in mind the following informal rule: Unless you establish otherwise, *assume* that every place from which you get data has its own point of view, which permeates any data from that source.

Estimate the Data's Accuracy. Once you have assessed the reliability of the data source you are looking at, you next estimate its accuracy. This can involve formally classifying the data you get as to relative degrees of accuracy or doing so on an informal basis, based on past experience. As you collect more data and involve others in collecting and analyzing it, you might find that you need some systematic way of labeling individual pieces of raw data to identify both their likely accuracy and the probable credibility of their sources.[6]

For example, information you get from the current distributors for a target firm may or may not be reliable. That data's reliability depends on the attitude of the particular distributors toward their supplier, their view of the use to which the information they are giving to you may eventually be put, and their access to current data of the sort you are getting from them. Similarly, data from a competitor's suppliers, even those with whom your firm also does business, may be influenced by conflicting factors. These influences include the desire to please you, reluctance to discuss other customers, or a lack of perception on the part of the individual providing you with the data.

The past track record, if available, of both individual and institutional sources of data is generally a good basis on which to estimate current reliability. A supplemental test is one dealing with the likelihood that your source could actually have the specific data you have obtained from it. That is, ask yourself whether, under the conditions facing the specific source, that source could have actually obtained the specific data within the limitations of time, access, and financing that it faced.

Eliminate False Confirmations. Confirming data from one source with data from another lets you assess the original data's accuracy. In the long run, it also helps you to be able to assess the reliability of its source. A false confirmation is a situation in which one source appears to confirm data obtained from another source. In fact, however, there may be no real confirmation, because the first source obtained its data from the second source or they both received it from the same third source.

Pseudo-Precision. Be careful that you understand exactly what a data source has said and has not said. Many businesses and industries use a private language. Sometimes, this provides real clarity and precision for insiders. In other cases, it only serves to keep outsiders, including you, from understanding what is actually going on. The jargon may even be intended to create desired impressions in targeted groups.

Assess the Consistency of the Data. Merely because you have consistent data does not mean that you can immediately draw a conclusion based on it. When your research seems to provide consistent estimates, it can mean one of several things:

- The data and your conclusions really are valid.
- No one ever questions this particular "revealed truth."
- All the data has a common source, so there is no real confirmation, merely a false confirmation.

Look at the data in question and analyze it, keeping all these possibilities in mind. Make sure you know why data is consistent before you rely on it.

In evaluating consistency or dealing with possible inconsistencies, one of the easiest mistakes to make is to confuse similar terms that are really used to mean widely differing things. You can avoid this by paying careful attention to definitions and terminology.

Anomalies. An anomaly is a situation when data does not fit. It is usually an indication that one's working assumptions are wrong or that an unknown factor is affecting the results you have found. Always review anomalies and try to figure out why they occurred. Something out of the ordinary should not be automatically rejected as an aberration or even a mistake.

If you spot a possible anomaly, of course you should first ensure that it is not actually a mistake in the way the data was presented or collected, such as transposed numbers or a misquotation. If it is not a mistake in that sense, look for other data to indicate that this is something that is true or could be true in the future.

What you are doing is actually attacking your assumptions by using the anomaly to test them. The existence of an anomaly may indicate that your basic assumptions about what is true or possible are not correct.

Keeping alert for anomalies has another benefit. Specifically, by doing so, you help prevent yourself from falling into a common trap for those involved in handling intelligence: the predisposition to subconsciously reject a deviation from a known trend or situation until a new trend or situation has been conclusively established.

Business disinformation. Because CI involves converting your data into a cohesive picture, you must beware of business disinformation, more now than ever.[7] Business disinformation is something that looks like information but is not. For CI purposes, business disinformation is defined as incomplete or inaccurate information designed to mislead others about your intentions or abilities. Business disinformation is, however, not the same as *puffing,* a generally accepted form of advertising "overstatement," which falls short of fraud. Business disinformation can be created intentionally, and aids in misleading competitors and others with erroneous or exaggerated information. It can be generated simply by concealing relevant information. In each case, the business disinformation is aimed at establishing false value judgments, creating erroneous impressions, diverting attention from defects or problems, or hiding facts. This is just a way of looking at business disinformation based on its content (or lack of content). It can also, but rarely, happen by accident.

Being aware that business disinformation really exists and trying to decide whether a competitor is using it can be complex.

- If you don't consider whether a key piece of data represents business disinformation and, in fact, it does, this failure can be destructive. Moreover, you may not recognize its destructive effect until it is too late to counteract it.

- If you look for the business disinformation, you may not spot it even if it is present. In that case, your intelligence analysis could be affected by the business disinformation, but in a direction and to a degree you cannot predict.
- You may find what you think is business disinformation when it is not really there. In that case, you simply become more suspicious about the credibility you assign to what is really accurate data and more reluctant to rely on it without further confirmation.
- You may be correct in spotting the business disinformation. In that case, handling it properly allows you to avoid its damaging effects on your CI analysis.

If you have identified data that appears to be business disinformation, you should handle it as follows:

1. Is the reason for your concern the source of the data or the nature of the data itself? If your concern is due to a questionable data source, you should look for other sources to verify the data, avoiding those that might a false confirmation. If your reason arises out of concern in the nature of the data itself, you should seek confirmation or contradiction from all sources, including the original source.
2. Seek alternative sources of data to confirm, or discredit, the possible business disinformation. Be very sensitive to the danger of false confirmation here.
3. If you are not sure whether the data is business disinformation, try to estimate the likelihood of its accuracy and then explicitly assign a probability of accuracy to it. This may allow you to use the data, even while there is a question about its validity.
4. Analyze why the potential business disinformation was created or allowed to continue. If you cannot see a reason why the source would have created it or permitted it to exist, it may not be business disinformation. On the other hand, if you can determine why it may have been created or allowed to continue, you may not only have identified it as business disinformation, but you may now understand what the source was trying to accomplish.
5. If there remains any question about critical, nonconfirmable data, it is generally better to treat it as business disinformation.
6. Don't overreact. Be sensitive to the distinction between a good image and business disinformation. Remember, the success of any business disinformation initiative requires that you, the target, be willing to be deceived; that is, you are looking at your competitor through your preconceptions rather than considering alternatives.

Organize Your Analysis

Manipulating and structuring research results can help you to put together seemingly isolated pieces of data and achieve an unexpected result.

Outlines and Templates. How are you assembling the data to help you produce your analysis? One way is to use an outline. The outline format is particularly easy to handle when you are using word-processing software.

- First, create an outline of the topic you are analyzing.
- Then, as you review the raw data, insert each piece of data as many times as needed under every appropriate heading.
- Do this for all your data.
- Then read the outline, section by section. What conclusions do you see? What problems and gaps do you notice?

Data versus Conclusions. Another tactic is to separate the raw data, visually or physically, from your conclusions. By doing that in the draft stages, you can then go back through it and make sure you have enough data to support each of the conclusions you have drawn. If you do not find enough support, you can then add the data you did not include in the right place or drop the conclusions as unsupported. In addition, you should read the analysis to verify that you have drawn conclusions from all the data you have included in it. If not, ask yourself why you included each piece of data in the first place.

Coverage. Typically, you will find that the raw data you collected on a competitor will fall into in one of three basic categories:

- what your competitor says about itself
- what one competitor says about another competitor
- what third parties say about your competitor

When you are starting an analysis, try organizing the raw data by area of coverage, that is, dividing it among report categories such as costs, markets, consumer relations, and financial strengths. If you do this, you may find that data in one category appears to be dominated by one of these three categories of sources. If that is the case, then consider whether that is significant. For example, if virtually all of the information about a competitor's supply chain comes from third parties that are not competitors or suppliers, this may suggest that you look more closely at the quality of the data. Among the potential conclusions could be that the data is not likely to be accurate because you can find no way in which outsiders could have derived it. Alternatively, it could mean that the third parties were provided data by your competitor, so that you have some data that is quite accurate.

Inferences. When you study raw data and try to come to a conclusion about what it all means, one tool you should use is to try draw inferences. That involves coming to a conclusion in light of both logic and your own past experience. However, that same process can mean that you fit incoming data into your own preexisting beliefs or even see what you expect to find. In other words, your own experience can act as a screen on the data as well as an aid in analyzing it correctly.

Just being aware of the difficulty of dealing with inferences can help you avoid the pitfalls. Use this simple test to see whether you are having a problem dealing with inferences. Ask yourself, as each new piece of data comes in, which of the following is your immediate reaction: "That fact *is* incorrect (or correct)," or "That fact *must be* incorrect." If your response is the second, and not the first, you may be fitting the data into your preexisting beliefs rather than testing it to see what it really means.

Omissions. Do not be afraid to say that you lack enough data on something to reach a valid conclusion. The presence of a gap may be significant, or it may simply represent an area where more work needs to be done. In particular, the presence of a major gap should be an alert of the need to develop or supplement that data.

What is *not* present after you have finished your research can often be as significant as what is present. For example, you may have found that a competitor is planning to spin off a particular operation. From previous analysis, you may have found that this operation is a highly profitable one. If you can find no reason for the proposed spin-off, you should consider that a significant omission.

Then try to establish what the most plausible reasons might be for this action. In this example, there may be two:

- a possible need by the parent company for cash for its other operations
- a technological breakthrough by a competitor that might soon make this operation less profitable or even obsolete

NOTES

1. (Upper Saddle River, N.J.: Prentice Hall, 2002).
2. (New York: John Wiley & Sons, 1999).
3. (Westport, Conn.: Quorum Books, 2000).

4. (Greenwich, Conn.: JAI Press, 1996).

5. According to one study of practitioners, academics, and others involved with CI, competencies such as analytical ability and the ability to examine both the big picture and small details are generally "inherent traits" although analytical ability "can be taught." Miller, "Competencies for Intelligence Professionals," *Newsletter of the Society of Competitive Intelligence Professionals*, November 1995, 2.

6. For more on this, including details of a formal two-character rating system, see John J. McGonagle and Carolyn M. Vella, *The Internet Age of Competitive Intelligence* (Westport, Conn.: Quorum Books, 1999), 106–7.

7. For an extensive discussion of business disinformation, see ibid., 103–13

12

Effectively
Communicating CI

EXPRESSING CONCLUSIONS

Regardless of the form in which you deliver the results of a CI assignment, you should always be careful to avoid the two most common problems in expressing the findings and conclusions: "group think" and the "Sherwin-Williams mentality."

"Group think" means there is often pressure among members of a team working on a project to compromise, find a common denominator among themselves, and reach a consensus, instead of stressing diversity or even dissension if appropriate. As has been noted in the context of governmental intelligence, "[b]ecause judgments by consensus are the lowest common denominator, they are often of poor quality."[1] Another critic, translating that phenomenon in the context of CI, has put it bluntly: they are "useless" to the end users.[2]

The "Sherwin Williams mentality" label was derived from the paint company's advertising slogan, "Covers the Earth", showing a can of paint being poured to cover the globe. A Sherwin Williams mentality means that a team works to provide analysis on every conceivable aspect of a topic, and to cover, if not predict, every possible action by a competitor, whether or not the end users ever specifically asked for such CI or not.[3] One consequence is that such assessments impacted by this mentality end up protecting the analysts from criticism from being wrong, by making sure every option is covered. But this is done at the expense of having the CI analysts ever be wholly right.[4] As a popular fiction writer described that perspective:

> What we provide people with, most of the time, is official guesses. . . . If you give people a firm opinion, you run the risk of being wrong. . . . People remember when you're wrong a lot more than when you're right. So the tendency is to include all the possibilities. It's intellectually honest, even. Hell of a good dodge. Problem is, it doesn't give people what they think they need. On the user end, people as often as not need probabilities rather than certainties, but they don't always know that.[5]

Each of these reflects the adaptation of intelligence analysts to a culture or organization which expects precision and penalizes "inaccuracy." However, if your end users expect a CI unit to be 100 percent accurate all the time, they are setting the stage for a truly ineffective unit.

Reflecting on these tendencies, when your end users expect perfection, they are actually asking for the unit to provide them with CI and draw conclusions of such substantial breadth and limited depth, subject to such qualifications, as to be virtually useless to them. That is because the CI staff will not be aggressive for fear of being "wrong," so their results will cover all potential options. On the other hand, if end users make it clear that perfection is not, and cannot be, expected from a CI unit, that may encourage it to take the small risks necessary to ensure consistent, high-quality, usable CI.

Here CI can learn from the medical profession. For years, hospitals used to review the records of physicians who had "too many" deaths from a statistical point of view. The goal was to make operations in hospitals safer by identifying medical personnel or procedures that were putting patients at excessive levels of risk. This was done with the clear realization that deaths in surgery, for example, will happen. That was accepted since, unfortunately, medical professionals cannot save everyone.

Over time, the medical profession began to appreciate that there was another, very different, problem. That is, in part because of these very reviews, there were medical professionals who did not undertake certain procedures or admit certain classes of patients to hospitals. They did this, in part, to avoid being called to account for deaths at some later time.

Eventually, hospitals began to review both physicians and procedures that seemed to have excessively high death rates, as well as those that were excessively low. The first were reviewed to make sure that the medical staff or procedures were not exposing patients to excessive risks. The latter were reviewed to make sure that the medical professionals were taking enough risks and were not having patients stay out of the hospital unnecessarily.

When translated to the realm of CI, that means that your CI unit must work to educate management—that is, more than all CI end users—that they first must accept that not every CI assessment will be correct. That is because you and your associates are making an assessment, or analysis, and that process is not a perfect science. In addition, sometimes even the most accurate and precise assessment will no longer be correct as time passes, for example when the target changes personnel, and so on. Second, to assure that it receives intelligence that reflects intellectual honesty, management end users must also expect assessments that are not always correct.

Your ultimate goal is to draw a conclusion. That conclusion should be logical, but it may not be in all cases. If, for example, you are trying to determine what a competitor will do under certain circumstances, your goal is to anticipate how that competitor thinks. That, in turn, is based on its track record, its corporate culture, and how it perceives its competitive environment. To you that perception may not be careful and realistic, but that is not the concern here. The issue is whether that is what the target perceives. And the target may not have a clear perception.

The lesson here is that if the CI unit does not have any failures or miscues, perhaps it is not taking enough risks in its analysis. To put it into simpler terms, *not only must end users accept a lack of perfection, they must expect it.* That is because the only way that a CI unit can always be "right" is never to give its end users a strong, detailed, specific assessment.

DEALING WITH CI'S HALF-LIFE

How do you handle CI that is, or will soon become, dated? As already indicated, the half-life of some CI can be very short. You should keep this in mind and consider protecting your end users from using dated CI. There are a variety of options available:

- First, delivering a finished CI analysis just when it is needed, and not weeks before, can eliminate the most common reason that end users use outdated CI.
- Second, consider dating each printed page or overhead. That should, at least subliminally, alter end users to the age of the data and analysis.
- Third, you may want to consider a note in major reports and presentations indicating your estimate of the half-life of the report.

- Fourth, if it can be determined with reasonable certainty, add a note stating when the analysis should be replaced, disregarded or updated. For example, if a firm will be releasing in 30 days financial data that you had to estimate from older data, tell the end users that.
- Fifth, if discussing the half-life of the data is likely to be potentially confusing, consider briefing end users on the limits of the analysis before they are added to the distribution list.
- And last, make sure to cover this subject in internal training of all end users.

LIKELIHOOD

One problem often associated with presenting intelligence conclusions is that there can be lacks of consistency in communicating how "good" or "strong" the conclusions are. For example, it is very common to include in a report a phrase such as, "it has been reported that. . . ." Such a phrase really provides no useful CI to the end user. That is because it fails either to identify the source (which could allow at least some determination of the likelihood that the data is correct) or to give the CI analyst's opinion on how accurate that report actually is.

TABLE 12.1   Likelihood Phrase Set

Probability	Expressed as	
	As "Odds"	In Words
Virtually certain	50:1 or more	Plain statement of fact
Almost certain[6]	9:1 or higher	I believe that . . .
		[Source] indicates that . . .
		It is evident that . . .
		It is apparent that . . .
		There is little doubt that . . .
		This undoubtedly will . . .
Chances are good[7]	3:1 in favor	It is probable that . . .
		It is fairly certain that . . .
		It appears to be . . .
		It should be . . .
		It is expected to . . .
		It is logical to assume that . . .
		It is reasonable to conclude that . . .
Chances are about even	1:1	. . . fifty-fifty . . .
Inconclusive	Unknown	It is possible that . . .
		It could have . . .
		It may/might be . . .

One way to overcome this problem is to develop, and then use with consistency, a standard set of phrases that establish a sense of likelihood for both the CI analyst, and for the end user reading that analysis. In addition, by forcing analysts to think in these terms, it helps them focus on their own conclusions as well as provide a more accurate sense of what they have found for the end users. Table 12.1 is merely a suggested way to deal with this.

ISSUES IN COMMUNICATING CI

Overall Drafting Suggestions

Every CI assignment is different because its audience is different and the CI to be communicated differs. However, there are several basic rules that apply to all communications. As a former CI director for Eastman Kodak noted, "CI analysts are in the consulting and communications business. They are not in the analysis business. The Best analysis is useless unless it is communicated, believed, [and] acted upon."[8]

There are a few tips that should be kept in mind when drafting any CI report or document:

- Try to tell the reader, hopefully the end user, when something happened as well as when it was reported to you or published, if the difference is critical.
- Assume nothing about your end users, or very little at best. It is always better to keep the materials simple rather than to use only technical nomenclature. Your end users may not all be conversant with the level of technical detail or nomenclature provided by a source, or the CI may be shared with others lacking that technical facility.
- If you need a sense of editorial direction, fall back on the newspaper editor's tools: tell the end users who, what, where, when, how, and why (especially why).
- Always identify facts in contrast to your, or someone else's, assumptions. Identify all intelligence gaps. Do not be shy about saying that there is no data available on which to draw a reasoned conclusion.
- Think about future end users, readers, and even indexers. That means you should use parallelisms (e.g., both trade name and chemical name) and always clarify acronyms, even if only in an appendix. What is crystal clear to your end users may become indecipherable nonsense to another audience or at a future date.

- Avoid floating comparatives, such as "a 40% increase." They can be confusing, or even misleading. Instead, note the start or end points to provide the end user with the right context. Alternately, you can provide the actual computations.
- Try to develop and maintain a consistent voice and style. It makes the end users more comfortable.
- Avoid the use of military terms, like *counter-intelligence.* They carry with them unwanted and unwarranted baggage. In addition, their use to emphasize a point can come back to haunt you.[9] For example, do you really want to explain away a memo which says "it's time to go to war and stop capitulating," or which refers to an officer's desire to "nuke" the competition?[10]
- Note if this report triggers a need for additional CI research.

If you are working with news-type documents, such as CI alerts, or are developing documents (as distinguished from presentations), you should think in terms of bringing the end users' attention to the core of the subject matter. This, in turn, often translates into style issues.[11] For example, one key to bringing readers into a passive system, such as Intranet posting of short reports, lies in the careful drafting of the headlines or titles of these documents (by whatever name they are called). Among the useful techniques in preparing a caption, headline, or abstract are these:

- Tell most of, or at least the best of, what is in the following text.
- Look to the end users' needs to generate headline phrases that trigger attention. Words like *decline*, *reversal*, and *threat*, if accurately reflecting the content, can do that.
- Choose the first two or three words very carefully. Experience with e-mail shows that it is these words that often are used as the basis for deleting e-mail without ever reading it. The same style of screening happens when an end users must decide whether to read a CI document.
- Make sure the headline makes sense, even if the end user never goes to the body of the document.

Selecting the Right Way to Present CI

As detailed in Chapter 13 and in *Bottom Line Competitive Intelligence*,[12] there is a very significant link between the orientation of CI that you are providing and the optimal ways to communicate that to the end users. However, regardless of the manner in which the CI will be communicated, there are trade-offs to be made in the way that you provide it.

Your decision about the appropriate manner of communication will always involve trade-offs among the following factors:

- being current or providing some perspective
- being easy to understand or perhaps being less precise
- being complete and thorough or avoiding subjecting the users to "information overload"
- being able to be absorbed rapidly or lacking in detail
- using "headlines" with short summaries or transmitting careful analyses
- providing free access to important CI or maintaining the confidentiality of the analysis and sources of raw data

The form you select for disseminating CI should transmit the conclusions reached to the end users in the most effective manner possible. There is no one right form. CI may be communicated orally, in writing, in graphic form, or in some combination of these. The key is to select the option or options will help the end users be most to receive, retain and understand the CI.

Oral Communications. An oral presentation, whether a formal briefing or just a conference call, is quick and permits CI to be communicated to a large number of end users at once. It also allows the analyst communicating the CI to keep it extremely current and, by answering questions, to cover areas not included in the original presentation. Its flexibility allows the CI professional to communicate in ways that a written document cannot.[13] However, it has a significant disadvantage because miscommunications can occur more easily with oral communications than with either written or graphic communications. In fact, it is sometimes argued that spoken communications are received differently than are written communications.[14]

Another disadvantage of an oral presentation is that usually there is no permanent record that the CI was provided to the end user nor any description of what that CI was. The lack of a record of the providing of the CI may make it difficult or even impossible to evaluate its effectiveness at a later date. The lack of any record may also hinder the end users seeking to use the CI because they may need to refer again to some element of the presentation. Retransmission of what was communicated in the first instance carries with it the high likelihood that important elements will be omitted and that errors will creep in. In addition, the presenter does not have an exact record of what was said. Finally, this lack of permanence makes it difficult for either the presenter or the end users to build on that CI in the future.

While the PowerPoint®-style slide presentation would, at first glance, appear to overcome many of the shortcomings of the purely oral presentation, that is not necessarily true, for several reasons:

- Preparing a PowerPoint presentation takes time, sometime more time than writing out a formal document.
- Communicating complex relationships and large amounts of detailed data, particularly financial data, is not always easily accomplished in this context.
- While end users do have a document to take with them, it is, in essence, only an outline. Either the presenter must put all key conclusions on the overheads, or the end users must rely on the notes that they take to complete the delivery of the CI.
- PowerPoint presentations are subject to their own rules for enhancing effectiveness.[15] Unfortunately, most people giving presentations do not follow these rules.

Written Communications. Written communications take longer than oral ones, if for no other reason than it takes longer to write something down than to say it. However, once it is in written form, the CI will not change its content when it is transmitted from one end user to another, unlike oral communications. Also, written communications can be reproduced or, in the case of e-mails, even be sent to many end users at once. However, keep in mind that the wider the distribution of written CI, the more likely it is that this CI will be available to persons, or even organizations, for whom it was never intended.

Written communications also can be extremely precise or easily read, depending on the analyst's choice. Written communications also have the advantage that they can be reviewed before communication happens, stored and retrieved, or even updated. They also create a permanent audit trail for those who want to evaluate the real impact of CI on a firm.

Graphic Communications. The use of graphics in communicating CI can sometimes be quite effective. In fact, using graphic aids such as charts or illustrations in a written report or as a part of an oral presentation can enhance the overall message.

- You can emphasize particularly critical points or concepts by presenting material in two different ways.
- You can make it easier to understand complex numeric comparisons.
- You can give individuals at a presentation something to take with them, such as a copy of the charts and graphics, without having to distribute the full text of the presentation.

The methods you select depends on the need for clarity, accuracy, speed, and security. An oral presentation, for example, may be quick to prepare and present, but it may be difficult to have end users grasp complex financial relationships merely by hearing a recitation of data. A graphic can help clarify comparisons of data, but preparing complete and understandable graphics may require more time than is available. In CI, as in many other areas of business, timeliness determines whether information is useful. Precise information that arrives late may be less desirable than a rough approximation that is available on schedule.

Regular Reports

Your presentation of your CI analysis and related data may not necessarily be a written report, but if it is, you should consider developing a format for the final report before you begin. For example, in developing a format for a regular CI report on each of a pre-selected set of competitors, you have several options:

- The first is to use a form that can apply to all situations, such as by adapting some of the forms set out in this section.
- The second is to organize each report so that its structure parallels that of each company being tracked.
- The third is to develop a report form that approximately tracks the responsibilities of end users of your CI, in other words, the internal structure of *your own firm*.

The key benefit of developing your own standard form is that each report has the same structure. That makes it easy for end users to find what they want when they want it. It also makes it easy to upload portions or even all of such documents to an Intranet. The primary disadvantage is that it may scatter data needed by one reader among several categories.

The major benefit of a tracking form paralleling the target is that each report can be prepared quickly by reference to the target company's own documents, advertising materials, Web pages, reports, and so on. You do not have to skip from place to place to insert new raw data as much as you might with other options. The primary disadvantage is that, unless each of your competitors is structured and managed similarly, each CI report will differ in structure and order, That will make it harder for your end users to find comparable CI about each firm.

The major benefit of the form that parallels your firm's organization and responsibilities is that it provides a uniform format where each end user always knows exactly where to look for key CI. One major problem with it is that such a format requires a substantial amount of effort to create and to keep up to date. Another problem is that end users may tend to read only "their" section, which means that they may miss key CI findings and trends mentioned elsewhere.

CI Report Form Templates. Following are examples of the three types of documents you can use to *communicate* the CI you collect, in writing, on individual firms. They are:

- competitor alert
- periodic competitor report
- full competitor profile.

Competitor Alert. From time to time, you may find that you need to communicate raw, almost unevaluated data on a specific competitor very rapidly to a number of end users. To do this, you should consider adapting the "Competitor Alert" form (see Table 12.2). Using this type of form, you would insert the following under each heading:

- *Competitor/Target:* Name the firm, or even SBU, you are tracking or the particular market in which your end users are interested.
- *Subject:* Use very brief titles that permit you to narrow the focus quickly, by limiting it to subjects such as "new products" or "pricing changes."
- *Raw data:* Describe what you found, such as the text of a local news story or a summary of an announcement at a trade show. The description is captioned "Raw data" so that those receiving it know immediately that it is unevaluated. Edit it if it is too long.
- *Source:* Show the data's source so that the end users can judge the reliability and accuracy themselves.

Table 12.2   Competitor Alert Form

Competitor/Target:	Subject:	
Raw data:		
Source:	Received:	Provided by:
Reliability of data/source:		

- *Date Received:* Indicate the date when you learned of this. You may also want to indicate when the event probably occurred, if that is very different. All this is intended to remind the end users that some CI has a very short half-life.
- *Provided by:* Add the names of those persons and organizations helping your CI program. That means to specify who or what brought this to your attention. This can also help your end users judge the accuracy of the data. It also assists your CI unit to track the units and people that are most helpful to intelligence efforts. In some cases, you may want to withhold the name to protect your source, as with a very co-operative retailer, who might face retaliation from a competitor.
- *Reliability of Data/Source:* You should provide a very quick and short estimate of how reliable the source and/or the data is. It is perfectly proper to say that the data is a rumor so that its reliability cannot be assessed.

If you are using a memo or e-mail, you might want to add a "distributed to" line, showing all of those to whom this is sent. This helps avoid having those receiving the Alert send copies to people who have already received it.

Periodic Competitor Report. Providing a higher level of CI analysis is one through the "Periodic Competitor Report" (Table 12.3). This differs from the "Competitor Alert" in that it is distributed on a regular basis and includes some analysis of the data's significance. When using this form, you would put the following information under each heading:

- *Competitor/Target:* Same as for "Competitor Alert."
- *Subject:* Same as for "Competitor Alert."
- *Competitor Information:* A summary of what you have learned about the target competitor or market. This is *not* just an accumulation of pieces of raw data. It reflect your evaluation and analysis.
- *Significance of CI:* This is a brief description of what you believe this data means to the target and to your firm.
- *Sources:* Same as for "Competitor Alert."
- *Date Prepared:* Same as for "Competitor Alert."
- *Reliability of Underlying Data and Sources:* This is an estimate of how reliable you think each of the pieces of data and their sources are. Usually, you can do this in the aggregate, noting something like, "Based on past experience with these data sources, we believe that the data they provided is . . ."

If you are using a memo, you may wish to add a "distributed to" line, just as in the "Competitor Alert."

TABLE 12.3   Periodic Competitor Report

Competitor/target: Subject:

Competitor information:

Significance of CI:

Sources: Date prepared:

Reliability of underlying data and sources:

Full Competitor Profile. At the top of this information pyramid is the "Full Competitor Profile," a form that stresses the analysis of raw data accumulated over a significant period of time. A "Full Competitor Profile" may be distributed in its entirety or in sections. Do not maintain this only for your own use. You do better to develop and distribute smaller versions of this if they are of value to your end users.

The sample "Full Competitor Profile" has two key aspects. First, it should be arranged in a way that tracks, at least approximately, a firm or SBU's *own* internal organization. Second, it should move end users upward from data to analysis. If mounted on an Intranet, this form can be the location of hyperlinks to other documents and resources.

Here are some tips to using a "Full Competitor Profile" (pp. 157–158):

- The heading and subheadings are strictly illustrative. Develop your own form based on the CI needs of your end users. For that you may want to refer to the Competitor Analysis checklist found in Chapter 9.
- Parts 1 through 4 are intended to contain CI analysis, while Parts 5 and 6 contain data and raw materials. In fact, Parts 5 and 6 are designed to capture some of the raw data supporting the analysis going into Parts 1 through 4. For example, 1.1 is a summary of Part 2, 1.2 is a summary of Part 2, and so forth.
- Parts 1 and 2 are typically regularly made available to all end users. The final form of their contents depends on the end user's own perceived needs.

Beyond Parts 1 and 2, the end users would usually only want to read the portions applicable to them. So, for example, a top marketing officer would read sections 3.3 and 4.3, and, if data is wanted in addition to analysis, Section 5.3. A sample profile outline follows.

Target Company Inc.

Part 1. Executive Summary
  1.1 Profile
  . . .
  1.3 Overall Strategy
  1.4 Operations
Part 2. Profile
  2.1 Product Line
        2.1.1 Key Products
        2.1.2 Comparison with Our Products
  2.2 Status in Industry
  . . . .
Part 3. Corporate, Management, and Organizational Structure
  . . . .
  3.3 Marketing and Customer Service
  3.4 Human and Physical Resources
  3.5 Financial and Legal
Part 4. Overall Strategy
  4.1 Product Development and Engineering
  4.2 Manufacturing
  . . .
Part 5. Operations
  5.1 Product Development and Engineering
        5.1.1 Product Specifications
        . . .
        5.1.4 Research and Development
  5.2 Manufacturing
        5.2.1 Manufacturing Facilities
        5.2.2 Operations
        . . .
        5.2.5 Key Suppliers
        5.2.6 Planned Improvements
  5.3 Marketing and Customer Service
        5.3.1 Customers
        5.3.2 Service
        5.3.3 Distribution Systems
        5.3.4 Pricing and Pricing Policies
        5.3.5 Warranties
  5.4 Human and Physical Resources
        5.4.1 Key Executive and Management Personnel

The key benefit of using the profile is that each report on each competitor has the same structure. The disadvantage is that it may scatter data vital to one end user throughout several rigid categories.

Intranets. A newer way of providing CI is now emerging. By exploiting the benefits of computer software like Lotus Notes, firms are adopting a passive, but technology-based, dissemination mode.

In these systems, CI analysts still establish the needs of their clients, as well as other potential readers of the analysis. They then develop reports of varying length, complexity, and frequency. What the reports all have in common is that, when completed, they are posted on a firm's Intranet. While not directly distributed, they are significantly more accessible as they are now "centralized rather than scattered, pigeon-holed, or otherwise hidden."[16]

The ideal is that those interested in the intelligence will seek it out. To date, the limited number of experiments with this seems less promising than many had expected. In particular, research indicates that companies using an Intranet for research purposes[17] are having poor results. A recent study concluded that there are "two underlying reasons why research Intranets fail:

- Many sites are poorly designed and just plain hard to use.
- Workers lack the experience to conduct research and use the specific resources made available to them on these systems." [18]

Experience also shows that, in the case of Intranets which are not designed for do-it-yourself research, significant efforts must be made to assure that the potential users of this intelligence actually take the time to read it. Like other forms of information, "[I]t also has to be 'promoted' and 'sold.' Information audits routinely reveal that many employees do not use existing information resources because they don't know they are available."[19] Realizing that these readers have numerous demands on their time, CI professionals are finding that they must prepare the reports to be more attractive, in a communications sense, than they might otherwise have to be.

NOTES

1. Michael Handel, "Avoiding Political and Technological Surprise in the 1980s," in Roy Godson (ed.), *Intelligence Requirements for the 1980s: Analysis and Estimates* (Washington: National Strategy Information Center, 1986), 103.

2. Herbert Meyer, *Real-World Intelligence* (New York: Grove Weidenfeld, 1987), 43.

3. Handel, "Avoiding Political and Technological Surprise," 103.

4. Meyer, *Real-World Intelligence*, 43.

5. Tom Clancy, *The Sum of All Fears* (New York: G. P. Putnam's Sons, 1991), 403–4.

6. For "Almost certain . . . not," use negatives of the same phrases.

7. For "Chances are good that . . . not," use negatives of the same phrases.

8. Ann Selgas, "Seven Success Factors for CI Today," in Society of Competitive Intelligence Professionals, *Conference Proceedings* (Alexandria, Va.: Society of Competitive Intelligence Professionals, 1999), 150–51.

9. For a more extensive discussion of this, see John J. McGonagle and Carolyn M. Vella, *Bottom Line Competitive Intelligence* (Westport, Ct.: Quorum Books, 2002), 231–233.

10. Bill Fiora, "Choose Your Words Carefully," *Competitive Intelligence Magazine* 6 (January-February 2003), 38

11. See, for example, Paul Waddington, "Effective writing: how good copy can make your information work harder," SCIP.Online 1, no. 21, December 17, 2002.

12. John J. McGonagle and Carolyn M. Vella, *Bottom Line Competitive Intelligence* (Westport, Conn.: Quorum Books, 2002).

13. For an example of this, see Leonard M. Fuld, "The Magic of Storytelling," in *Society of Competitive Intelligence Professionals, "Conference Proceedings"* (Alexandria, Va.: Society of Competitive Intelligence Professionals, 1996), 243–55.

14. Tomas J. Walters, Jr., "High Impact Presentation Tactics to Improve the Intelligence Experience," in Society of Competitive Intelligence Professionals, *"Conference Proceedings"* (Alexandria, Va.: Society of Competitive Intelligence Professionals, 2001), 363, 375.

15. For example, there should never be more than three points on each overhead.

16. Bart Victor and Andrew C. Boynton, *Invented Here* (Boston: Harvard Business School Press, 1998) 39–40, describing Monsanto's experience.

17. These typically "feature a combination of research resources ranging from company-generated content (company news and directories) to links referencing outside sources (e.g., commercial databases such as Hoovers, Dow-Jones, and other research Web sites)." Alison J. Head, "Why research intranets fail," SCIP.Online 1, no. 28, March 25, 2003.

18. Alison J. Head, "Why research intranets fail," SCIP.Online 1, no. 28, March 25, 2003.

19. Jean L. Graef, *Executive Briefing: CFO's Guide to Intellectual Capitol* (Montague, Mass.: Limited Edition Publishing, 1997), 41.

13

Dissemination of the Finished CI

TIMELINESS

As indicated in Chapter 12, CI does not age well. When an end user needs CI, he or she often needs it by a certain time, *not* a day or two later. But because the data on which final analysis is based should be as current as possible, you may find some analysts who are tempted to wait "just a little bit longer" for that one key piece of data to complete an analysis. If the CI unit has done its work and obtained a real deadline for the work, it cannot, and must not, try get an extension. Unfortunately, no matter how good your CI is or how critical it could be in decision making, if it arrives the day after a crucial decision had to be made, it is of no use whatsoever.

HOW IS CI MADE AVAILABLE?

"The CI process contains user-friendly and organizationally wide accepted forms of communication to disseminate information."[1]

The fourth step of the CI cycle requires that the results of the research and analysis be actionable, able to be acted upon. And that, in turn, requires that the results be delivered to the end user, in a timely manner and in a form the end user can utilize.

Over the past fifteen years, the form in which CI is delivered to its end users has changed. In the mid 1980s, the majority of CI communications were made in one of three forms: the occasional written report, the periodic—that is, regularly scheduled—report (written or oral), as well as making files of research materials available as needed.[2] Considering that the internal database is another form of passive access, a significant majority of the CI was not truly communicated, but rather just collected.

The manner in which CI is communicated has gradually, but perceptibly changed for two reasons (see Table 13.1):

- One is the rise of Internet-based technologies, such as e-mail and Intranets.
- The other is due to the interconnected changes in the types of CI being communicated and the audiences to which it is being communicated.

While the amount of CI provided in the form of files and internal databases has fallen sharply, a part of what had formerly been provided in those ways is now just posted on firm Intranets. The underlying philosophy is still not significantly different: many CI units still merely collect data and develop CI and then let the users access it when and as needed.

HOW SHOULD CI BE PROVIDED?

What *is* being done is not what *should be* done. There are two issues involved in determining the best ways to communicate particular types of CI:

- the form of communication of, or manner of access to, the CI
- the frequency of communication

TABLE 13.1   Forms in Which CI Is Made Available: 2003

Form	Percentage
Occasional written reports	65%
Periodic reports	60%
Occasional presentations	40%
Intranets	40%
Periodic presentations	25%
Newsletters	20%
File materials available on request	10%[3]

There are only a limited variety of intelligence outputs that are typically being provided, and there are only a limited variety of patterns for distribution or access.

Typical CI Outputs

Newsletters
Source data and raw inputs

Flash alerts

Face-to-face briefings and presentations

Written reports

Forecasts, modeling, and scenario development

Gaming and shadowing exercises

Internal training on CI

Each of the forms through which CI is delivered to end users has its own unique characteristics, strengths and limitations. While every CI professional may handle them in a different manner, understanding their characteristics can help you decide when they are best used to communicate particular types of CI.

This is not to say that a particular kind of CI can only be delivered in these ways. The goal must always be to see that the CI reaches the end user in time for it to be useful and in a form that the end user can deal with. Given a choice between taking additional time to communicate critical CI in the "right" form or sending it in the "wrong" way, always keep in mind that *form is never more important than substance.*

The following sections highlight some of the key characteristics of each delivery vehicle.[4]

Newsletters

Purpose: Provide short, current reports of particular changes, usually of the competitive environment or in particular competitors

Manner of Communication. Hardcopy, e-mail, and Intranet distribution, typically weekly or biweekly

End User Participation. Most end users will quickly scan shortly after receipt.

Currency. Tends to be no older than one to two weeks.

Ability to be Updated. Any changes must be captured and noted in succeeding issues.[5]

Balance of Data versus Analysis. Tend to be heavily weighted toward relatively raw data.

Source Data and Raw Inputs
Purpose. End user can see the original inputs, documents, interview notes, and so on.

Manner of Communication. Usually by e-mail, as well as in hard copy form

End User Participation. End user provides virtually all of analysis.

Currency. Depends on the frequency with which it is collected and archived

Ability to Be Updated. Can be updated as often as needed.

Balance of Data versus Analysis: These tend to be almost exclusively raw data.

Flash Alerts
Purpose: Communicate new, important events as soon as they are known

Manner of Communication: E-mail and voice mail are the most common, typically on a sporadic basis.

End User Participation: None[5]

Currency. Extremely current

Ability to Be Updated: None

Balance of Data versus Analysis: Tend to be almost exclusively reports of raw data

Face-to-face briefings and presentations
Purpose: Present end users with findings as well as with access to those who did the analysis

Manner of Communication: Typically PowerPoint-style, that is the use of overheads with summary points, accompanied by oral presentation, often followed by question and/or discussion period

End User Participation: The format allows significant participation

Currency: Somewhat dated, given the fact that the presentation is prepared and duplicated in advance of what is often a scheduled meeting

Ability to Be Updated: Presenters can do this in their oral presentation, but the materials may not reflect updates

Balance of Data versus Analysis: Tend to be more heavily oriented toward analysis and conclusions

Written Reports

Purpose: Provide a detailed, highly documented report of both the analysis and the underlying data

Manner of Communication: Written document. May also be made available on an Intranet

End User Participation: Depends on issues end user's available time. Sometimes only conclusions and recommendations are read.

Currency: Given the long lead time, can be dated

Ability to Be Updated: Updates can be provided easily.

Balance of Data versus Analysis: Typically heavily weighted toward analysis and advocacy

Forecasts, Modeling, and Scenario Development

Purpose: Provides end users with the tools and ability to predict changes in markets, in competitor behavior, and even in macro-level cultural and political trends. It may also provide the predictions themselves

Manner of Communication: Forecasts are typically communicated in the form of a report or presentation or integrated into another product, such as a strategic plan, a strategic intelligence report, or a market projection. Models are created and then results are generated that are also communicated to management. Scenario development involves detailing competitive environments and what could happen under them. Any one may produce an analysis of "alternative" futures

End User Participation: Varies widely

Currency: Due to their complexity the underlying data and work are often dated.

Ability to Be Updated: Can be updated, at considerable effort

Balance of Data versus Analysis: While often based on vast amounts of raw data, the end products are heavily, almost exclusively, analysis and conclusions

Gaming[7] and Shadowing Exercises

Purpose: Provide an interactive way for end users to work out the impact of decisions. Both involve individuals playing out the role of competitors

Manner of Communication: Usually face-to-face over an extended period of time, but there are some Internet- and Intranet-based options that do not require all players to be present

End User Participation: Rarely effective without the personal participation of key decision makers

Currency: Due to their complexity, the underlying data and related work are often dated.

Ability to Be Updated: Underlying process can be updated, but it takes a considerable effort.

Balance of Data versus Analysis: While based on vast amounts of data, the process requires the articulation, and then application, of analysis to generate conclusions.

Internal Training on CI

Purpose: Stated purpose is to train end users to be betters clients, by creating an understanding of how CI really works and of its ethical and legal limitations.

Manner of Communication: Usually face-to-face, although there are multi-media course materials available.

End User Participation: Typically passive, although good trainers and materials will affirmatively generate participation.

Currency: Fairly current

Ability to be Updated: Fairly easily updated

Balance of Data versus Analysis: Not applicable

FREQUENCY OF DISTRIBUTION OF, AND ACCESS TO, CI

Having established the most common forms of CI outputs, it only remains to define the small number of frequency options. There are really two major divisions of distribution: active and passive, and for each there are only a limited number of variations.

Active

Active distribution of CI can be broken down into three separate alternatives:

- as requested
- occasional
- regular

As Requested. This is the case where the CI is provided to the end user *if and when* the end user asks for it. When it is once provided, it is not again provided again until the end user asks for it again. This can mean that the end user requests, for example, a report on a specific competitor's product development and distribution capabilities. It can also mean that an end user has requested a flash alert if certain narrowly defined factual circumstances, such as the opening of a new distribution facility, change.

Occasional. This is the case where the CI is provided to the end users more than once, but not on any regular or preset schedule. Typically, the decision to provide the CI, if it is dealing with an emergent matter, is made by the CI professional rather than the end user. That is because the CI professional is more likely to know of the change, and the end user is relying on that work by the CI professional. On the other hand, the end user may sometimes initiate a onetime CI request, which the CI professional then works to track and report on, as developments require.

Regular. This means that the CI is provided to the end users on some predetermined schedule. That schedule may be weekly or even daily, or it may be annual. It is usually set by the end user, but also may be set following consultation with the end user. This usually occurs when the end user and CI professional have already identified and agreed on a series of CI tasks and targets.

Passive

As with the active distribution of CI, there are really only two methods of passive distribution: on Intranets and in files and databases.

On Intranets. This means that CI professionals post, often on a regular basis, both finished CI (and data) and third-party reports on an internal Internet, usually called an Intranet. End users can then access this to use the intelligence and underlying data themselves. In many cases, access to the site is limited through security protections. Usually, the Intranet site provides some way to connect to a CI analyst for further assistance.

The selection of the materials and topics placed on the Intranet may be made in any number of ways. Most common are these:

- CI professionals, working from approved KITs and KIQs, select content that meets their profiles.
- End users identify data and CI that they want available, but do not wish distributed to them.
- End users identify data that they might need to locate but do not need collected and updated on any regular basis. The Intranet can provide hyperlinks to such data.
- CI professionals load abstracts or even entire reports from assignments completed for internal clients for the use of other employees.

They may also upload onetime reports prepared by outside CI firms.

In Files and Databases. This applies to finished intelligence as well as data and, to a lesser degree, third-party reports. It means that CI professionals collect, and either input (for databases) or collate (for files) them, usually on a regular basis. End users are then free to access the files or databases for their own use.

The selection of the materials placed in the files or databases may be made in any number of ways. Most common are these:

- CI professionals work from KITs and KIQs to select materials that meet these profiles.
- End users identify data and intelligence to which they want access, but that they do not wish distributed to them on a regular basis.

IN WHAT FORM AND HOW SHOULD YOU DISTRIBUTE EACH TYPE OF CI?

Strategy-Oriented

In general, end users of strategy-oriented CI need deliverables that do the following:

- stress analysis over data
- are provided to them on a fairly predictable basis
- may provide ways for the end users to probe further and develop their own understanding of the analysis and recommendations

Passive programs almost never produce CI on which strategy-oriented users can act, so the delivery of the CI must rely exclusively on active approaches.

Target-Oriented

In general, end users of target-oriented CI need deliverables that do the following:

- provide a wide rage of data and analysis
- capture both baseline analysis and current new pieces of data

Passive programs rarely provide actionable CI for target-oriented CI end users, so the delivery of the CI must heavily rely on active approaches.

Technology-Oriented

In general, end users of technology-oriented CI need deliverables that allow them to have direct access to the underlying data and other raw materials. While active delivery systems are in widespread use, the end users of technology-oriented CI are, in many cases, still content to have passive delivery systems. These are accepted as long as the data and other contents are constantly refreshed.

Tactics-Oriented

In general, end users of tactics-oriented CI need deliverables that stress immediacy and currency over those that provide long-term and highly refined analyses. They rarely, if ever, avail themselves of passive channels.

Table 13.2 (page 170) summarizes the most effective match of CI outputs, distribution, and orientation being provided.[8] Of course, regardless of how you distribute CI, in what forms, and on what basis, those decisions should be reviewed on a regular basis (probably annually). In addition, whenever the orientation of the CI being provided may change, the CI unit should immediately review its CI products with an eye toward changing them to reflect the changes in its future mission.[9]

Security

While you want your firm to make the widest use of your CI, you should be sensitive to security issues. You must balance distribution with the need to ensure that your CI results, as well as some of the sources of data for that CI, are kept confidential. The reasons for the concerns about security about the CI, as well as about the targets you have focused on, are self-evident. If a competitor knows that you are conducting CI against it, that is, in and of itself, competitively valuable information, which could trigger defensive efforts not put into place in the past. If that same competitor learns the object of your particular CI efforts, it will have gained an important insight into your probable strategy or plans. If it knows the results of your CI efforts, then it also knows what intelligence you were unable to generate and can proceed accordingly.

That means you may want to label the CI reports as "confidential," "proprietary" and the like. However, unless it really is a trade secret, you should not use that label. Also, you should include in your internal training some time on the importance of protecting the results of the firm's CI efforts. If any of this does reach a competitor, it is more likely to have done so due to the oversight of an end user than due to the negligence of a member of the CI unit.

TABLE 13.2 Table of Typical Intelligence Outputs

	Orientation of CI			
	Strategic	Target	Tactics	Technology
Newsletters		▲	▲	▲
Occasional		▲	▲	▲
Regular		▲	▲	▲
On intranets		▲	▲	▲
Source Data and Raw Input				
As requested	▲	▲	▲	▲
Occasional event		▲	▲	▲
Regular event			▲	▲
On intranets		▲	▲	▲
On file or database				
Flash Alerts				
As requested		▲	▲	▲
Occasional event	▲	▲	▲	▲
Regular event	▲	▲	▲	▲
On intranets		▲		▲
Face-to-Face Briefings and Presentations				
As requested		▲	▲	▲
Occasional event?	▲	▲	▲	▲
Regular event	▲	▲	▲	▲
On intranets		▲	▲	▲
Written Reports				
As requested	▲	▲	▲	▲
Occasional event	▲	▲	▲	▲
Regular event	▲			
On intranets				▲
On file or database	▲	▲	▲	▲
Forecasts, Modeling, and Scenario Development				
As requested	▲	▲	▲	▲
Occasional event	▲	▲	▲	▲
Regular event	▲			
On intranets				▲
On file or database	▲	▲	▲	▲
Gaming and Shadowing Exercises				
As requested	▲	▲	▲	
Occasional event	▲	▲	▲	
Regular event	▲			
Internal training on CI				
As requested				▲
Occasional event	▲	▲	▲	▲
Regular event		▲		▲
On intranets		▲		▲

The reasons for keeping the sources of data confidential are less clear, but may be compelling. There are situations when confidentiality could be vital. It would be embarrassing and potentially damaging if, for example, a list of distributors who cooperated in providing data for a CI report reached the competitor targeted in your project. To minimize the chances of such a mishap, you may want to keep the list of cooperating sources separate from your report.

Determinations of what should be kept confidential, whether the distribution of a particular assignment should be limited, and how that should be accomplished should be made, if possible, at the initiation of each assignment. In addition, every time you change the distribution systems or recipients of your CI efforts, you should review these issues. Do not overlook removing names from distribution, particularly mailing lists. One of the common mistakes firms make is to put off purging employee and external mailing lists.

NOTES

1. Society of Competitive Intelligence Professionals, *Team Excellence Award Booklet* (Alexandria, Va.: Society of Competitive Intelligence Professionals, 2002), 11.

2. The Conference Board, Inc., *Competitive Intelligence, Research Report No. 913,* (New York: The Conference Board, 1988), 6.

3. Helicon Group estimates. These are supported by limited surveys such as that reported in Jane Marin, "The gathering and internal dissemination of CI," SCIP.Online 1, no. 19, November 8, 2002, which indicated that 88% of the respondents distributed CI by e-mail, 85% in reports as requested, 74% on an Intranet, 43% via newsletters, and 21% "other."

4. For more on this, see John J. McGonagle and Carolyn M. Vella, *Bottom Line Competitive Intelligence* (Westport, Conn.: Quorum Books, 2002), 115–26.

5. Noting how well past estimates of competitor behavior track with actual behavior can help in promoting CI.

6. Reading an alert may prompt some end users to ask additional questions.

7. The term *gaming* includes what some call *war games*.

8. Adapted from the table originally appearing in McGonagle and Vella, *Bottom Line Competitive Intelligence*, 123–24.

9. For more on this, see ibid., chs. 5, 11.

14

Growth and Development

TIME FRAME FOR DEVELOPMENT

While every CI unit is different, the issues underlying success and failure or growth and decline, are relatively similar. For example, regardless of industry, it takes about three months to set up a basic CI unit. That time is needed to define the CI unit's mission, establish its end users, and provide staff. However, it takes up to two years to really establish a CI unit. The significant difference in time is due to several factors:

- Once established, the CI unit must really focus on defining the real needs of its end users.
- It can take up to a year to get the new unit into the overall budgeting process.
- Assignments at the beginning tend to produce more general, and often historical, intelligence. That typically is of less value than the predictive and micro-level intelligence it can generate in the future, after the end users are educated.
- Efforts to evaluate the CI require that the CI unit have actually completed projects, that the decisions being supported have been made, and that enough time has passed to be able to evaluate how well the unit performed.
- Many units find that their input, particularly in providing strategy-oriented and target-oriented CI, is controlled by internal plan-

ning and marketing cycles within their own firm. As a result, it can take one, two, or even more cycles for the CI unit's input to achieve full integration.

Following the two-year establishment period, in the third or following years, there can arise a potentially fatal problem: that of uncontrolled end user expectations.

GROWTH AND DEVELOPMENT

Integrating CI in a business firm takes a lot of time, and is a continuous process, independent of any individual. It requires that the CI personnel continuously identify their own firm's strategic goals and changes in them, and then create and maintain ongoing links to them.

An element critical to institutionalizing CI, according to the experience of Best Practice CI firms, is to affirmatively develop the CI process. That means that *all* CI personnel must develop, maintain, and then follow, an underlying, affirmative promotional plan. For example, institutionalizing CI can be aided by "seeding" the firm with a variety of products, services, and practices. These range from holding "road show" presentations illustrating CI unit's capabilities to conducting ongoing training of *all* employees in CI techniques. However, to be accomplished effectively, they must be planned. And once planned, they must be done on an ongoing basis. Onetime efforts are not sufficient.

For the firm that has formal CI units, affirmatively developing the CI process means a formally planned evolution, planned from the first day of operation, if not earlier. The experience of Best Practice firms is that CI units "evolve or dissolve," or put another way, either "grow or go."

A critical element in this is the ongoing affirmative development and maintenance of a high level of awareness of the role of CI. Experience shows that this is best accomplished through internal training. Another element in the institutionalization process is to integrate across the entire CI cycle. In particular, Best Practice CI programs work affirmatively to integrate three of the CI cycle processes:

- needs assessment
- taking action
- feedback and evaluation

The reason for this integration effort is that, without it, there is an almost inevitable series of events that lead to the demise of the CI unit. First, poorly defined intelligence requests, which are the result of problems in the area of needs assessment and feedback, eventually result in unfulfilled end user expectations. The end users did not get what they needed; they got only what they asked for.

Regardless of the cause, these internal customers then implement few, if any, CI project deliverables. Over time, less and less action by the firm is based on the efforts of the CI unit. Finally, the CI unit then loses its credibility and influence, first gradually and then rapidly, as end users see no value in the process. The final step is that the CI unit ultimately ceases to exist.

When dealing with planning for institutionalization, you should keep the following in mind:

- As the CI staff gets better in determining what its *best* customers need, it can, and must, provide better products.
- As the CI staff upgrades and refines products and services, ultimately it must become involved with key strategic and tactical teams.
- The resulting staff involvement leads to a high level of influence, which supports further improvement.
- The long-term goal is to link CI activity to actions of decision makers to achieve organization's goals or objectives.

The objectives of institutionalization efforts are to heighten sensitivity among all employees, not just your current end users, to the need for and value of CI. In addition, in doing that, you should always take the opportunity to demonstrate the capabilities, as well as the past successes, of your CI unit. Remember, you are not only looking to make you current end users into better clients, you are also looking for additional end users for the future. That means this process is independent of any individual end user or CI professional.

The institutionalization process requires also that the CI unit identify, and then monitor, the firm's strategic goals and any changes in them. To put it bluntly, a CI unit and the CI process cannot provide the maximum benefit to the firm if it is not supporting the most important elements of that firm, those in pursuit of critical goals and targets. As a part of that process, the most effective CI units have aggressively used both training and networks to provide access and lines of communication to help their firms survive and thrive. However, CI units and CI personnel should have a vision of where and how CI, in all of its forms, can fit into their firm. And we have a way to help them do that.

POTENTIAL PENETRATION OF CI IN THE "QUALITY" ORGANIZATION[1]

How and where should CI be involved in the workings of the modern business? That analysis requires that we have a way to describe the dynamic relationships that make up the way any well-run business operates. For modern companies, we have been provided with a set of such dynamic relationships, through the efforts of the Malcolm Baldrige National Quality Award Program (MBNQA or Baldrige Program). That program offers annual awards to U.S. companies of all sizes and in both the services and goods categories for business excellence and quality achievement.

To evaluate competitors for this award, the public-private partnership administering the MBNQA has developed and refined a set of guidelines to help the applicants document and demonstrate excellence in performance. Significantly, these guidelines are also designed with the hope that they will serve as a working tool for managing performance, planning, training, and assessment. Each year, the experts administering this program finetune the guidelines, thus assuring an instrument reflecting the "best practices" in management analysis, as well as one applicable to virtually any company.[2] We use these guidelines to illustrate the ways in which CI can potentially be involved in the functioning of the modern enterprise.

First, the overall Baldrige Criteria are broken down into seven major categories:

1. Leadership
2. Strategic Planning
3. Customer and Market focus
4. Measurement, Analysis and Knowledge Management
5. Human Resources Focus
6. Process Management
7. Business Results

The Baldrige Award process visualizes that every one of these seven categories, which embody what the MBNQA program calls the Core Values and Concepts, is linked to every other one, directly or indirectly, in a dynamic system. Categories 1 through 3 denote a "leadership triad," which is intended to "emphasize the importance of a leadership focus on strategy and customers."[3] Categories 5 through 7 represent the "results triad," showing that an organization's "employees and its key processes accomplish the work of the organization that yields business results."[4]

At first glance, it would seem that CI might be directly involved only with the "Measurement, Analysis and Knowledge Management" category. CI is obviously involved there, but its impact is much more pervasive than that. In fact, as a part of the assessment process, the MBNQA application now includes a "Preface," with two parts:

• Organizational Description
• Organizational Challenges[5]

This Preface is designed to set the context for the way the firm operates and to "serve as an overarching guide for your organizational performance management system."[6] Organizational Challenges asks that the firm "[d]escribe your organization's competitive environment, your key strategic challenges, and your system for performance improvement."[7]

The MBNQA Criteria note that the Organizational Profile is "critically important" for several reasons, including the fact that it "may be used by itself for an initial self-assessment. If you identify topics for which conflicting, little or no information is available, it is possible that your assessment need go no further and you can use these topics for action planning."[8] The firm is then directed to include answers to a set of questions, including these two groups:

> What is your competitive position? What is your relative size and growth in your industry or markets served? What are the numbers and types of competitors for your organization?

> What are the principal factors that determine your success relative to your competitors? What are any key changes taking place that affect your competitive situation?[9]

In other words, a quality organization must be able to answer these two questions, which require the extensive use of Active CI, before it can even begin to measure itself against the MBNQA criteria.

Going through each of the seven categories and eighteen associated "items," we will summarize the scope of each item and briefly note the roles played by active and defensive CI. For each section, we note only how and to what extent CI *directly* impacts the category. This is because CI *indirectly* impacts every one of them in some way:[10]

- By a "low" level of impact, we mean that the particular kind of CI is involved, on a sporadic basis, in the implementation or execution of the particular Core Value and Concept.
- By a "moderate" level of impact, we mean that the particular kind of CI is involved on a frequent, recurring basis in the implementation or execution of the particular Core Value and Concept.
- By a "high" level of impact, we mean that the particular kind of CI is involved on a continuous and ongoing basis in the implementation or execution of the particular Core Value and Concept.

This will help show you how pervasive CI can be in a quality organization and thus help you to set the course for the long-term development and integration of CI within your firm. It can also be used to demonstrate to management that effective CI benefits the entire firm.

Leadership (Category 1) requires that the firm address "how . . . senior leaders guide your organization in setting organizational values, directions, and performance expectations."[11]

Item 1.1, Organizational Leadership

> examines the key aspects of [an] organization's leadership and governance systems. . . . It focuses on the actions of [its] senior leaders to create and sustain a high-performance organization. [That includes] how [the] senior leaders set and deploy values, short- and longer-term directions, and performance expectations and balance the expectations of customers and other stakeholders.[12]

Strategy-oriented CI could have a high level of direct impact on this item by supporting senior management's understanding of the current and future competitive forces that the firm will face.

Item 1.2, Social Responsibility

> examines how [an] organization fulfills its public responsibilities and ensures [behaving] ethically, and encourages, supports, and practices good citizenship. . . . An integral part of performance management and improvement is proactively addressing . . . legal and regulatory requirements and risk factors. Addressing these areas requires establishing appropriate measures/indicators that senior leaders track in their overall performance review.[13]

Strategy-oriented and target-oriented CI could have a moderate level of direct impact through support for the assessment of the impacts of legal and regulatory requirements on competitors and on the overall marketplace.

Strategic Planning (Category 2) has the firm address

> strategic and action planning and deployment of plans. . . . The Category stresses that customer-driven quality and operational performance are key strategic issues that need to be integral parts of your organization's overall planning. . . . The requirements in the Strategic Planning Category encourage strategic thinking and acting—to develop a basis for a distinct competitive position in the marketplace.[14]

Item 2.1, Strategy Development, "examines how [an] organization sets strategic directions and develops [its] strategic objectives, guiding and strengthening [its] overall performance competitiveness and future success."[15] In explaining this item, the MBNQA Program specifically notes that

> [a]n increasingly important part of strategic planning is projecting the future competitive environment. Such projections help to detect and re-

duce competitive threats, to shorten reaction time, and to identify opportunities. . . . [O]rganizations might use a variety of modeling, scenarios, or
other techniques and judgments to anticipate the competitive environment.[16]

Firms are then asked to outline how they gather and analyze data to
address a number of issues including the "competitive environment
and your capabilities relative to competitors, [and] technological and
other key innovations and changes that might affect your products/ser-
vices and how you operate."[17]

Strategy-oriented, technology-oriented, and target-oriented CI all
could have a high level of direct impact on this item. They can support
assessments of the competitive environment, technology trends, and of
the possible actions and intentions of major competitors.

Item 2.2, Strategy Deployment, "examines how [an] organization
converts [its] strategic objectives into action plans to accomplish the
objectives [and] how [the] organization assesses progress relative to
these action plans."[18] Among the questions an applicant firm is expected to answer is "[h]ow does your projected performance compare
with competitors' projected performance? How does it compare with
key benchmarks, goals, and past performance. . . ?"[19]

Strategy-oriented and target-oriented CI each could have a moderate
level of direct impact on this item by assisting in developing critical
data on the performance of major competitors.

Customer and Market Focus (Category 3) makes a firm address "how
[its] organization seeks to understand the voices of customers and of
the marketplace. . . . [C]ustomer satisfaction and dissatisfaction results
provide vital information for understanding your customers and the
marketplace."[20]

Item 3.1, Customer and Market Knowledge,

examines [an] organization's key processes for gaining knowledge about
[its] current and future customers and markets, with the aim of offering
relevant products and services, understanding emerging customer requirements and expectations, and keeping pace with marketplace changes
and changing ways of doing business. . . .[21]

The requirements specifically state that firms should be

asked how you keep your customer listening and learning methods current with your changing business needs and directions. . . . Some frequently used modes include focus groups with key customers; close
integration with key customers; interviews with lost customers . . .; use of
the customer complaint process . . .; win/loss analysis relative to competitors; and survey/feedback information.[22]

Target-oriented and tactics-oriented CI could each have a moderate to high level of direct impact on this item in their development of CI on marketing and related areas of activity.

Item 3.2, Customer Relationships and Satisfaction,

> examines [an] organization's processes for building customer relation-
> ships and determining customer satisfaction, with the aim of acquiring
> new customers, retaining existing customers, and developing new market
> opportunities. . . . This Item emphasizes how you obtain actionable
> information from customers. . . . In determining customers' satisfaction, a
> key aspect is their comparative satisfaction with competitors and compet-
> ing or alternative offerings.[23]

Target-oriented and tactics-oriented CI could have a low to moderate level of direct impact on this item by developing information on how competitors' customers see the firm and the competitors.

Measurement, Analysis, and Knowlege Management (Category 4) is

> the main point within the [MBNQA] Criteria for all key information about
> effectively measuring and analyzing performance to drive improvement
> and organizational competitiveness. . . . Central to such use of data and
> information are their quality and availability. Furthermore, since informa-
> tion, analysis and knowledge management might themselves be primary
> sources of competitive advantage and productivity growth, the Category
> also includes such strategic considerations.[24]

Item 4. 1, Measurement and Analysis of Organizational Performance,

> examines [an] organization's selection, management, and use of data and
> information for performance measurement and analysis in support of
> organizational planning and performance improvement. The Item serves
> as a central collection and analysis point in an integrated performance
> measurement and management system that relies on financial and nonfi-
> nancial data and information. The aim . . . is to guide [an] organization's
> process management toward the achievement of key business results and
> strategic objectives. . . .[25]

Among the key requirements of Item 4.1 are that firms indicate how they

> gather and integrate data and information for monitoring daily operations
> and supporting organizational decision making and how you select and
> use measures for tracking those operations and overall organizational
> performance. You also are asked how you select and use comparative data
> and information to support operational and strategic decision making and
> innovation.[26]

In this context, "[t]he use of comparative data and information is important to all organizations."[27]

Target-oriented CI could have a moderate level of direct impact on this item, and technology-oriented CI could have a low level of direct impact on it. Target-oriented CI can provide information on the performance of competitors, and technology-oriented CI can help to determine technology trends.

Item 4.2, Information Management and Knowledge Management, "examines how [an] organization ensures the availability of high-quality, timely data and information for all your key users—employees, suppliers and partners, and customers."[28] Specifically, the firm is "asked how [it] make[s] data and information available and accessible to your user communities [and] how you ensure that the data, information, and organizational knowledge have all the characteristics your users expect: integrity, reliability, accuracy, timeliness, and appropriate levels of security and confidentiality."[29]

Defensive CI could have a low level of direct impact on this item by alerting those dealing with this information to the ways they can protect competitively sensitive data from the CI collection efforts of competitors.

Human Resource Focus (Category 5) requires an examination that "covers human resource development and management requirements in an integrated way, i.e., aligned with [the] organization's strategic objectives."[30]

Item 5.1, Work Systems, "examines [an] organization's systems for work and jobs, compensation, employee performance management, motivation, recognition, communication, and hiring, with the aim of enabling and encouraging all employees to contribute effectively and to the best of their ability."[31] Neither active nor defensive CI would have any direct impact on this item.

Item 5.2, Employee Learning and Motivation, "examines the education, training, and on-the-job reinforcement of knowledge and skills of [the] organization's workforce."[32] Neither active nor defensive CI would have any direct impact on this item.

Item 5.3, Employee Well-Being and Satisfaction, "examines [the] organization's work environment, [its] employee support climate, and how [it] determine[s] employee satisfaction, with the aim of fostering the well-being, satisfaction, and motivation of all employees while recognizing their diverse needs.[33]" Neither active nor defensive CI would have any direct impact on this item.

Process Management (Category 6) involves a review of "the central requirements for efficient and effective process management: effective design; a prevention orientation; linkage to customers, suppliers and partners and a focus on value creation for all key stakeholders; operational performance; cycle time; and evaluation, continuous improvement, and organizational learning."[34]

Item 6.1. Value Creating Processes, "examines [an] organization's key product, service, and business processes, with the aim of creating value for your customers and other key stakeholders, improving your marketplace and operational performance."[35] Technology-oriented and target-oriented CI could each have a low level of direct impact on this item by providing information on current product or service process management and supply chain practices in the marketplace.

Item 6.2, Support Processes, "examines your organization's key support processes, with the aim of improving your overall operational performance."[36] Neither active nor defensive CI would have any direct impact on this item.

Business Results (Category 7) makes sure that the firm "provides a results focus that encompasses your customers' evaluation of your organization's products and services, your overall financial and market performance, your governance structure and social responsibility, and results of all key processes and process improvement activities."[37]

Item 7.1, Customer-Focused Results, "examines your organization's customer-focused performance results, with the aim of demonstrating how well your organization has been satisfying your customers. . . ."[38] A part of this involves collecting "current levels, trends, and appropriate comparisons for key measures and indicators of customer satisfaction and dissatisfaction, including comparisons with your competitors' levels of customer satisfaction."[39] Target-oriented CI could have a moderate level of direct impact on this item by providing critical data to allow needed comparisons with competitors.

Item 7.2, Product and Service Results, "examines [the] organization's key product and service performance results. . . ."[40] Neither active nor defensive CI would have any direct impact on this item.

Item 7.3, Financial and Market Results, "examines your organization's financial and market results, with the aim of understanding your marketplace challenges and opportunities. . . . Overall, these results should provide a complete picture of your financial and marketplace success and challenges."[41] Among the data to be provided are "levels, trends and appropriate comparisions for key financial, market, and business indicators."[42] Strategy-oriented CI and target-oriented CI could each have a moderate level of direct impact on this item by allowing accurate and realistic comparisons with competitors and an assessment of the overall market environment.

Item 7.4, Human Resource Results, "examines your organization's human resource results."[43] This includes "appropriate comparisons for key measures/indicators of employee well-being, satisfaction, dissatisfaction, and development."[44] Neither active nor defensive CI would have any direct impact on this item.

Item 7.5, Organizational Effectiveness Results, "examines your organization's other key operational performance results [those not covered above], with the aim of achieving organizational effectiveness and attaining key organizational goals."[45] Neither active nor defensive CI would have any direct impact on this item.

COMMON CAUSES OF FAILURE AND HOW TO HANDLE THEM

It is critical that CI professionals, particularly managers, be aware of the causes for failure of CI units:

- How management is educated to understand the likelihood of failures in analysis
- The cost and turf threats that face a new CI unit at the very beginning
- A failure of the CI unit and management to plan for success
- Three separate threats to survival faced by newer units
- A separate set of threats to continued survival facing established CI units

Failures in Analysis

As has been reiterated throughout this book, for a CI unit to be successful, it must do more than merely provide raw, unevaluated data for its internal customers, its end users. If it does only that, and only that, the CI unit is little more than a newsletter publisher. And, as we know, subscriptions to newsletters are often canceled when they are not seen as immediately and consistently productive. The same can happen to a CI unit that is merely producing a staff "newsletter."

Given that the well-run CI unit provides analysis, not raw, unevaluated data, both the unit and senior management must face the fact that, for the CI unit to be successful in the long run, it must also fail from time to time. This apparent anomaly is called the "expect/accept" failure problem.

There are several reasons why a CI unit must sometimes fail if it is to do a first-rate job overall:

- The CI unit is often asked to analyze "moving targets," that is dynamic situations and targets. When the analysis is finished, the targets do not then conveniently stop moving. That means that the analysis can be correct as of the date it was done, but it may not necessarily be so when the end user actually reads it, much less uses it.

- The CI unit is usually asked to provide a precise output in a world of imprecise inputs. Mistakes in interpretation and analysis are almost inevitable in this context.
- The CI unit can be asked to provide specific intelligence, often reflecting an evaluation of the target's intentions as distinguished from its assets or capabilities. The end product may be in error, for it is ultimately very hard to predict with certainty how someone else, in a different environment and with access to different facts, will act at some point in the future.

It is for these reasons that management should expect failure. However, it must do more: management must not only expect failure, but affirmatively accept it. That is because pressure for perfection in CI can actually be counterproductive.

Management must be understanding of the likelihood of some failures in CI, since they reflect the limits inherent in the intelligence process itself. But, management must also be suspicious of a CI unit that is never wrong. That is because a CI unit that avoids being wrong usually ends up providing intelligence of such generality and subject to such qualifications that it ultimately becomes unusable. In other words, in an effort to avoid being wrong, it may also never be right in the sense of giving the end user focused intelligence on which to act.

Sometimes, the CI unit must "reach" in order to form a conclusion from the analysis. Without this reaching, and possible failure, the unit is not functioning properly. For example, when a CI unit has been following a specific target for a period of time, the CI professionals may draw conclusions based on the way they feel the target will react. They may have no hard data upon which to base their decision other than their intimacy with the target. However, these apparent hunches may nonetheless yield valid results.

Immediate Failures

The most common reason given for companies establishing and running an internal CI unit, instead of relying exclusively on outside providers for all their CI, is that the more formal the process for producing CI is, the better the resulting product will be. This can be true. However, where such units have not proven successful in a very short time, experience indicates that there are several reasons contributing to immediate and rapid failure. First, cost can be a very large factor. Creating a CI unit involves set-up costs, ranging from obtaining office space and equipment to training the new CI team. It also may entail operating costs that appear to be much higher than for operating under a more informal system, that is one where CI is obtained, usually from outside (or from insiders), only on an as-needed basis. Usually the problem is not the total fixed and operating costs of the CI unit, however, but rather management's failure to anticipate the full scope of such costs, both in the short term and in the long term. While these costs may appear to be high, the benefits to the firm from having such a unit should quickly eliminate any such considerations.

Second, creating a new, specialized CI unit may result in conflict with existing departments within the firm. A new CI unit might be perceived as a threat to existing units, such as marketing, planning, finance, and legal. That is because they may perceive that some of their functions are being, or may soon be, usurped by the new unit. In addition, creating a formal CI unit has, on rare occasion, given rise to erroneous objections from management, stockholders, or the public that that business now uses "spies." Fortunately, the latter problem is becoming less and less frequent as businesses, shareholders, and the media have become more sophisticated and knowledgeable about CI.

Failing to Plan for Early Successes

How will you and the CI unit handle its success? To do so effectively, you must plan for it at the beginning. Experience shows that a successful CI unit is very often flooded by assignments, requests, and demands beyond what its creators anticipated. Most CI units will seek to respond to these because they rely on the good will of many managers making requests to provide raw data needed for other CI assignments. While this may seem a good idea, in fact, it can quickly undermine the effectiveness of the CI unit by overloading it with tasks that are not central to its mission.

Another problem of success is that it quickly means that the CI unit must plan to deal with the collection and storage of increasing, potentially excessive, amounts of raw, unevaluated, and unsolicited data. That happens because departments and executives throughout the firm, whether or not now using CI, begin to see its effectiveness. Then, they may try to cooperate, perhaps too much, by providing what they see as the necessary raw data for the CI unit. It is very embarrassing to have to turn off the data flow after literally begging for it to start. Remember, too, that success can have an impact on how future CI reports are regarded and the risks faced by the CI unit. As one observer noted, "[T]he more successful an intelligence organization becomes, the less are its reports questioned and the greater the chance that it will fail."[46]

Two European consultants recently made the following chilling observations about their experience with CI units:

CI is under-resourced in 90% of companies.

Few companies have more than 5 people in dedicated CI roles [presumably analysts, staff, researchers, and managers].

However, these small teams are expected to deliver multiple products to multiple audiences.

New competitors, new products, new markets—everyday!

They can't cope, they get overwhelmed, they get shouted at, they get disillusioned, they leave.[47]

Failures of Newer Units

Boehringer Ingelheim Pharma, Inc., in reviewing its efforts to create a CI unit, recently provided its own subjective look at the key lessons learned.

1. Establish the intelligence process first—how you will operate.
2. Begin with clearly defined roles and responsibilities—what you do and whom you will serve.
3. Establish a seamless intelligence communication strategy within the company.
4. Build awareness slowly with key successes.
5. Don't get caught in the activity trap of answering everyone's questions.[48]

The studies conducted by AP&QC of Best Practice CI firms included an inside look at those which are not Best Practice, but rather have failed to grow and thrive, or have even been closed down. CI units that fail in the early stages of their development generally do so for one of three major reasons:

- the usual "big mistake"
- changes in top management
- change in the CI unit's leadership

The "big mistake" is self-explanatory. Here a new CI unit has typically been given an assignment that has major significance to the firm. Unfortunately, however, the assessment of the CI unit turns out to be wrong. If the CI unit has not undertaken to educate management about the requirement that it accept and expect failures, the unit's fate is sealed. It is usually dissolved and the firm then tends to reject CI as an appropriate function, at least until senior management changes. The only way to forestall this is to make sure that senior management is aware, at the very beginning, of the accept/expect failure process in CI. They should also be educated about the dangers of punishing the CI unit for such a failure. In many cases, the blame often lies with management, which either should have been seeking such CI at a significantly earlier date or should not have overtaxed the new CI unit.

The second common cause of failure in the early stages involves a CI unit whose creation and operation are dependent on the decision of one or a few members of the firm's senior management. In such cases, these constructed CI units may vanish along with their champion. [49] If the CI unit has not been in existence long enough to have begun its own marketing and integration campaign, such a fate is unavoidable.

The third common cause of failure in the early stages is caused by the departure of the CI unit's manager. Typically, the first CI manager is not only managing the unit but is usually an advocate for the entire CI process. New units rarely worry about succession planning when they are first created. However, in the case of the CI unit, succession planning is one of many options that should be dealt with before, or at least while, the unit is being formed.

Threats Facing More Established Units

Failure to Continue to Advance the Program. One concern for CI managers is that they must never lose sight of the mid- and long-term future of CI and the CI unit (and these can be separate) when enjoying short-term successes. That is, the development plan for every CI unit must provide not only for the unit to provide actionable CI for its key end users in the near term, but it must also be designed to be sustainable for the mid- and long-term. That may involve aggressive "colonization," that is, looking for units or areas within the organization where the seeds of a new CI unit can be planted.

Not only can such new units increase the efficiency and reach of existing units, they can provide something else. That is a place for the CI process to find a new home if, for any reason, its current site becomes inhospitable. For example, if the CI unit is located in an SBU that is facing a major reduction in force, it can be very useful for the CI professionals to know that there are other units, outside the impacted unit, where CI is appreciated and in use.

Failure to Control End Users' Expectations. We are increasingly seeing end user dissatisfaction with the output of previously well-regarded CI units. In addition to the problems mentioned elsewhere in this book, we now know that there are other factors that almost inevitably contribute to this.

In its first years, the CI unit typically is involved in providing substantial amounts of raw data, often with minimal analysis. That data is sufficient for the new end users, for, until that point, they have been relatively ignorant of many of the facts now being provided by the CI unit. However, the end users, who are becoming sophisticated due to exposure to the CI unit's output, will soon be able to see where analysis is minimal or lacking and will, rightly, come to expect better. If the CI unit does not affirmatively plan to increase the amount of analysis and to decrease, or even eliminate, the provision of raw data, over time it will surely face problems with its end users.

In the early months and years, the CI unit is usually involved in responding to numerous requests for historical CI. That is, its end users are focusing on issues such as production capacity, budgets, and long-range plans of key targets. Over time, however, these end users will become more sophisticated and begin asking for more current, rather than historical CI. This should be expected, for the CI unit itself will have already done the spade work by giving its end user the historical materials on which it can now base its requests for "current" CI.

However, current CI is more difficult to collect and analyze than is historical CI. Not only are there often fewer sources for it, but it is a much more mobile target. In addition, as the end users have built up their own understanding of the target and the industry segment, again thanks to the work of the CI unit, over time they will almost inexorably shift their requests from the macro-level CI (such as industry capacity) to more micro-level requests, such as production capabilities at a particular plant. This is often done at the same time that the requests begin to reflect a shift in time perspective demanding more current information and predictions of future actions.

As time passes and the end users become even more comfortable with the capabilities of the CI unit, and more conversant with the historical and current CI that has already been made available, the end user requests will again materially change. From that point, they will tend to be even more micro-level in nature (output for a production line in a specific plant) and more current (as of last week). That time shift can become even more significant. Over time, the end user requests will then tend to shift again, from the current (last week's output) to the future (next months' planned production).

Thus, over time the CI unit will almost certainly see the end users' requests shifting forward in time, from the historical to the current and then to the prospective, and, at the same time, shifting downward in terms of level of detail, from the macro to the micro level. One final shift inevitably occurs, often at the same time these two others do—from the prospective to the predictive (what will they do if we do this?).

To put it another way, as the CI unit does its job well, its tasks will inevitably change over time. Typically, the CI professionals will begin by developing macro-level, often historical, CI. Then, over time, they shift more to micro-level CI and to "current" or real-time CI. Finally, they will see little other than requests for projections or "estimates"—bluntly put, for guesses. At the same time, the extent and importance of the analysis they provide will also increase.

All during this time, the internal end users will have the accumulated benefit of all of the CI collected in the past. They will now be used to getting good CI, usually relatively inexpensively and quickly. They expect, reasonably they think, that as the CI unit develops and matures, it will do its job better, faster, and cheaper. However, this predictable change in expectations will almost certainly generate conflict between the CI unit and its end users. The end users, increasingly appreciating the benefits of CI, will seek more CI to better assist them. However, the ability of the CI unit to provide the same quality of CI at the same price, in the same time frame, and with the same accuracy and precision, inevitability must decline. In other words, the better a job the CI unit does in serving the end users, the tougher it will be for the CI unit to maintain the same level of production and efficiency in the future.

If the end users are not expecting this trend, the CI unit will soon hear the cry, "Why can't you do as good a job as you did in the past?" The answer should be, "We can't *because* we did so such a good job in the past." However, waiting until the question arises is to wait too long. The end users of CI must therefore be educated, and early on, both that CI will, inevitably, be wrong in some instances, and that, over time, their expectations with respect to accuracy, cost, and speed will probably outpace the ability of the CI unit to perform. These are odd, but real, consequences of success.

NOTES

1. This is updated and substantially revised from its first expression in John J. McGonagle and Carolyn M. Vella, *A New Archetype of Competitive Intelligence* (Westport, Conn.: Quorum Books, 1998), Ch. 4.
2. Baldrige National Quality Program, *2003 Criteria for Performance Excellence* (Milwaukee, Wisc.: American Society for Quality, 2002), 1.
3. Ibid., 5.
4. Ibid.
5. Ibid., 10–12.
6. Ibid., 4.
7. Ibid., 12.
8. Ibid., 10.
9. Ibid., 12.
10. While these reflect our perception, your own experience may lead you to see other direct linkages.

11. Baldrige National Quality Program, *2003 Criteria*, 36.
12. Ibid.
13. Ibid.
14. Ibid., 36–37
15. Ibid., 37.
16. Ibid., 38.
17. Ibid., 15
18. Ibid., 38.
19. Ibid., 16.
20. Ibid., 39.
21. Ibid.
22. Ibid.
23. Ibid., 39–40.
24. Ibid., 40.
25. Ibid., 41.
26. Ibid.
27. Ibid.
28. Ibid., 42.
29. Ibid.
30. Ibid., 43.
31. Ibid.
32. Ibid., 44.
33. Ibid., 45.
34. Ibid., 45–46.
35. Ibid., 46.
36. Ibid., 47.
37. Ibid.
38. Ibid., 48.
39. Ibid.
40. Ibid.
41. Ibid.
42. Ibid.
43. Ibid., 49.
44. Ibid., 48.
45. Ibid., 49.
46. Richard H. Giza, "The Problems of the Intelligence Consumer," in Roy Godson (ed.), *Intelligence Requirements for the 1980s: Analysis and Estimates* (Washington: National Strategy Information Center, 1980),189–206.
47. Ted Howard-Jones and Fiona Walker-Davis, "Delivering and Maintaining Tactical Intelligence," in Society of Competitive Intelligence Professionals, *Fifth Annual European Conference and Exhibit: Conference Proceedings* (Alexandria, Va.: Society of Competitive Intelligence Professionals, 2000), 93, 100.
48. Sharlene Zagozewski, "Business Intelligence: An Emerging Practice at Boehringer Ingelheim." (presentation at the SCIP Annual Meeting, Seattle: April 2002), 2.
49. See Chapter 4 for more on this type of CI unit.

15

Going Outside for Help

WHAT DO YOU NEED, AND WHEN?

CI Research and Analysis Work

How should the research and analysis work of your CI unit be divided between your own personnel and outside providers? Over the long run, it is extremely unlikely that any internal CI unit will always be able to handle all of your firm's CI needs at the time those needs arise. But what research and analysis tasks, or combination of tasks, are best contracted out will vary from firm to firm.

For example, Visa International has recently identified the "key drivers" it considers in deciding to contract out CI research and analysis:

- Need difficult-to-get information that is not available through secondary sources.
- Can't easily approach competitors, analysts, suppliers and other target competitor stakeholders.
- Need data quickly and reliably.
- Do not have wide, well-cultivated range of relevant interview contacts.
- Need a neutral, "objective" 3rd party investigation and analysis.[1]

Another firm expressed it as follows:

The Best Use of Intelligence Contractors

- *Operational Performance Benchmarking*. Firms must compare their current operations performance and costs compared with direct competitors, customer expectations and best-in-class companies to learn what to do differently to improve effectiveness & efficiency.
- *Understanding Strategic Plans*. Strategic plans of competitors (direct, latent & parallel) as well as the firm's customers can provide an understanding of comparative opportunities for the client.
- *Specialized Collection/Analysis*. Intellectual property, vulnerability testing, legal/regulatory environment, war games, selling tools, etc.[2]

Experience shows that the following cover most of the situations facing firms with regard to the decision to contract out:

- Using an outside firm for CI research and analysis may be appropriate to let your CI unit handle overwhelming peak work loads. That is, there will be brief times when the unit, whether one person or a dozen, may be overwhelmed with requests. Alternatively, you may find, from time to time, that you are short of available staff, either because of hiring restrictions or financial limitations. An outside firm can help to supplement your CI staff and other resources. At that point, contracting out may be an appropriate option.
- Utilizing an outside firm to test the utility of developing an internal CI function. In other words, the outside firm is expected to demonstrate whether or not CI provides enough benefit for the firm to justify bringing that function inside.[3]
- You may want some CI research and analysis work to be contracted out only in special circumstances, such as dealing with potential merger and acquisition transactions, when the internal security of sensitive information may be especially important.
- You may need to contract out a part of your CI research and analysis involving demands that do not fit with its base load. For example, a CI unit that is involved in producing tactics-oriented CI may want to consider contracting out tasks that do not fit, such as occasional technology-oriented CI research and analysis.
- Your company lacks expertise or lacks experienced personnel to handle a particular project, *and* the nature of the project does not warrant hiring full-time, or even temporary, personnel. An outside firm can offer a concentration of specialties and experienced analysts that makes its use a relative bargain.
- You are short of time and cannot meet the timetable established for the CI project without some outside assistance. An outside firm can

be a useful resource that can focus substantial resources on that particular project in a very short time.

- You believe that your end user needs or wants an "objective" or "outside" point of view. For internal reasons, it might be preferable to have someone who is not enmeshed in your own firm's management or policies and who can bring fresh insight, guidance, and analysis, or even to have someone not on staff deliver an unwelcome message. Sometimes, in particularly sensitive situations, you may prefer to have the CI provided by an outside firm on a "cut-out" basis. The cut-out means that the CI is given directly to someone other than you, usually to an intermediary working for the ultimate end user. While it can occasionally be useful, your firm should resort to this option only in the most extreme situations. That is because CI analysis is most accurate and useful when the analyst is aware of all the key facts. Sometimes it is vital for a consultant to know the identity of the client and to deal directly with them. The cost of concealment is often a lack of completeness.

In any case, it is always much easier, and highly desirable, to set a policy on when and what types of CI research and analysis to contract out *before* a CI unit begins its operations. Like any other business unit, a CI unit's staff may see as a threat to growth, or even its existence, efforts to contract out what is regarded as its personal research and analysis work. Making these decisions as early as possible and with the input of the staff will minimize such conflict.

Non–Research and Analysis Tasks

Shadowing and Gaming. The question of when, or even whether, to use an outside firm is less clear when you are involved with processes like shadowing or working with related concepts such as gaming.[4] When you are involved in shadowing, it might be more cost-effective for you to do the all of the work inside, for several reasons:

- Because shadowing is often an ongoing operation, you and your staff will benefit most by doing it again and again. That means that the long-run cost of doing it inside may be lower than the costs of contracting it out, even if the short-run costs are not.
- You may want to be able to continue to call on those who are role playing your competitors at any time after the exercise, so these people can answer current "what if" questions from you or your end users right away.
- It is easier to prevent your own personnel from working for competitors in the future, by the use of employment contracts, than it is to control outside consultants and all of the consultants' personnel.

On the other hand, it may be wiser to use an outside consultant to help develop a shadow market plan, a document, as distinguished from conducting shadowing, for these reasons:

- You do not have to train your own CI personnel in shadowing techniques. By going to outsiders, you are buying the time of trained personnel, not paying for training insiders for what may be a onetime event.
- You can minimize the total number of people who know about the shadow market plan project. For defensive CI reasons, you may want to be extremely careful that competitors do not suspect your firm's involvement with such a detailed probe of their plans.
- The final shadow market plan may well include conclusions about the capabilities of or estimates of future probable actions of a competitor at odds with your own firm's conventional wisdom. It could be significantly easier for an outsider to deliver and defend this conclusion than it might be for insiders, such as your CI staff.

Training and Advocacy. While a CI unit should be actively engaged in conducting its own training, as well as training other, non-CI personnel, at the firm, outsiders can be a very important source of such training. For example, outside firms can often provide training superior to that available in a public large meeting in areas such as the following:

- improving interviewing skills, particularly on the telephone
- practicing techniques such as elicitation
- initiating defensive CI programs
- explaining how to locate currently unused sources of raw data
- showing how to improve CI output by learning to "push back" with end users to sharpen the focus of CI assignments

The reasons for this superiority are the following:

- The group being worked with is typically much smaller than would be found in a large public meeting. That allows one-on-one interaction.
- The presentation and training can be customized to the groups' unique needs, as well as the current competitive context in which it operates.
- The contract with the firm can include allowing the CI staff to call upon the consultant, for a limited time, with follow-up questions that arise as the staff implements its training.

Outside firms can also be very effective in helping a CI unit develop and integrate an existing CI program. In this role, they are serving as advocates. The most effective use is to have these firms present open meetings for all employees, or at least CI end users, to explain the potential that CI can provide their firm. In that context, they are a source of success stories, a good use of their experience to expand a firm's understanding of CI. Alternatively, such firms can be used, selectively, to provide training on CI, data gathering, and related subjects.

The overall goals of such activities are three:

- to build internal confidence in CI and in the firm's existing and future CI program
- to stimulate and support the development in internal networks
- to help develop future end users and to make both present and future end users into better clients, which is accomplished by underscoring what CI can and cannot do

Other Tasks. Outside consulting firms can also be used to help manage outside firms. While this may sound circular, in fact, this is a very effective mission. Specifically, if your firm is considering retaining an outside firm to conduct complex, long, or costly research and analysis, hiring a firm to help you could be very cost-effective.

The typical mission for a firm in this category is to serve as an advisor to your firm, and not to compete for the assignment in question. Selecting a firm that is familiar with your firm and with CI in general can allow you to do some or all of the following faster and/or cheaper than you can do it yourself:

- Develop a Request for Proposal (RFP) or Request for Quotation (RFQ). The key here is to describe, in terms clear to CI researchers, what your firm wants, what it does not want, what your firm intends to do with the output, when it needs the research, and how it expects a budget to be presented.
- Advise your firm on what range of quotations it can expect to receive. This can help your firm avoid asking for proposals or quotations that, when received, will clearly exceed the expected or available budget.
- Help your firm break the deliverables down to control costs. For example, a firm can help you define which deliverables are most critical and which can be let go if there are time or budget limitations.
- Review the work product at regular intervals to make sure it is really proceeding as you and your end user expect.

What Outsiders May Do Better

The services an outside CI professional will offer to provide will depend on what you ask to have done. In deciding whether to seek outside assistance, you should be aware that, *in general,* a CI specialist is able to develop certain types of data and analysis on competitors better than you can. In such cases, the CI specialist can even be seen as the primary source of your CI. In other cases, however, you can better use your own CI staff for a CI task and so should consider using the CI specialist firm to supplement your own research and analysis work.

In general, if your CI staff is focused on a specific orientation, such as providing only tactics-oriented CI, it will be more efficient for you to retain an outside firm to provide CI where there is little or no overlap, in terms of data sources and deliverables, with what you are doing. In. this case, it could be wise to use outside resources to develop strategy- or tactics-oriented CI.[5]

Outsiders should be able to significantly contribute to developing CI in the following broad areas of competitor analysis:

- owners and managers of the competitor, including information on how decisions are made, who makes them, and corporate politics
- emerging technology, research and development, current manufacturing methods and processes, and access to outside technology
- your competitor's personnel, resources, and facilities, including its sources of raw materials, the level of its quality control, and planned facilities
- your competitor's strategies, objectives, and self-perceptions, including how strategy is made and implemented, what markets it is targeting, and how the company sees itself
- how other competitors and customers see the targeted competitor
- how the targeted competitor sees you

In the following broad areas, outsiders providing CI will probably be able to make significant contributions to developing CI on competitors, but in some cases, that contribution may only be supplemental to what you can develop from your own CI efforts:

- products and services offered by competitors, including customer service and performance, and products or services likely to be introduced or eliminated
- marketing, including market shares by product lines, marketing approaches, and probable future changes in marketing directions
- sales and pricing policies, including topics such as pricing strategy; price levels and flexibility; and credits, discounts, incentives, and special pricing policies

- competitor's sales force and customers, including the type of sales force, its organization, training, and compensation; the number of customers; and an analysis of the most important customers

The following broad areas are ones for which outside sources of CI will be most often tend to be most effective if used to supplement, rather than develop, research and analysis. That means, in the following cases, you are usually better off developing CI from your own CI staff first:

- the overall competitive environment, including the industry's structure, potential entrants and future competitors, and market shares and profits of existing competitors
- your competitor's financial and legal positions, including sources of financing, profitability, and major lawsuits and regulatory actions affecting it

FINDING CONSULTANTS AND CONTRACTORS

Particular Types of Outside Firms for Particular Tasks

As businesses have increased their use of CI over the past twenty years, they have come to appreciate the need for assistance in finding raw data, as well as in analyzing it.[6] As a result, many firms seek out CI specialists to locate competitive data, analyze or to evaluate it, draw conclusions from it, and even merely prepare it for presentation, even when they have their own CI capabilities.

Turning now to this issue from the perspective of the outside contractor or consultant, you must keep in mind that each outside source of raw data and analysis (finished CI), as well as of other services, has its own pros and cons, its unique set of strengths and weaknesses. No firm can do everything equally well. For example, in the case where you are seeking an outside firm to do research and analysis, one of the major distinctions you should try to make is between firms whose primary interest and strengths lie in the mere collection and processing of data and those that have different interests, and expertise. Another is where that firm's focus lies in providing strategy-oriented, target-oriented, tactics-oriented, or technology-oriented CI.

Before contacting a firm to conduct CI research and analysis, you may feel you want to consider using some of the following people and companies already working with your firm to help you find at least some of the raw data you will need. These sources include:

- distributors
- advertising agencies
- marketing and marketing research firms

While these sources can be of some assistance, they are all most efficient in helping you locate raw data only as that data or its access directly pertains to their profession. Getting CI is not their primary expertise, so their ability or willingness to help you get the data will be uneven at best. And the resulting analysis, if any, will probably not be up to your expectations. Given that, these firms should be considered only to help reduce the amount of research work you will have to contact out.

In general, the most effective and impartial CI will be obtained from sources that do not have any other interest in your business. That means your sources for CI should have no financial interest in seeing that a particular transaction goes forward, such as an acquisition being reviewed, and that other relationships, such as auditing, may not be conditioned on the work they do or conclusions they draw. This is not to question the objectivity of professionals such as attorneys, accountants, investment bankers, and banks. Impartiality, however, is both an objective and a subjective matter. An outsider with no financial or collateral interest in a particular transaction or decision may provide a needed and desired level of impartiality, both actual and perceived.

Obtaining Raw Data

If you are simply looking for raw data, consider focusing on firms specializing in obtaining business data. These are known variously as information brokers or document retrieval services, depending on their reliance on on-line databases or on hard-copy material filed with government agencies.

Whatever the source of the data, the strengths of such specialists lie in obtaining, but *not* in analyzing, the data. Once they have provided the raw materials you seek, you should then have the data and documents evaluated and analyzed, either inside your business or by outside experts. However, you will probably find that using the specialists for such tasks is considerably more cost efficient than using a full-service research and analysis firm. In fact, such full-service firms often rely on information brokers and document retrieval firms to help them in the early stages of their non–interview-based research.

Providing CI Analysis

The most reliable method of obtaining finished CI (which entails the production of analysis, and not just the location of raw data), from an outside source is to hire a firm that engages in CI research and analysis as a specialty. This is not to say that non-specialist firms, such as the global management consulting firms, cannot offer do this. They can, but the evidence is that such programs are significantly less mature than those of specialist CI firms. For example, a recent analysis of *internal* activities at such firms noted, in passing that "[m]ost [large management] consulting firms are running reactive and tactical CI activities on an ad-hoc basis (for their largest pitches)."[7] In addition, experience shows that the individuals assigned to such projects tend to be less experienced than those assigned to considerably higher-value projects.

SELECTING THE RIGHT CONSULTANT

Overview

In selecting and using any outsider for your CI work, you must first understand that how you proceed and how you define the end task have a major impact on what the outside firm does and how it can and will respond to you. This is true not only during the assignment, but during any review process as well.

The major steps you face are the following:

1. Honestly define your problem, what you need, and what you can expect to get. The answers may differ.
2. Locate several potential firms that appear to be qualified.
3. Conduct a threshold review, eliminating firms that are not qualified or available.
4. Evaluate the firms. Then look at their proposals, if you are having them compete, and select your firm.
5. Monitor how the firm carries forward your assignment.
6. Evaluate the results of the assignment.

What Do Clients and Consultants Each Want?

As a potential client, you should keep in mind that the average consultant, whether providing CI or any other service, wants to contract and deal with "F-U-N" clients if possible. A F-U-N client is one who:

- has both the *Funds* and the authority to spend them
- *Understands* what is involved in working with a consultant and
- *Needs* the services that the consultant can provide

As for the consultants, they will do well to keep in mind that you, the potential client, tend to look for a consultant who is a J-O-Y to work with. That consultant is one who:

- has done this type of *Job* before and will do it personally, if necessary
- can *Obligate* his or her firm to the retention under discussion

- listens to *You* when you describe your firm's needs and any associated problems[8]

Defining the Problem

In defining what you expect a CI consultant to do, you first have to settle upon the following. Is the consultant to carry out the assignment alone or is the consultant to carry out the assignment while working with you? In either case, you should identify what data you have already collected and what, if any, you will be releasing to the consultant.

Then you will need to be able to explain what kind of CI you need, why you need it, and when you need it. Also identify exactly what form or forms in which you expect the consultant to provide the finished product. It may be any or all of the following:

- ongoing advice
- a written report
- interim written or oral reports
- copies of specific materials, such as product brochures
- all notes of interviews
- a formal presentation

Then use the tools and techniques outlined in Chapter 9 on needs determinations.

Costs

In evaluating the potential cost of outside CI services, you must keep in mind several factors:

- CI services are intangible products. That means they cannot be turned on and off or accelerated or decelerated without causing problems, which means additional costs.
- The costs of CI services are driven by what you seek.
- The costs of CI services are also heavily influenced by when you need the CI.

This means that the better you define your problem and what help you need, the better you will be able to control the cost. You must be frank with a CI consultant about the terms of the services needed, the time frame of the project, your budget, and the nature of the final product. If you try to go in "cheap," you will often find that you have cost your firm more money, not saved it.

This also means you are buying something before you or the consultant knows exactly what the result will be (and whether you can get it). If you are not satisfied, the consultant cannot "repossess" the CI and recover its costs; once completed and provided to a client, CI is out of the consultant's control forever.

Some tips are in order:

- Determine what you can afford to spend for the CI you need and figure out what the absence of that CI could cost your firm, as well as what its presence could mean in terms of profits and benefits. Then you can do a cost/benefit or cost/risk of loss analysis to see if you are being realistic.
- Target what you would like if you could get everything you wanted. Then establish what will be "enough" for you to get in order to be able to operate. If the ideal is unattainable or too expensive, shift to the fallback position.
- Consider breaking an assignment into tiers. That is, when you have the results of the first tier of work, you can narrow down what you need in the second tier, and so on.
- Arrange to keep in close touch with your CI consultant.
- Establish how much data already on hand the CI consultant can access and use.
- Consider using the CI consultant only as a guide or coach, while you and your own CI personnel do most of the work.
- Get a written proposal with a quotation covering a range of fees. In general, try to avoid any research proposal or quotation given in terms of dollars per hour plus costs. In that case, you have little or no control over the final cost.
- If that type of pricing is unavoidable, such as with on-site consulting services, work with the consultant to establish formal or informal controls, such as having the consultant call you before fees and costs exceed a predetermined level.
- Consider sharing the costs of a CI consulting assignment with other units in your company who can use its services, particularly if the services you are obtaining may benefit several units.

Finding Firms

In seeking a CI consultant, you might be surprised to find that the process is subject to constraints you may not always face in searching for other consultants. For example, you or your internal client may not wish to advertise openly for a firm with CI expertise, because this will alert your competitors about your future business intentions and capabilities. Alternately, you may find that your firm is unwilling to distribute an RFP, as it will detail what you want and why you want it.

CI consultants should be identified and located through a combination of the following:

- Use a broad directory, such as the SCIP on-line membership directory, but do not restrict yourself to this (or any other) source alone.
- Read recent books and articles written by CI consultants. These can lead you to their firms. However, you should first read what each says and their rationale for that. Do their experiences and points of view match your needs?
- Research the trade press covering your own industry, as well as the more general business press, for discussions of the activities of consultants and consulting firms working in CI. But keep in mind that being quoted may only mean that the consultant was available to the press, not that this is the foremost expert.
- Review directories of research, and related service organizations for leads. If you already use such firms, contact them to ask for their suggestions.
- Survey key employees for their suggestions. Include in this sweep members of other CI teams within your firm, if there are any. Exchanging positive and negative information on CI consultants is a valuable dividend of such internal networking.

Each of these steps should turn up some names. But your search should not stop there. Always work to expand that list before you close it. For example, individuals identified with one CI firm several years ago may now be with another CI firm, making that new firm a candidate for your consideration. That also may remove the first firm from your consideration.

In looking for names of CI consulting firms, as with the search for any consulting firms, avoid the trap of going only for the "old, established consulting firm," with a general practice, rather than to a specialist. Just because a management consulting firm is large and has been around a long time does not mean that it provides any CI services or that it can provide the quality of services you want on a cost-effective basis.

There is another pitfall to avoid: you should never assume that every firm does everything well. Rather, look at the types of CI services you may need as falling into one of four broad categories:

- *Raw data:* Reprint and clipping services, information brokers, document retrieval services, and directory publishers
- *Processed data:* Prepackaged reports and public seminars

- *Custom analysis services:* Collecting and analyzing data and helping individuals
- *Training and consulting services:* Enabling companies to improve the way they perform, including collecting data and producing finished analyses

Once you have developed a list of potential CI consultants, then you can begin to evaluate them. That means generating some background information from Web pages, followed by contacting the targeted CI firms for indications of their qualifications to conduct the kind of research you want and their ability to consider taking the assignment within the time and cost constraints that you face. If appropriate, consider entering into a simple nondisclosure agreement so that your discussions about your needs are protected from retransmission.

Before going further, each of these firms should be told immediately about any special limitations, such as important time constraints, a requirement to work at a specific location, or the requirement that the CI be based only on interviews, not on secondary research. If you wait until later in the process, you may find you have wasted your time and their time. In addition, this is a good time to make sure that your potential consultant is not "conflicted out." That means that it cannot bid on or accept an assignment since it is, or will be in, a conflict of interest situation (see the following discussion).

Shorten the List

After you clarify the qualifications, availability, and interest of the firms on your list, review them to decide which firms should be contacted for additional discussion. If you have too many firms on your list, you may find that you are actually spending more time selecting one than that firm might spend on the potential assignment.

Start Discussions

These discussions may be as elaborate as interviewing key members of the firm or requesting each firm to submit a complete proposal and price for the assignment. The follow-up may be as simple as sending a contract to one firm and asking whether the firm will sign it and start to work. Unless the fit between the assignment and the potential consultant is overwhelmingly tight, you should not move to this step.

In initial discussions with potential CI consultants, begin by presenting your problem or the scope of the assignment directly to the consultant. It is not enough to have a consultant state that he or she understands the problem and that he or she can provide the needed services. You should obtain clarification on several key items before you decide whether to retain a particular consultant, including the following:

- General information on the consultant and its (his or her) experience: How relevant is that experience to your needs? Have the individuals likely to be assigned to your project worked on similar projects?
- Specific information on key individuals employed by the consultant who would probably be working on the project: It cannot be overemphasized that if you are hiring a firm because of the particular experience or expertise of one or more individuals, you should always ensure that the specific individuals will be working on your assignment. Moreover, that should be done in the final contract.
- What references can the consultant provide? Do confidentiality concerns mean that some of your potential consultants cannot provide you with the names of past clients or details on completed projects? Is so (and that can be very common in CI), what kind of references do you want?

Your goal is to get information so that you can knowledgably compare one consultant with another. You and each consultant should discuss openly exactly what the consultant will need from you. That means you must be ready to discuss, not only fees and costs, but also your firm's commitment of other resources, such as your time or the time of other key employees and executives. You must be very frank in deciding whether you are willing and able to commit your time or that of others, particularly if you are overcommitted already.

In many cases, you may want to go into detail on how the consultant will handle the assignment, whether it is research or training. A trap to avoid, and one not always easy to spot, is the retention of consultants with prepackaged approaches. In such cases, you will typically find that the consultant is very assertive, pointing to how it handled similar problems for other clients with the same approach time and time again. Determine whether the approach suggested to each of these is basically the same, regardless of the unique characteristics of each assignment. If that is the case, the consultant is probably selling its own predetermined approach and not a way to handle your task in the best and most cost-effective way.

Another key point is to deal with reporting and communication. You should be wary of a consultant who indicates that he or she will take a research and analysis assignment and then report back to you at the end, but does not see any need to provide interim communications, progress reports, or other feedback. Be particularly wary if the consultant appears reluctant to keep in regular communication with you. That may mean any one of a number of things, none of them positive.

Avoiding Internal Legal Problems

One way to handle problems created by the need for internal legal review of terms which might offered by a consultant is to ask each consultant with whom you *may* work to provide you with its set of standard terms and conditions. Then you can take this to your own legal department and get feedback before you get a proposal you want to accept. Then, you should go over that legal review with the consultants. When you are ready to use that firm, you can then give the legal department the terms of the particular proposal, reminding it that the balance of the terms of the offer have already been cleared by it.

Client Records and Information

In working with a CI consultant, a critical issue should be what access the consultant will have to your own competitively sensitive information and how the consultant will handle that information. A related issue is how the consultant will treat the results of your assignment.

To perform effectively, in many cases a CI consultant may have to have direct, continuing, and unimpeded access to corporate records, key personnel, and internal information that is highly sensitive. The issue, then, is not merely protecting the confidentiality of your information while the assignment is being conducted, but in some cases protecting your information from being disclosed after the fact.

The key here is to establish, at the beginning, a clear understanding between you and the consultant that the data you provide will be kept confidential *and* that the assignment being conducted for you will also be kept confidential. In addition to language in the consultant's proposal or agreement covering this point, look for the following as evidence of the consultant's ability and willingness to keep this kind of commitment:

- How many people in the consultant's organization will actually know the identity of the client? How many will now the actual scope of the work? How many will have access to the project files or the final work product?
- If you provide the consultant with materials during the assignment, what will happen to them? Ideally, they should be returned to you un-copied.
- Do client names appear on copies of work kept by the consultant? Do you have a problem with that?
- What does the consultant do with the work files accumulated during an assignment? Are they kept intact or destroyed? What about working files on a server or on individuals' computers?

- Does the consultant name other clients and describe assignments conducted for them in detail? Will it refrain from doing that with your company's name and its assignment?

Identification of Former Clients. The question about descriptions of past assignments raises what is an often-ignored issue: the identification of former clients by a CI specialist firm. Some firms involved in CI research and analysis will disclose past and even current clients. Obviously that is done in the hopes of generating additional business, by showing potential clients how well known past clients have been.

The reasons that this practice is not widespread are two. First, the agreement with the client prevents the disclosure of confidential information with respect to the assignment, or even the identity of the client; and second, that many in the CI community regard such a disclosure, except at the express request or express consent of the client for whom the work was done, as improper and unethical.

Legal Limitations. In an increasing number of situations, clients and consultants alike commonly use some sort of confidentiality agreement covering the retention. That usually says something like the following:

> The consultant will not disclose to any person, firm or corporation any confidential information regarding the Client, this Assignment, or the business of the Client received or developed in connection with this Assignment without the Client's consent.

But this kind of clause rarely covers the identity of the Client. Why do some clients ask for such coverage? As one client put it to your authors years ago, "the very fact that we are using or have hired a firm like yours is, in our mind, competitively sensitive information. It is not the sort of thing we want our competitors to know." That attitude has not changed significantly in over fifteen years.

But what about today? A couple of years ago, we asked current and past clients whether they had a problem if we deleted this clause from our confirmation:

> The consultant will not disclose to any person, firm or corporation, the identify of the Client without the Client's consent.

The majority felt that they still wanted this kind of clause. It appears that firms are becoming more sensitive to the effectiveness of the CI activities of their competitors. They feel that competitors assume that they are doing CI, and may be using outsiders to do it or to help them. But now they feel that the disclosure of their identify as a current or past client of a CI firm still reveals something that is competitively sensitive, but in a way that differs from the situation fifteen years ago. By listing ABC Corporation as a client, they feel that a CI firm is telling competitors about the client's level of CI sophistication, or about the types of CI and methodologies they employ.

Trust. There is also another underlying issue, one of trust. While firms understand that consultants of all sorts will seek continually retentions within the same industry, there are some that concerned about a CI consultant who approaches them saying, in essence, "Hire me; I am a proven commodity, for, you see, I was good enough to be hired by your competitor."

Why is there such concern? The problem is that information is a strange commodity. It is, as economists say, "sticky." That is, once having received a bit of information, you can not eliminate your mental retention by returning the paper from which you derived it. You still keep some of it, if only a little. And you do not need access to confidential information to develop good CI. So these firms may rightly be concerned that even the receipt of a lot of nonconfidential information from a past client has potentially provided a foundation for developing CI against them in the future.

Questions to Ask a CI Consultant. The following ten sets of questions help you to get important information that you will require from a CI consultant

1. Who will be doing this work? If not you, who? Can we replace that person? Will any of it be subcontracted?
2. Do you adhere to ethical standards? Are they written? May we see them?
3. What is your policy on conflicts of interest? Are others at your firm working for a target of this project? Did you do so in the past? Will you be available to do so in the future? When?
4. What does your confidentiality policy cover? Who does it cover? Do you make copies of what we give you? What do you do with them?
5. What happens to the research materials and files you generate on this project? Are they destroyed? Will they be returned to us?
6. Can you give us references? Do you disclose the names of all former clients? If not, who and under what circumstances?
7. What happens to the report you do for us? Is it contributed to a knowledge management base? If so, how are our interests in the CI protected?
8. What are your usual payment terms? Do you understand ours? Will that change the price or other terms?

9. Do you need/want access to information we have previously generated? If so, why? If not, why not?
10. Do you have any other standard contract terms? What are they?

Questions a Consultant May Ask You. Just as you want to learn about a firm and its capabilities through interviews, increasingly, CI firms are seeking opportunities to learn how they are perceived by potential clients. For that reason, they may contact firms that asked for a formal proposal to ask for a debriefing following the award to another firm. They ask questions like these:

- Was the proposal responsive to your perceived needs?
- Was the statement of work clear?
- Was the price competitive?
- Was the methodology appropriate?

The goal is not to resell the lost potential client; rather it is to finetune the way in which they present what they have to offer to meet what these companies think they need. While you are under no obligation to respond, courtesy does indicate that you should take a few minutes to respond to the needs of a consultant that took hours to respond to your needs.

EXPERT TESTIMONY ON CI

As competitive intelligence grows and matures, the question will inevitably arise: can someone testify as an "expert witness" about competitive intelligence? At least Pennsylvania trial courts have faced the issue of whether or not competitive intelligence is a subject about which one can be an expert witness, and their answer is "yes."

What is an Expert Witness?

Rule 702 of Federal Rules of Evidence provides that

> If scientific, technical, or other specialized knowledge will assist the trier of fact to understand the evidence or to determine a fact in issue, a witness qualified as an expert by knowledge, skill, experience, training, or education, may testify thereto in the form of an opinion or otherwise.

This rule, and its equivalents under state law, creates what we know as the "expert witness."

This person, the expert witness, should be distinguished from a consulting expert. In trial practice, this is an individual who assists trial counsel to prepare an expert witness for trial.[9] In general, since they work with trial counsel preparing the case for trial, what they produce for a client is not subject to discovery. In the federal court system, discovery, the pre-trial process whereby the parties exchange information, specifically applies to expert witnesses. They generally do not apply to those working with the trial counsel, usually including a consulting expert.

What Does an Expert Witness Do?

Basically, an expert witness provides an unusual input into a trial. The general rule in a civil trial is that a witness may testify only as to what he or she has seen or heard. While, in some cases, the emotions of the witness may be a subject for testimony, the average witness is not permitted to offer an opinion or to discuss an event which he or she did not actually see. The formation of an opinion, based on the facts in evidence, is traditionally the responsibility of the jury, or of the judge when there is no jury.

The use of an expert witness is an exception to this rule. The reasoning for this exception is that some situations are so complex that an expert must be brought in to explain the significance of what is in evidence to a jury. However, since the American common-law based system still places ultimate responsibility for the finding of facts with a jury, the expert comes in as another type of witness. That means the jury must evaluate the expert's testimony, particularly his or her conclusions, as it would that of any other witness. The jury is not required to accept what the expert says as its own conclusion. Therefore, the jury must also be told the facts on which the expert's opinion is based, as well as the special qualifications that the expert has to be able to draw the conclusion advanced.

How is Someone Qualified as an Expert Witness?

An expert witness is typically presented to the court by one of the parties. The party presenting the expert must satisfy the judge as to the following issues:

- that there is some specialized area of knowledge that will help the jury understand the case before it
- that this area has a reasonable foundation as the subject of activities such as formal research, academic courses, professional education or licensing, trade or professional groups
- that the person offered as an expert has a foundation in the specialized area of knowledge, such as having publications in the area, experience, honors, academic posts, etc.

The way this is usually done is by having the witness being offered as an expert directly testify as to these points. Then, the witness can be considered as qualified. At that point, the expert is permitted to testify on the matter before the court. This is done by having the attorney present the expert with specific facts. Customarily, a question is presented to the expert in a form like this:

Assuming that the facts that have been presented to you are correct, have you drawn any conclusion about them, based on your expertise?

When the answer is "yes," then and only then can the expert offer his or her opinion as to the meaning of the offered facts. But it is still for the jury (or judge sitting in place of a jury) to determine whether or not to accept the testimony and opinion offered.

The process does not end there. The opposing trial counsel has the right to do several things. They include:

- challenging that the area of testimony is a legitimate area for expert testimony
- arguing that the expert presented is not really qualified to draw a conclusion
- asking the expert questions based on different assumptions, to elicit different conclusions
- offering up opposing expert witnesses

How Might a CI Professional's "Expert" Testimony Be Presented?[10]

Here, we will take you through how expert witnesses have been used in two cases[11] in which one of the co-authors was involved.

First, as noted, the trial counsels had to establish that that there is, in fact, some specialized area of knowledge that would help the court understand the case before it. As part of this same effort, counsels had to show that this area has a reasonable foundation in terms of being the subject of activities such as formal research, academic courses, professional education or licensing, trade or professional groups, etc. To meet this standard, lawyers in each case had to first establish the existence of competitive intelligence as a distinct discipline or, alternatively (a common way in which law suits often go) that it was a part of some other recognized discipline.

This was accomplished by bringing several different matters to the judges' attention:

- that competitive intelligence was a subject encompassed in Professor Michael Porter's 1980 book *Competitive Strategy*,[12] a foundation book for corporate planning. And that corporate planning was recognized as being a specialized area of knowledge

- that competitive intelligence is being been taught in universities
- that an international society, SCIP, existed, whose focus was the advancement of competitive intelligence
- that both juried and non-juried publications have published articles on competitive intelligence
- that the subject was covered in both popular and technical or scholarly books.

Having established to the court, in essence, that competitive intelligence existed as a separate discipline, in which a person could develop expertise, the lawyers then had to pass the next step: to establish that the person being offered as an expert had a foundation in the specialized area of knowledge. This was accomplished by offering up testimony on books and articles co-written by the proposed witness on competitive intelligence, workshops presented (particularly outside of the United States), and courses on the subject which the witness had taught. At that point, the expert witness can begin to present his or her expert opinion.

CONTRACTING

Why Have a Written Contract?

The consulting relationship means you are dealing with an outsider who has agreed to provide services to you that you, and no one else, can use. In light of the special nature of the consulting relationship, several key topics should be always considered in the creation of the consulting relationship, and thus, ultimately, in the consulting agreement itself. Of course, not all of these will appear in every contract, but their place should always be considered:

- the nature and scope of the services to be performed
- details on payment of compensation and costs
- the length of the relationship or of the assignment
- how, when, and by whom the relationship can be terminated
- how the work to be performed can be changed, if at all, and by whom
- a statement that the consultant has the status as an independent contractor, including in the handling of the final work product
- special requirements (covenants) to protect the firm, such as handling of confidential information and avoidance of conflicts of interest
- how to handle any disputes

- what remedies are available and to whom on default or failure to perform, and what remedies are not available
- how formal notice is to be given, such as how changes in the scope of the assignment are to be memorialized, and so on.

Because of the complexity of these elements, you should never enter into a CI consulting relationship, or any consulting relationship, orally.[13]

Some Key Contracting Issues

Conflicts of Interest. This is an extremely important issue for CI specialists, but one where very little guidance can be given. That is because the facts of each case have a powerful influence over defining what constitutes a conflict of interest.

An ethical CI consultant should avoid any conflict of interest as well as the appearance of a conflict of interest. Although most people think of a conflict of interest in the context of being hired by one firm to develop CI about another firm which is currently a client, it is important to appreciate that this issue can emerge in many other, less-direct areas.

Thinking about avoiding a conflict of interest means dealing with the following issues. If they are of potential concern to your firm, they should be raised before entering into any retention. Later is too late:

- A CI consultant should not use the consequences of any work done for one client as data in any work for another. For example, if a CI assignment has resulted in the first client changing its marketing plan, that result should *never* be disclosed to a competitor, a later client, unless it has first been made public.
- A CI consultant should not use any information received in confidence from one client as data for work done for another. For example, if a client has developed internal cost data on its own operations that it provided to the consultant, that data should never be revealed to any other firm.
- A CI consultant should not disclose the analysis or conclusions it has given to one client to any other client. For example, if you have advised Company, Inc., that a particular market is vulnerable to imports, you should not tell Industrial Concern, Inc., that you have drawn that conclusion and given it to another business.
- A CI consultant should not be involved in both sides of a transaction. For example, the consultant should not work for one corporation that has targeted a client for a takeover.

The lesson is that you must be clear in your own mind what problems a potential conflict of interest might produce, and then deal with them directly. Merely to say that the CI consultant must not have a conflict of interest is to scratch the surface.

RFPs and RFQs. Some firms erroneously label some RFPs as RFQs. This happens often when the firm has a fairly detailed statement of its needs, and even of deliverables, but where it is asking for information on a firm's qualifications in addition to its pricing. Implicit in this is that the decision is to be made on price and qualifications. Properly, a process that asks for anything more than pricing and related terms is not an RFQ.

Request for a Proposal. An RFP is a request for a proposal. It is usually used when you, the client, have already determined exactly what you need done, at least in terms of the desired end result. In it you describe, in detail, the desired results, provide information about your business and other related issues, outline the way the project will be managed, and ask for a response.

Before drafting an RFP, think about *who* should be doing this work. For example, if you are planning to ask only one consultant for a proposal for a retention, consider asking that consultant to help *you* draft a statement of the scope of the work. That way both you and the consultant are, quite literally, on the same page, when the retention goes forward. In this situation, make sure you make the consultant aware of any special terms and conditions that will apply to it.

The response to an RFP is a document in which the consultant typically, but not always, provides you with the following:

- A description of the qualifications and skills the consultant will bring to the assignment. While this is not always a formal requirement, expect that most experienced consultants will include assuming that their proposal may be reviewed by persons unfamiliar with them.
- Information on the individuals who will work on the project.
- A statement of what the consultant intends to do, including how it will approach the project.
- Any special terms that are a part of its offer, such as payment terms, and the need for client cooperation.
- Pricing for the project. If you do not specify, this may be a fixed price, estimates of low and high costs, hourly rates with estimates of hours to be utilized, details on potential disbursements, and so on.

Your RFPs must include a response date after which proposals will not be accepted. Usually RFPs provide that a proposal submitted to the firm must stay open for some period. These time frames should be reasonable. If you ask for a response to your RFP in a short period of time, you should be prepared to respond just as quickly and not require that proposals be kept open for an excessive period of time.

While it is not required, some firms have developed the good practice of providing those firms who are given the RFP a copy of the guidelines that the soliciting firm will apply to the final proposals.[14] This is the same document that will guide those reviewing it. If your firm is reluctant to do this, it would be appropriate to provide extracts from the guidelines to help assure that the proposals are fully responsive to your RFP.

You then will review all of the RFPs you get back. It is your option to send an RFP to one firm to three or to dozens. Keep in mind that not every firm you ask to propose may do so. Then, based on your review of the responding proposals, you would usually award the contract to one firm. Sometimes, you may wish to go back to one or two firms, the finalists, and ask that they re-propose. This is costly for the consultants and time-consuming for you, so you should do it only infrequently. Unless those responding to the RFP are told, in advance, that their response may be shared with competitors, you should not show a response from one firm to another.

The final terms of the agreement between your and the consultant are typically made up of the terms you have already included in the RFP. To that are added:

1. the pricing and other individualized consultant responses to your request for a description of services
2. any new terms and conditions requested by the consultant, if you agree to them

Experienced clients provide in the RFP that, on acceptance, all the terms and conditions will be incorporated into one final document. Taking this approach allows both sides to make sure that they understand what the client has agreed to, and what it will hold consultant responsible to do.

Request for a Quotation. The RFQ is a request for a quotation. Technically, it should be a document that sets forth, in detail:

- what you need done
- what you expect a consultant to do
- all other terms and conditions, such as payment terms and required insurance, that will apply to the project

An RFQ is usually sent to firms that have been pre-cleared as qualified. That means that a responding firm just sends in pricing information. As with the RFQ, unless you say how that pricing is to be expressed, it can be a fixed price, an hourly rate, or some other option. Typically, the terms of the RFQ require that the pricing be kept firm for a set period of time.

Once you have decided, a process which should be based on price, you notify the winning firm. The reason the decision should be based on pricing alone is that all competing firms have already been pre-qualified. Usually, the winning firm just signs a contract, which was a part of the RFQ, and can begin.

Handling Written Proposals from Consultants. While a consultant may submit an unsolicited proposal to you, more often you, following discussions with a consultant, may ask the consultant for a "proposal on this." In either case, you should exercise care in handling this document.

- If your firm has standard terms that apply to all contracts for consulting services or if the services will be governed by a purchase order, get these to the consultant now if they were not provided earlier. The consultant should be given the opportunity to revise its proposal in light of any of these terms or conditions.
- If the proposal is unsolicited, and you do not want to consider it, return it as quickly as possible to the consultant.
- If the proposal interests you, quickly review it for anything you must deal with up front. For example, if the proposal expires within a short time and you need more time to review it, take care of that at once. In addition, if all discussions must be under your confidentiality agreement, get that taken care of before spending time in reviewing the proposal.
- Now look at it again, with care. Is it really responsive? Are the terms clear? If any points need clarification, those explanation should be made by the consultant, in writing.
- If the proposal is just not acceptable, either tell the consultant that promptly, or ask for a revised proposal, pointing out what else you want or need. Set a reasonable deadline.
- If the proposal is acceptable, communicate that. If there are no changes needed, say that. If the proposal is acceptable, but only with changes, do *not* say the proposal has been approved. Rather, you should say it *can* be approved if certain changes are made. Once the changes have been made, then, and only then, should you accept.
- Be prompt. If a proposal is not satisfactory, get that message out as quickly as you can. If you have asked for a proposal in a very short time, be prepared to respond equally as fast. A good rule is that you should take no longer to respond to a proposal that you solicited than you gave the firm to prepare it.

- The proposal should never be shown to any firm in competition for this same retention, nor should it be used as the basis for soliciting proposals from other firms. If you need help in soliciting proposals, or developing an RFP, hire someone for that. Do not exploit the work put into developing a proposal by a consultant.

KEY ISSUES IN MANAGING CONSULTANTS AND CONTRACTORS

A discussion of all of the issues related to the effective management of consultants and contractors is beyond the scope of this book. (It is the subject of our *How to Use a Consultant in Your Company: A Managers' and Executives' Guide*.)[15] But we can touch on a few key issues here.

Planning

While you have probably expended a lot of effort in selecting a consultant, establishing your needs, communicating them to the consultant, establishing a budget, and arranging for the assignment to be undertaken, there is more to do. Above all, in the case of CI, as with all other consulting relationships, those who plan for the management and for the end of the assignment gain more from it than do those who do not do so.

Dealing with End User Concerns about Consultants

How do you deal with an end user when the outside consultant or consultants you have selected indicate that they cannot or will not carry out the assignment as the end user has stated it? That is, it is the consultant's opinion that the sought-after CI cannot be provided, perhaps for legal and ethical reasons.

The SCIP Code of Ethics requires a CI professional "To provide honest and realistic recommendations and conclusions in the execution of one's duties." That requirement certainly carries with it the implication that the consultant should not promise that which he or she cannot deliver, for whatever reason.

There are several reasons why an end user may have a problem with accepting or even receiving CI on such limitations. Among the most common are the following:

1. The end user is planning action premised on getting *exactly* this bit of CI.
2. The end user believes that he or she already knows the answer, so the CI being sought serves only to validate the client's own conclusions.

3. The end user is not aware of the specific limitations—legal, ethical, financial, or otherwise—on the CI project being discussed.
4. The end user is not really aware of what CI can (and cannot) do.

There are a variety of ways you can try to handle these problems, as follows.

Case 1. If the end user is planning some action premised on getting exactly this bit of intelligence, not much can be done here. You should try to elicit from the end user some acknowledgement that he/she is in this situation. Then you need to identify what other *obtainable* CI could be provided that would help in this decision-making process. Oddly, you may find that the end user has asked for this CI in the mistaken impression that it is easy to get. There have been many cases where an end user was told some other CI was obtainable, and has responded, "Well, that would be even better. I just did not think you could get that." Another option is to get the end user to describe the decision-making process and issues he or she is facing. You will also get a sense of what is needed and when. You goal is to get to the underlying decision, and to get past the end user's personal perception of what is needed to make that decision.

Case 2. The end user believes that he or she already knows the answer, so the CI is really being sought to validate the client's own conclusions. This is not a very good end user. Do what you can, but try to work with other end users. Just as in private practice, you will find that a small percentage of your end users are very good ones (active, inquisitive, understanding, cooperative), a small percentage of them are very poor, and the balance are in the middle somewhere. Serve all of them, but, in the long run, cultivate the best and try to turn the middle ones into good clients, through training.

Case 3. The end user is not aware of the specific limitations, legal, ethical, financial, or otherwise, on the CI project being tasked. If you are already in this situation, then you (or your CI process) may already have a major failure on your hands. One of the keys to success, to development, to growth, and to survival, is that a CI unit undertakes *and maintains* an ongoing and ever-expanding internal education process. That means training and other sessions that include your CI team, its direct customers, its indirect end users, and even potential internal sources of raw data. The training, as noted, should probably cover, in order, the essentials of CI, legal and ethical issues in data collection, and analysis techniques most often used in your industry, and then move to advanced issues such as defensive activity. You cannot possibly cure such an oversight at once. One option is to turn the problem on its head. Try to see if your end user understands how difficult it would be for your competitors to develop this very CI on your firm under the same limits of time, laws, and so on. That very often provides a quick wake-up call. If you must, ask an outside consultant to evaluate the request from this point of view. But do not wear out your welcome. While consultants are happy to help clients, there are mixed feelings over telling a potential client "no" again and again because the consultant is willing to review these difficult projects.

Case 4. The client is not really aware of what CI can (and cannot) do. This is sort of a combination of Cases 3 and 1 above.

Overall, the key to dealing with all of this is to be frank while being diplomatic, particularly when you feel that you cannot be very frank:

- Instead of saying that the end user does not really need this intelligence, say: "If we had the answer here today, how quickly would we act on it? And what would the results be if the answer were other than you expect? How will that change what we are doing? All of this will help us find what we need better and faster."
- Instead of saying something is illegal, say: "I am sure you did not realize this, but doing it this way would violate the Economic Espionage Act [or whatever]. So our only legal option is to do it this other way [explain]. Now we can expect it will take xx weeks, cost \$$Y$, and deliver about 60 percent of what you wish [not what you say you need]. Will that work for you?"
- Instead of saying it is impossible, say: "Well, if our competition tried to get this from us, where would they find it?—Oh, only you know that? Then there is no way they could learn this until it is too late to act on it. They don't operate much differently from us on this, do they?"
- Instead of saying you will ask an outside firm to look at this, knowing they will pass, say: "We can retain [a named firm] to review this for overall cost, timing and feasibility so that we can restructure it properly. Since they cannot then bid on it, how do we cover their fee?"
- Instead of saying there is not enough time, say: "Since a full assault on this would take much longer than you have, we can either cut back on the deliverables or raise the budget. Which option fits better here?"
- Instead of saying that there is not enough budget, say: "We expect that the cost of this work would be \$$xx$,000. How do we go about getting a budget transfer for that?"

Monitoring the Assignment

If you are working with a consultant for the first time or the assignment is one that will take a long time to complete, you may want to monitor the assignment as it is being done. However, if you anticipate doing this, make certain that the consultant is aware of this *before* the assignment is finalized.

Remember, from the consultant's point of view, your firm's monitoring activities, such as a need for regular reports, written or oral, may significantly increase the time the entire project takes, the complexity of managing the work production, or the out-of-pocket costs the consultant faces incurring. That all impacts the consultant's profits by increasing costs. For this reason, it is not fair to impose any substantial monitoring or reporting requirement *after* an assignment has begun.

If you will be monitoring the assignment, decide how and when that will happen. For example, if you require regular monthly reports, you should understand that the consultant may actually have to slow things down, or even stop them, in order to take the time to give you a report. In addition, there is always the indirect pressure on the consultant to revise the way in which work is done so that there is something to include in each report.

Evaluating the Results of an Assignment

To evaluate results, always make sure that you compare what you expected to receive from the consultant with what you finally received. The best way to do this is to compare the final report (if any) with the written proposal given you by the consultant at the beginning of the assignment. However, always make sure that *you* take into account any later changes in the assignment due to requests that you made, interim results, and so on.

The simple question is, "Do they match?" If they do not match, then you should determine in what ways they do not match and why. In doing that, always keep in mind that CI is not an exact science. A research and analysis assignment may not produce satisfactory results for one of more of a wide variety of reasons unrelated to a failure in effort by the consultant, including:

- You were seeking CI on, for example, what a target was planning to do, but the target has not yet made that decision.
- If you were seeking financial or production data, that data was provided but is incompatible with your own.
- Your statement of needs was not sufficiently precise.

It is important to be frank in making this evaluation.

If the consultant is providing services, rather than a report, the way to start the evaluation process is to find out from those with whom the consultant worked whether they were satisfied with the consultant. That includes assessing issues such as the following:

- Was the consultant cooperative, prompt, and effective?
- Did the services provided match those in the contract?
- How did individuals working with the consultant rate the consultant in comparison with others from who they have also received, for example, training?
- Did the consultant stay within budget estimates or limits? If not, why not?

Evaluating or Valuing Your Work Product

The next stage in the evaluation should be an effort to evaluate or value the work product, whether services or a report, delivered by the consultant. As we have detailed elsewhere, this can be done, so long as you are using the right measures, or metrics, for the type of CI you are providing, the way you are delivering it, and the way that you are collecting the underlying data.[16]

There are several reasons why you should consider adding this step:

- Valuing the work product requires that the end user or end users be a part of the evaluation process, adding another perspective. In the long run, it may be a powerful tool in controlling end user expectations.
- The time when this can be done may not be at the end of the assignment. That means that you have an opportunity to revisit the evaluation process after some time has passed.
- At this point, you are better able to use the process to see if your own needs determination process was sufficient.
- These efforts help in validating your own CI program, at least in terms of your use of and the value of outside service providers.

Valuation of each assignment can involve answering a variety of questions:

- What was the financial value of the assignment to the firm?
- How does that compare with any estimates made of that value at the beginning?
- How does that compare with the cost of the project?
- How much would it have cost to do this internally, if that was possible?

- If that was not possible at the time, have you learned enough that you could do this the next time it is needed? How much would you save by doing that?

Do not stop with the mere completion of the valuation and evaluation process. It is important to use these, not only to see what you and your firm did correctly, but to see what you and your firm did wrong. Also, alert others within the CI community in your firm that these exist. A review of some of these when other are considering this very firm can materially improve the way others, as well as you, utilize the firm in the future.

On occasion, consultants may ask you for a copy of such evaluations. Whether or not they get this is a matter is be dealt with at the beginning of the relationship, and covered in the final consulting agreement. In addition, your firm should not share with a firm the internal valuation aspects of the review. If you share anything, it should be on how well the firm worked with you and how well the final product conformed with the work initially sought.

Misusing Consultants and Contractors

As with the entire issue of managing them, misusing CI consultants is a broad issue. Its causes, from your perspective as a potential client, are numerous, including:[17]

- a failure by a potential client to understand the business perspective of consultants
- consultants' inability to understand the management perspective of potential clients
- a reluctance by one side or both sides to communicate completely, fairly and accurately, particularly with respect to potential problems

The majority of the most important, and difficult, causes fall into one of two categories:

- You, the potential client, were not frank with the consultant at all stages. For example, do not try to use a consultant you are hoping to retain to provide help in selling the entire project to those who must approve. At least, tell the consultant your problem first and ask if the consultant will help; and
- You are not being fair. For example, you provide one or more consultants with an RFP without telling them that the project is political dynamite, in internal terms, at least, or, you use an outside

consultant, who turns down an assignment on ethical grounds, to make that very point to an internal client.

APPENDIX: SAMPLE CONTRACT CLAUSES

Throughout these sample contract clauses, the parties are called "the Client" and "the Consultant." In drafting an agreement, you, the client, should *never* be called "the Employer," because even the mere use of this term could undermine the independent contractor status of the consultant.

Keep in mind that these clauses are samples; they are not models. A contract should reflect the agreement of the parties, and, ideally, be prepared at the end of discussions and negotiations. But realistically, both consultants and the firms retaining them often start that process with prepared terms and conditions.

Amendments Must Be Written

Any waiver, alteration, or modification of any of the provisions of this Consulting Agreement will not be valid unless they are in writing and are signed by both the Client and the Consultant.

Assignment Can Be Modified by Client as It Proceeds

The Consultant will perform [describe the Assignment]. These services to be performed by the Consultant may be changed by the Client from time to time by letter requests [or work orders, or change orders] sent to the Consultant by [name of authorized person].

Best Efforts Will be Used

The Consultant will use its best efforts in carrying out this Assignment and will retain control over the means and manner in which it performs this Assignment.

Billing, How Conducted

Bills shall be delivered to the Client on a monthly [or quarterly] basis. All bills shall show the nature of the work performed on the Assignment, the individual(s) performing the task, the title of such individual(s) and the days [or hours] involved. Such bills shall also include, in itemized form, the Consultant's reimbursable costs arising out of its performance of the Assignment. The Client agrees to pay Consultant the amount of such bills within thirty (30) days after receiving them.

Complete Agreement, Contract Contains

This document contains the entire Agreement between the Client and the Consultant. Any agreement or representation respecting the duties of either the Client or the Consultant not expressly set forth in this document is null and void.

Confidentiality with Respect to Your Information

In performing the Assignment, the Consultant may acquire or be made aware of certain confidential information, in particular, but not limited to, confidential information relating to the Assignment, regarding products, processes, and operations as well as present and contemplated activities of the Client. The Consultant, its employees, and others whose services may be procured by the Consultant to assist the Consultant in the performance of the Assignment shall not divulge or disclose such confidential information to others without first having obtained specific written permission from the Client to do so. The term "confidential information" as used here means information disclosed to the Consultant by the Client or information obtained by Consultant for the Client in the course of performing the Assignment, excluding (a) information previously known to the Consultant or information that is publicly known (except through disclosure by the Consultant in violation of this paragraph) or (b) information that comes to the Consultant from a third party without confidential commitment.

Confidentiality with Respect to Retention

The Consultant will not disclose to any person, firm or corporation, [the identify of the Client or] any confidential information regarding the Client, this Assignment, or the business of the Client received or developed in connection with this Assignment without the Client's written consent.

Confidentiality with Respect to Trade Secrets

In performing the Assignment, the Consultant may acquire or be made aware of trade secrets of the Client. The Consultant, its employees, and others whose services may be procured by the Consultant to assist the Consultant in the performance of the Assignment shall not divulge or disclose such trade to others. The term "trade secret" as used here shall mean any information, including a formula, pattern, compilation, program, device, method, technique, or process designated by the Client as a trade secret.

Conflict of Interest during the Assignment

The Consultant represents that, during the course of the Assignment, it will not be working for [named direct competitor of the Client] or [any of the following firms: list of firms].

Conflict of Interest Following the Assignment

During the term of this Agreement [and for zzz months thereafter], the Consultant shall not accept similar employment from, or serve in a similar capacity with, any other concern that is at such time engaged in a business of a like or similar nature to the business now being conducted by the Client [or from any of the following listed firms: list of firms].

Cooperation with the Consultant

The Consultant will be permitted to utilize materials and data already in the Client's possession. The Client will provide, on a timely basis, any additional materials or data requested to assist the Consultant in connection with this Assignment.

Expenses

The Consultant will receive reimbursement for the actual cost of reasonable expenses arising out of the work performed under this Agreement [not to exceed $yyy], subject to the approval of the Client. The Consultant shall deliver an itemized statement to the Client on a monthly [quarterly] basis that shows fully the work being performed under this Agreement and all related expenses. The Client will pay the Consultant the amount of any authorized expenses within [thirty (30)] days of the receipt of the itemized statement of all expenses submitted, together with receipts for all hotel, car rental, air fare, and other transportation expenses and for all other expenses of $25.00 [$50.00] or more.

Expert Witness

The Client, or its Attorney, will:

1. Provide full instructions in writing, supported by good quality copies of all relevant documents.
2. Deal promptly with every reasonable request by Consultant for authority, information and documents.

3. Not alter or permit others to alter the Expert Reports, that is any report or statement supplied by Expert Witness in connection with instructions received from the Client.
4. Give immediate written notice of every hearing, meeting, or other appointment at which Expert Witness' attendance will or may be required.

Expert Witness will:

1. Use its best efforts in carrying out this Assignment and will retain control over the means and manner in which it performs this Assignment. In all respects, its relationship to the Client is that of an independent contractor, not an employee.
2. Use reasonable skill and care in the performance of the Client's instructions.
3. Act with objectivity and independence with regard to the instructions.
4. Undertake only those parts of a case in respect of which Expert Witness considers that he/she has adequate qualifications and experience.
5. Promptly notify the Client of any matter including a conflict of interest or lack of suitable qualifications and experience which might disqualify Expert Witness or render him/her undesirable to continue involvement in the case.
6. Endeavor to be available for all hearings and meetings and other appointments of which adequate notice has been received.
7. Not, without good cause, resign from the appointment. Fees and disbursements to the date of resignation may be charged in full.
8. Not negotiate or communicate with any opposing party or attorney unless specifically authorized by the Client to do so (and in any event to act within the scope of the Client's instructions at any meeting of Experts).
9. Upon receipt of any materials and knowledge of a confidential or sensitive nature (the Information) Expert Witness will: -
   • acknowledge that all the Information provided is the property of the Client.
   • acknowledge that all the Information is provided by the Client in confidence.
   • undertake to keep the Information secret and confidential and not disclose all or any part thereof to any third party and not allow any third party to have access to it, other than those persons authorized by the Client or its Attorney.
   • undertake to keep in a safe, secure and confidential place all materials forming part of the Information supplied, together with any copies, notes or records made by Expert Witness.

- undertake not to make use of or permit others to make use of the Information or any part of it except for the purpose of preparing Expert Reports as instructed by the Client.

Fee, Retainer, Plus Costs

The Client will pay the Consultant for the Work performed under this contract as follows: (a) a fixed monthly fee of —— thousand dollars ($xxxxx) and (b) the reimbursable costs listed in Schedule A, which is attached and incorporated in this agreement.

Fee, Flat

The Consultant will be paid $xxxxx (US) for all work performed under this Agreement.

Independent Contractor, Status of Consultant as

In all respects, the Consultant's relationship to the Client is that of an independent contractor, not an employee.

Insurance Coverage Required

The Consultant will take out and maintain all insurance required by any governmental unit to meet any statutory requirement and to protect the Consultant and the Client fully from and against any and all claims arising out of the Work performed hereunder. The Consultant will supply the Client with satisfactory evidence thereof.

Integrating a Consultant's Proposal into Your Contract Form

The Consultant will provide the services as described in [identify the proposal document specifically, including at least the date and title], which is attached to and made a part of this contract. The terms of this contract, where in conflict with the [attachment] will apply.

Subcontracting, Limitations on

This agreement is personal in nature and is not assignable by the Consultant. Consultant may subcontract portions of its requested work or services on approval of the proposed subcontractor by the Client. Such approval shall not relieve the Consultant of its responsibility under this agreement for the Assignment.

NOTES

1. Julie Boland and Marc Limacher, "Actionable CI at Visa International—A Real-Life Case Study," (presentation at the SCIP Annual Meeting, Seattle, April 2002), 6.

2. Arik R. Johnson, "Best Practices in CI Consulting and Research Subcontracting." (presentation at the SCIP Annual Meeting, Seattle, April 2002), 7.

3. Bill Fiora, "Best Practices Forum: Outsourcing the CI Function," *Competitive Intelligence Magazine* 5, no. 6 (November–December 2002), 38–39.

4. For more on these concepts, see John J. McGonagle and Carolyn M. Vella, *The Internet Age of Competitive Intelligence* (Westport, Conn.: Quorum Books, 1999), ch. 10 and *Bottom Line Competitive Intelligence* (Westport, Conn.: Quorum Books, 1999), 53–56.

5. For more on the significant differences among all of the orientations of CI, see McGonagle and Vella, *Bottom Line Competitive Intelligence*, chs. 4, 6, and 7.

6. For a much more extensive look at all of the issues involved in hiring and using consultants, see John J. McGonagle and Carolyn M. Vella, *How To Use a Consultant in Your Company: A Managers' and Executives' Guide* (New York: John Wiley & Sons, 2001).

7. Philippe Ruttens, "Management Consulting's CI Elevator: Still at Ground Level," *Competitive Intelligence Magazine* 5, no. 3 (March–April 2002), 28.

8. Adapted from McGonagle and Vella, *How to Use a Consultant*, 31–32.

9. For contract language dealing with the retention of an expert witness, see the appendix to this chapter

10. For more on the general subject of the control of expert witnesses by the trial court, see *Kumho Tire Co., Ltd. v. Carmichael*, U.S. Supreme Court, No. 97-1709 (1999), which is one of the few cases where the U.S. Supreme Court has discussed this.

11. *Blasting Analysis International Inc. vs. Mark E. Mammele*, Court of Common Pleas of Lehigh County, Pennsylvania, No. 89-E-122, final order published in 44 Lehigh County Law Journal 675-81 (1991) in which expert testimony was offered that information sent to over 100 recipients was "information that had value to competitors of the plaintiff" and that it was information which was of a "confidential" nature; and *Crossroads Rehabilitation Systems, Inc. v. Alexandra Vickers et al.*, Court of Common Pleas of Montgomery County, Pennsylvania, No. 92-02933 (1992), case dismissed by order signed October 2, 1992, where expert testimony was presented as to the ability of a party to generate commercial information using lawful competitive intelligence means.

12. Michael E. Porter, *Competitive Strategy: Techniques for Analyzing Industries and Competitors* (New York: The Free Press, 1980). At the time this is written, it is in its 58th printing.

13. It may be virtually impossible to create and enforce an oral—that is, nonwritten—consulting agreement. The chief problem in enforcing such a relationship is a legal principle known as the statute of frauds. That provides, in broad terms, that an oral contract is void if, by its terms, it cannot be performed within one year after the contract is made. See McGonagle and Vella, *How to Use a Consultant*, 59–90.

14. See the Coca-Cola Company, "Request for Proposal," in Society of Competitive Intelligence Professionals, *Conference Proceedings*. (Alexandria, Va.: Society of Competitive Intelligence Professionals 1998), 301–308.

15. McGonagle and Vella, *How To Use a Consultant*, chs. 8–11.

16. McGonagle and Vella, *Bottom Line Competitive Intelligence.*

17. See, for example, McGonagle and Vella, *How To Use a Consultant*, chs. 2, 9, and 10.

Measuring CI's Impact on the Firm

There is no single perfect metric for CI.[1] It is up to a CI manager to understand all the metrics that are available and to select the best for the particular situation from among them. To aid in considering the choices, we have summarized the situations in which these metrics tend to work best. From there, it is up to you to select a small number to adapt to your unique context.

When deciding which among these metrics are the most appropriate for your firm and your CI unit's situation, keep in mind the following guidelines:

- Aim at creating and capturing a small number of key measures on a limited group of activities.
- The measure you select should be tied to the significant underlying strategies, tactics, and operations of your firm. In other words, if these factors change, so, too, should your CI program and the way in which you measure its impact.
- Find ways to measure what you have done, what you are doing, *and* what you will do in the future.
- Ideally, the measures you select should provide information to everyone deeply involved with the CI process. That includes not only the CI unit and its end users, but also those providing raw data and those authorizing the budget.
- While anecdotal support, such as interviews, may provide powerful indications of the effectiveness of a CI program, it is always

better to have some quantitative measures supporting these key qualitative findings.

- Recognize that CI units that develop close working relationships with their end users tend to find they have less need to use such metrics. For example, research indicates that end users may tend to prefer qualitative metrics rather than quantitative metrics.[2]
- Just as what the CI unit does will change, as will the perspective of its end users, will change, so also should you be ready to change the measures you are using. (See Chapters 4, 5, and 9 on change and end user perceptions.)

METRICS FOR ACTIVE CI PROGRAMS

The following tables summarize those metrics that are most often useful by the type of CI process.[3] On Table 16.1, identify those potential metrics that usually fit your individual CI situation. So, if you, for example, use a combination of tactics-oriented CI and target-oriented CI, you would check the metrics that are usually relevant in the table. Then remove those that are clearly not relevant, given the way in you communicate with your end users as well as the kinds of raw data you typically collect. For example, if you provide your CI on a daily basis, in the form of daily briefings, then metrics tied to projects with specific time lines are not relevant. Similarly, if you provide a significant amount of tactics-oriented CI that entails providing substantial raw data, then metrics measuring suggestions submitted are not appropriate. Then rank the remaining measures in order of the number of "hits." From that list, you can identify those measures most likely to be relevant to the CI processes in your firm or unit.[4]

TABLE 16.1   Potential Metrics

CI Orientation	Strategic	Tactics	Target	Technology
Assignments and Projects				
Meeting objectives	•	•	•	•
Number completed	•	•	•	•
Number completed on time	□	•	•	•
Number requested	□	•	•	•
Number requested—increase by end users	•	•	•	•
Number of follow-up assignments	•	•	•	•
Number of projects assisted	□	•	•	•
Number of suggestions submitted	□	•	•	•
Budget				
Comparative costs savings				
Compared with cost of outsider	•	•	•	•
Compared with cost of untrained person	•	•	•	•
Meeting project and function budget constraints	•	•	•	•
Efficiency				
Accuracy of analysis	•	•	•	□
Data quality	•	•	•	•

TABLE 16.1   continued

CI Orientation	Strategic	Tactics	Target	Technology
First time results (no reworking)	•	•	•	•
Meeting project time line	•	•	•	•
Time for research versus time for response	▫	•	•	•
End users				
Creating compelling reasons to use CI	•	•	•	•
Effectiveness of implementation of findings	•	▫	•	▫
Meeting needs	•	•	•	•
Number of referrals	▫	•	•	•
Number served	▫	•	•	▫
Feedback				
Written	•	•	•	•
Oral	•	•	•	•
Financial				
Cost avoidance	▫	•	•	•
Cost savings	▫	•	•	•
Goals met	•	•	•	•
Linking CI to specific investments	•	▫	•	•
Linking CI to investment enhancement	•	▫	•	•
Linking CI to specific savings from unneeded investments	•	▫	•	•
Revenue enhancement	•	•	•	•
Value creation	•	▫	▫	•
Internal Relationships				
Building strong relationships with end users	•	•	•	•
Formulating relevant strategy and tactics	•	•	•	▫
Quality of relationship with end users	•	•	•	•
Quality of participation on cross-functional teams	•	•	•	•
New Products and Services				
Number developed due to use of CI	▫	•	▫	•
Cost savings/avoidance in development from use of CI	▫	•	▫	•
Performance				
Growth, profitable for the unit or firm	•	•	•	•
Impact on strategic direction of unit or firm	•	•	▫	▫
Market share gains for unit or firm	•	•	•	•
Report and Presentations				
Number	•	▫	•	▫
Number of follow-ups	•	•	•	•
Production of actionable CI	•	•	•	•
Sales effectiveness				
Customer satisfaction	▫	•	▫	▫
Linking to specific customer wins	▫	•	▫	▫
Number of customers retained	▫	•	▫	▫
Number of leads generated	▫	•	▫	▫
Repeat business	▫	•	▫	▫
Improvement in win-loss ratio	▫	•	▫	▫
Surveys				
Written	•	•	•	•
Oral	•	•	•	•
Time				
Gained by CI input	▫	•	•	▫
Projects delivered on time	▫	•	•	•
Saved by CI input	▫	•	•	▫

• Usually relevant; ▫ Rarely relevant.

METRICS FOR DEFENSIVE CI PROGRAMS

The basic methodology set out above applies to defensive CI programs. However, given the nature of its mission, defensive intelligence is much more difficult to measure than active CI.

- First, the role of the CI professional in defensive CI is one of education and awareness: The job is to teach others to be more careful.
- Second, the more effective a defensive CI program becomes, the less often its competitors can find competitively sensitive data.
- Third, defensive CI often deals with avoiding the negative: a lost opportunity, lost initiative, and the like.

As a result, of the wide variety of options available for measuring the bottom line impact of active CI of all types, only a limited number are at all useful in working with defensive CI. Table 16.2 summarizes your options.

TABLE 16.2   Potential Defensive CI Metrics

Assignments and Projects	
Meeting objectives	•
Number completed	•
Number completed on time	•
Number requested	•
Number requested—increase by end users	•
Number of follow-up assignments	¤
Number of projects assisted	¤
Number of suggestions submitted	¤
Budget	
Comparative costs savings	
Compared with cost of outsider	•
Compared with cost of untrained person	¤
Meeting project or function budget constraints	¤
Efficiency	
Accuracy of analysis	¤
Data quality	¤
First time results (no reworking)	¤
Meeting project time line	¤
Time for research versus time for response	¤
End-Users	
Creating compelling reasons to use CI	•
Effectiveness of implementation of findings	¤
Meeting needs	•
Number of referrals	¤
Number served	•
Feedback	
Written	•
Oral	•

TABLE 16.2 continued

Assignments and Projects	
Financial	
Cost avoidance	¤
Cost savings	¤
Goals met	¤
Linking CI to specific investments	¤
Linking CI to investment enhancement	¤
Linking CI to specific savings from unneeded investments	¤
Revenue enhancement	¤
Value creation	¤
Internal Relationships	
Building strong with end users	•
Formulating relevant strategy or tactics	¤
Quality of relationships with end users	•
Quality of participation on cross-functional teams	•
New Products and Services	
Number developed due to use of CI	¤
Cost savings/avoidance in development from use of CI	¤
Performance	
Growth, profitable for the unit or firm	•
Impact on strategic direction of unit or firm	¤
Market share gains for unit or firm	•
Reports and Presentations	
Number	¤
Number of follow-ups	¤
Production of actionable CI	¤
Sales effectiveness	
Customer satisfaction	¤
Linking to specific customer wins	¤
Number of customers retained	¤
Number of leads generated	¤
Repeat business	¤
Improvement in win-loss ratio	¤
Surveys	
Written	•
Oral	•
Time	
Gained by CI input	¤
Projects delivered on time	¤
Saved by CI input	¤

• Usually relevant; ¤ Rarely relevant.

NOTES

1. See John J. McGonagle and Carolyn M. Vella, *Bottom Line Competitive Intelligence*, (Westport, Conn: Quorum Books, 2002) especially chapters 8, 9, and 14.
2. American Productivity & Quality Center, International Benchmarking Clearinghouse, *User-Driven Competitive Intelligence: Crafting the Value Proposition.* (Houston: American Productivity & Quality Center, 2003), 12.

3. Adapted from John J. McGonagle and Carolyn M. Vella, *Bottom Line Competitive Intelligence*, 164–78 and 228–30. For detailed explanations of the metrics, see chs. 9 and 14.

4. For more sophisticated ways to handle the issues concerning how the CI is delivered, and the kinds of data used, see McGonagle and Vella, *Bottom Line Competitive Intelligence*, chs. 6 and 7.

17

Special Cases

THE ONE-PERSON CI UNIT

As we indicated in Chapter 2, the most common staffing profile for a CI unit is to have one full-time CI professional. In fact, over 50 percent of the CI units surveyed in a 2000–2001 study had no employees reporting to the respondent.[1] And experience shows that managing the one-person CI unit is perhaps the most difficult scenario. That is because such a unit does not have fewer responsibilities than does a larger unit. Rather, the one-person unit has additional special problems not always found in larger units.

For example, as noted in Chapter 2, it is usually more effective for a CI unit to divide the work of data gathering and dissemination from needs determination and analysis. That is because these tasks rely on different types of skills. But in the one-person unit, that option does not exist. The one person must serve in both capacities, no matter how different they are. For that reason, it is advisable for a one-person CI units to make a very frank assessment of his or her skills, as well as shortcomings. Then, he or she should consider seeking assistance, outside if necessary, to supplement those shortcomings.

That suggestion highlights another responsibility: the CI manager in the one-person unit is also a contracts manager. That is, the manager will be, or at least should be, the focal point for all outside contracting efforts. That means that he or she must work with internal end users to determine the unit's true needs to communicate them effectively to an outside research firm and then supervise, to one degree or another, the outside firm.

The one-person CI manager cannot skip the development of a plan for the future growth and direction of the CI unit, even if there seems to be no likelihood that the CI unit will ever be expanded. The reason is that, even, or perhaps especially, in the case of the one-person CI unit, experience shows that the unit, and the entire CI process must evolve or die.

Of all of the tasks we dealt with earlier, which is the most important? It is serving as the marketing arm for CI within the firm. And that process entails all of the following:

- obtaining and providing training
- creating, managing, exploiting, and expanding internal and external networks
- developing a plan for improving the quality of the output of the unit
- aggressively expanding direct contact with the real end users of the CI
- reviewing the types of data collected and CI generated with an eye to changing it
- constantly upgrading the final output of the CI unit

SMALL AND MEDIUM-SIZED ENTERPRISES (SMEs)

Why Separate Out SMEs?

There are four reasons to look at SMEs separately:

1. SMEs seem to have a lower likelihood of having a formal CI program than do their larger competitors. But the degree of need is there, with only the focus being different.
2. SMEs are the driver of economic growth. In spite of the economic focus on the profitability and employment of large enterprises, SMEs usually account for the vast majority of positive job growth in the United States.
3. It is much easier for a SME to create and exploit a formal CI unit. Unlike the bureaucratic situations in the largest enterprises, at many SMEs the creation and integration of a new function, or the designation of individuals to carry on new duties, does not take one or more years to fully accomplish. While the managers/ owners of a SME may not have the power to say "So let it be written, so let it be done," usually they are much more agile than

their larger brethren. And that agility is one of their competitive advantages.

4. SMEs have, particularly in their first five years, a high failure rate, probably higher than that of their larger competitors. And this is true even if we eliminate those businesses that close due to the death/retirement of the owners/founders. Is there a connection between this and the lower utilization of CI? There are no studies on that, but the lessons from the Malcolm Baldrige National Quality Award Program set out in Chapter 14 should lead us to see that there may be a strong connection.

Should a SME Run a CI Program?

In most situations, a SME should run one. But, anecdotal evidence indicates that the smaller the enterprise, the less likely it is to be involved in any sort of CI.

Why SMEs Have a Greater Need for CI

In fact SMEs not only need CI, there are very good reasons why they should be involved in CI that their larger competitors do not have. The facts are that many owners and principals of SMEs possess a kind of tunnel vision. That is, they are certain that, as regular participants in the industry, they must necessarily *know* what is going on.

That is not the case. There are a very significant number of ways in which managers, owners and founders, particularly in SMEs, do not see what is going on. Three examples of this are the following attitudes:

- Then is still now.
- I am always on top of stuff.
- Even if I know something what can I do about it?

"Then is still now." What is that? Outside of business, the most common example is of the loyal college graduate seeking to steer teenagers to attend good old Alma Mater, from which he or she graduated 20 years earlier. He or she talks about Alma Mater as if nothing has changed, as if he or she is still is daily touch with it. But they are not.

That attitude exists in business too. For example, find someone who came to work for you from another firm. Let a year or so go by, and then ask him/her "what is going on over there at Another Firm?" The answer you get will most often be, "well, they *are* doing [this.]" But, unless they are still in daily contact with Another Firm, they are guilty of making their past observations "current"—a very common and significant error. Actually what they are doing is assuming what has happened (and why) in the past is still true unless they affirmatively know to the contrary.

"I am always on top of stuff." This is another very common syndrome in the SME. An example of this came from our practice. At one time, our firm worked on a government-sponsored trade impact project. The terms of the help were that the applicant had to get an industry/marketing assessment from a firm with which it had not worked before. The goal being to provide a fresh, and independent, assessment.

In our research, we found that a joint venture of several large oil refiners in Europe had just patented a new process which used one of the client's outputs as a key ingredient. This meant a potentially new market. However, we also found that medical research, in two different countries, would soon be released showing a strong link between that same product and brain cancer. So now, the firm faced both a new marketing opportunity as well as a new, health-related threat. Not only was the firm not aware of the research results, it was not even aware of the existence of this research. In fact this firm, which had been in the business for 25 years, was aware of—neither. One development might create markets in Europe; the other might shut them down—permanently.

Why did this happen? The founders, who were still running the business, kept their focus within the industry niche that they served, the same way they had done for years. They never raised their sights to look at the competitive environment, at the ingredients (intermediate products) they produced, and so on. In other words, if it data did not deal with making sales to existing customers and markets today, they did not seek it out, or worse, they subconsciously ignored it.

"If I know about it, what can I do about it?" That is often expressed in the statement that "I am a SME, so what can I do if Microsoft, or ExxonMobil or Unilever is going to do something! They are big and I am so, so small!"

Even in the worst case there are things you can do. One final example will illustrate this. Years ago, several former marketing managers from a major consumer product firm formed their own firm. They came up with a great new cleaner. They did really well. Now, the Big Product Firm saw how well they were doing. They learned of that threat. They quickly adopted some short-term responses to slow down, but not stop, the entry of the Big Product Firm into this category. They were able to stall the early success of the Big Product Company long enough—to sell out.

For the SME, the lesson is that, at a minimum, you may be able get out of harm's way. Sometimes success for the SME is not measured by profit or growth, but by survival.

Does Every SME Need CI?

No. But, *almost* every one of them should be involved with it.[2]

How to determine if a SME does not need CI. How does a SME determine if it does not need CI? Here we will apply the analytical framework we developed in *Bottom Line Competitive Intelligence* and indicate when that situation might occur. We will quickly look at these broad areas:

• The environment in which the SME operates
• The products/services the SME produces
• The companies the SME faces
• Production and supply chain issues
• Marketplace dynamics

First, look at the overall competitive environment in which a SME is now competing. If a SME is in a highly regulated environment, that is with respect to the *company,* in particular one with high barriers to entry, that firm is probably able to continue with whatever CI it is now doing.

Then look at the specific products (or services) that a SME and its competitors provide and which they bring to the marketplace in which they all are now competing. If the SME's product or service is one with a small number of substitutes, subject to a lot of product or service regulation, with a long lead time to market, and/or a long product life cycle, that SME probably does not need CI—at least for the present.

Try next to evaluate the firms with which the SME directly competes in its market or markets. Our experience indicates that CI is less critical, and sometimes much more difficult to develop in contexts where a SME's direct competitors are decentralized in management terms, and are not likely to be cooperative with each or (or in alliances outside of the industry). If this particular niche does not have a small number of firms which dominate the niche in terms of market share, and which also do not have high levels of knowledge intensity, CI is not likely to be a real priority—today.

Production and supply chain issues are increasingly important. And as companies seek to control and to redefine their own supply chain as well as the way they produce their goods and services, they are actually changing the very nature of the firms you compete with. So, if a SME competes in an environment which is marked by low levels of technology, numerous suppliers, and low levels of innovation, its need for CI is probably a lot lower than that of other SMEs.

The last diagnostic tool is marketplace dynamics—that is, the way the marketplace appears to the SME and its competitors. If a SME sees a lot of actual and potential customers, which are fairly concentrated geographically, feedback from its regular sales efforts is probably providing most of the tactics-oriented CI it needs.

In sum, SMEs with a very, very localized market, such as plumbers, can probably be run without it. Also, firms in a true monopoly situation are probably safe. However, keep in mind that, as we have seen in many markets and industries, having or being a monopoly does not guarantee long-term existence, much less long-term success.

Which Type of CI is Most Valuable to the SME?

There is no one type of CI which is best for all SMEs. However, experience and analysis indicates that the typical (if there is such a thing) SME, will benefit from CI in the following order of priority:

1. Target-oriented CI
2. Tactics-oriented CI, and then, probably much lower down on the list,
3. Strategy-oriented CI.

Why in that order? Again, generalizing excessively, the typical SME faces many other SMEs. And many of them are private, not public firms. That means they have to keep a focus on them not only in terms of what they are now doing in the market (tactics-oriented CI), but also in terms of what each of them is doing and is capable of doing (target-oriented CI). This order reflects not only what you need, but the ease in which you can develop these as well.

This list does not even include technology-oriented CI. That is because if a SME, its industry and/or its customers can be considered as impacted by changes in some underlying technology or technologies on an ongoing basis, then technology-oriented CI should be an addition to, and not usually a replacement for, one of these other types of CI.

Special Issues in Defensive CI for the SME

In larger organizations, the people who provide CI do not "provide" defensive CI services. That job is rather the job of all employees of the firm. The role of the CI professional in such organizations is to enlighten all employees as to the need for this, the ways in which competitors develop CI, and how to protect the firm. In other words, the CI professional manages the active CI process and is responsible for its success. However, the CI professional is a teacher, a facilitator, and an advocate with respect to defensive CI.

In the SME, there is often a very significant difference from this model. In the SME, quite often the CI professional is providing CI for him/herself and/or staff and subordinates. In other words, the provider and the end user of the active CI are the same, or almost the same. In the SME, in addition, it very often falls to that same person to assume the role of the cheerleader for a defensive CI program. So, not only do they conduct the CI, they must alert fellow employees as to the need to protect competitive information, what that is, and what protection means.

So, here is the core of what you must learn, communicate—and also adhere to:

- Identify what data to protect—and what not to bother with.
- Protect that information most difficult for a competitor to develop on your firm
- Protect sensitive information only for as long as necessary. You don't have to protect everything forever.
- Protect that competitive data that is crucial to completing a profile on your firm.
- Protect data that is already partially protected. For example, if you have a trade secret embedded in your equipment, make sure publicity photos in the local chamber of commerce magazine do not use that equipment as the background.
- Identify and protect information that is critical to your operation as a business. Which is more important, your list of customers or the names of your suppliers?
- Review the CI you are collecting on your competitors. If you need it on them, they probably want it on you. Be forewarned.
- Identify the data analysis techniques most likely to be used in your industry. Then figure out which piece or pieces of data are vital to completing those analyses. Protect them.

Do not forget that it is very likely that the very person who is now, or will be, doing these tasks will be assuming an additional, involuntary, role. That role is as one of the primary targets of competitor CI activities.

NOTES

1. Society of Competitve Intelligence Professionals, *2000/'01 Competitive Intelligence Professionals Salary Survey Report and Reference Guide on Analyst Job Descriptions* (Alexandria, Va.: Society of Competitive Intelligence Professionals, 2001), 52.

2. For more on how to manage a CI unit in a SME, see Amy Berger, "Small but Powerful: Six Steps for Conducting Competitive Intelligence Successfully at a Medium-sized Firm," *Competitive Intelligence Review* 8, no. 4 (Summer 1997), 75–77; Jean Brandau and Andrea Young, "Competitive Intelligence in Entrepreneurial and Start-up Businesses," *Competitive Intelligence Review* 11, no. 1 (2nd quarter 2000), 74–84; Jonathan Calof, Bon Fox and Dzung Nguyen, "Making

Intelligence Grow for Small and Mid-Sized Companies: A Mentoring Approach," *Competitive Intelligence Magazine* 5, no. 3 (May–June 2002), 9–11; and Jerry P. Miller, "Small Business Intelligence—People Make It Happen," *Competitive Intelligence Magazine* 3, no. 2 (April–June 2000), 22–27.

Glossary

Action plans Specific actions that respond to short- and longer-term strategic objectives. Action plans include details of resource commitments and time horizons for accomplishment. Action plan development represents the critical stage in planning when strategic objectives and goals are made specific so that effective, organization-wide understanding and deployment are possible.

Active CI Competitive intelligence operated by and for the benefit of a particular unit, firm, or organization.

Alignment The consistency of plans, processes, information, resource decisions, actions, results, analysis, and learning to support key organization-wide goals.

Analysis In general, an examination of facts and data to provide a basis for effective decisions. Analysis often involves the determination of cause-and-effect relationships. Overall organizational analysis guides process management toward achieving key business results and attaining strategic objectives. In competitive intelligence, analysis involves evaluating and interpreting the facts and raw data, thus providing finished intelligence to support effective decision-making.

AP&QC American Productivity & Quality Center.

Assessment A means of measuring and reporting, less formal than an audit.

Audit Independent, structured, and documented evaluation of the adequacy and implementation of an activity to specified requirements. An aduit may examine any element of management control, such as financial, environmental, or quality aspects.

Benchmarking Analyzing what you do, quantifying it, and then finding ways that other firms do it better, or better and differently (if at all). Then, you adapt (not simply adopt) what you have learned to your own firm. Organizations engage in benchmarking activities to understand the current dimensions of world-class performance and to achieve discontinuous (nonincremental) or breakthrough improvement.

Benchmarks The processes and results that represent the best practices and performance for similar activities, inside or outside an organization's industry.

BI Business intelligence.

Business Intelligence An old term for CI. Also used in knowledge management (KM) to describe the product of KM activities.

CI Competitive intelligence.

CI audit A review of your current operations to determine what you actually know about your current competitors and their operations. A CI audit also helps you focus on what kind of CI you currently need.

CI cycle The process of establishing CI needs, collecting raw data, processing it into finished CI, and distributing it to the end users (who then use it). It also includes feedback among the various phases.

Cloaking Protecting competitively sensitive information from the CI gathering and analytical efforts of competitors.

Competitive intelligence Competitive intelligence consists of two overall activities. First is the use of public sources to develop data (raw facts) on competition, competitors, and the market environment. Second is the transformation, by analysis, of that data into information (usable results).

Competitive scenario An analysis of what one or more competitors can be expected to do in response to changes in market and other conditions affecting their activities. The analysis is based on a profile of each competitor, including estimations of its intentions and capabilities and stemming from a study of its past actions and of the perceptions, style, and behavior of its present and future management. Each competitor's actions are studied against the same set of expected market conditions and changes.

Competitive technical intelligence Those intelligence activities that allow a firm to respond to threats, from and/or identify and exploit opportunities, resulting from technical and scientific change.

Corporate security A process aimed primarily at protecting and preserving all corporate assets, both tangible and intangible. Typically it operates to set up protections for assets (such as databases or automobiles), to determine potential threats, and to provide a barrier. In some corporate security operations, a special focus is on the identification and protection of Trade Secrets. This is also one of the units (information technology is the other) involved with protecting against "hacking".

Counter-intelligence A military term, it refers the process of identifying and then foiling intelligence activities. It can involve measures such as military assaults on opposing "spies." When used in the business context, it entails identifying and then foiling a specific competitor's intelligence activities aimed at your firm. More correctly known as defensive competitive intelligence.

Crisis management program A formal method of developing, updating and implementing crisis management plans.

CTI Competitive technical intelligence.

Current data Data that deals with a relatively short period of time, centered on the present. Examples of this might be sales figures for the past three-month period for one competitor.

Customer A person or organization, internal or external, that receives or uses outputs from one group or division. These outputs may be products, services or information. *See also* End user.

Cycle time The time required to fulfill commitments or to complete tasks. *Cycle time* refers to all aspects of time performance.

Data Raw, unevaluated material. Data may be numeric or textual. It is the ultimate source of information, but becomes usable information only after it has been processed and analyzed. *See also* Current data, Historic data, Macro-level data, and Micro-level data.

Data mining The process of sifting through massive amounts of data (in computer readable form) to reveal intelligence, hidden trends, and relationships between customers and products.

Data warehousing The ability to store large amounts of data by specific categories, so that it can easily be retrieved, interpreted, and sorted (data mining) to provide useful information, typically about customers and products.

Defensive competitive intelligence The process of monitoring and analyzing your own business's activities as your competitors and other outsiders see them. You can then protect your firm's competitively sensitive information from being accessible to your competitors.

DI Defensive competitive intelligence.

Disinformation Incomplete or inaccurate information designed to mislead others about your intentions or abilities. When used in the arena of international politics, espionage, or intelligence, the term also means the deliberate production and dissemination of falsehoods, fabrications, and forgeries aimed at misleading an opponent or those supporting an opponent.

Economic Espionage Act of 1996 A U.S. (federal) criminal statue, P.L. 104-294 of Oct. 11, 1996, which criminalizes, at the federal level, the misappropriation of trade secrets. It provides additional penalties if such misappropriation is conducted by foreign entities.

EEA Economic Espionage Act of 1996.

Empowerment Giving employees the authority and responsibility to make decisions and take actions. Empowerment results in decisions being made closest to the "front line," where work-related knowledge and understanding reside.

End users Persons or organizations that request and use information obtained from an on-line search or other source of CI. See also Customer.

Espionage Either the collection of information by illegal means or the illegal collection of information. If the information has been collected from a government, this is a serious crime, such as treason. If it is collected from a business, it may be a theft offense.

Fraud An act that involves distributing erroneous or false information with intent to mislead or to take advantage of someone relying on that information.

Gaming An exercise that has people either acting as themselves or playing roles in an environment that can be real or simulated. Games can be repeated but cannot be replicated, as is the case with simulations and models.

Historic data Data that covers a long period of time. It is designed to show long-term trends, such as gross sales in an industry over a five-year period. This may include projections made covering a long period of years.

Home page An Internet site owned by an entity that permits the user to obtain and view information about the owner.

IBC International Benchmarking Clearinghouse, a division of the American Productivity & Quality Center (AP&QC).

Inductive methods Problem-solving methods that involve reasoning from particular facts or individual cases to a general conclusion.

Information The material resulting from analyzing and evaluating raw data, reflecting both data and judgments. Information is an input to a finished CI evaluation.

Information broker A person involved in obtaining data on many subjects, including businesses, from public sources. The sources relied on are, exclusively or predominantly, public on-line databases. The data is provided without significant screening or analysis. The term originated because such businesses were seen as "brokering" the raw data found in on-line databases, by extracting it and reselling it to people who did not use these databases themselves.

Integration The harmonization of plans, processes, information, resource decisions, actions, results, analysis, and learning to support key organization-wide goals.

Intelligence Knowledge achieved by a logical analysis and integration of available information data on competitors or the competitive environment.

Intranet An internal or limited access Internet.

IT Information technology.

Key intelligence questions (KIQs) These are developed from KITs when the KITs are very broad.

Key intelligence topics (KITs) A process, adapted from the governmental process model of National Intelligence Topics, to identify and then prioritize senior management's key intelligence needs.

KIQ Key intelligence question.

KIT Key intelligence topic (or target).

KM Knowledge management.

Knowledge management The combination of data warehousing and data mining, aimed at exploiting all data in a company's possession.

Macro-level data Data of a high level of aggregation, such as the size of a particular market or the overall rate of growth of the nation's economy.

Market intelligence Intelligence developed on the most current activities in the marketplace.

Micro-level data Data of a low level of aggregation, or even unaggregated data. This might be data, for example, on a particular competitor company's profit margin for one product.

Mirror-imaging Assuming that your adversary can or will do what you could or would do in its place.

Mission statement The mission statement answers the question, "What is this organization attempting to accomplish?"

Modeling Representing an entity, such as a competitor, or a situation, such as a particular market's dynamics, in such a way that the representation has the relevant features or properties of the original. Usually used to help predict future actions.

Process Linking activities with the purpose of producing a product or service for a customer (user) within or outside the organization. In some situations, processes might require adherence to a specific sequence of steps, with documentation (sometimes formal) of procedures and requirements, including well-defined measurement and control steps.

Profiling Process of developing personality and psychological profiles of key individuals to help an analyst predict future behavior.

Qualitative In measures, this refers to evaluating the basic nature or attributes of a process or event.

Quantitative In measures, this refers to the accurate measurement of the components or consequences of a process or event.

SBU Strategic business unit.

Scenarios *See* Competitive scenario.

SCIP Society of Competitive Intelligence Professionals.

Shadowing A process of closely following a defined activity of a competitor. It has four differing aspects: shadowing specific markets; developing a shadow market plan; shadow planning as an ongoing process; and shadow benchmarking

Simulation Representing a system or an organism, such as a business firm, by use of another system or model that is designed to have a relevant behavioral similarity to the original. Very often this involves a computerized model. Often used to generate complex, financial responses to changes in underlying forces.

Strategic business unit One of several operating entities making up an enterprise.

Strategic intelligence Competitive intelligence provided in support of strategic, as distinguished from tactical, decision making.

Supplier A company or person that provides inputs to tasks or jobs, whether inside or outside the company.

Surveillance A continuous and systematic watch over the actions of a competitor, aimed at providing timely information for immediate responses to the competitor's actions.

Target A specific competitor, or one or more of its facilities, SBUs, or other units.

Trade Secret Protection This is the use of contracts, civil litigation, and even criminal prosecution, under both state and federal law, to prevent trade secrets from being used by competitors. Trade secrets are a very narrowly defined type of information. For example, trade secret protection is available only if the firm treats specific information differently from all other information, and it may be lost if the information becomes public, even if by accident.

Uniform Trade Secrets Act   A model law, drafted by the National Conference
        of Commissioners on Uniform State Laws, dealing with the civil penalties
        for misappropriation of trade secrets. Last amended in 1985, it has been
        passed, in one form or another, in forty-one states.

UTSA   Uniform Trade Secrets Act.

War game   A simulated military operation using gaming techniques. *See* Gaming.

Key References

American Productivity & Quality Center, International Benchmarking Clearing-house. *Competitive and Business Intelligence: Leveraging Information for Action*. Houston: American Productivity & Quality Center, 1997.

American Productivity & Quality Center, International Benchmarking Clearing-house. *Managing Competitive Intelligence Knowledge in a Global Economy*. Houston: American Productivity & Quality Center, 1998.

American Productivity & Quality Center, International Benchmarking Clearing-house. *Strategic and Tactical Competitive Intelligence for Sales and Marketing*. Houston: American Productivity & Quality Center, 1999.

American Productivity & Quality Center, International Benchmarking Clearing-house. *Developing a Successful Competitive Intelligence Program: Enabling Action, Realizing Results*. Houston: American Productivity & Quality Center, 2000.

American Productivity & Quality Center, International Benchmarking Clearing-house. *Using Science and Technology Intelligence to Drive Business Results*. Houston: American Productivity & Quality Center, 2002.

American Productivity & Quality Center, International Benchmarking Clearing-house. *User-Driven Competitive Intelligence: Crafting the Value Proposition*. Houston: American Productivity & Quality Center, 2003.

Baldrige National Quality Program. *2002 Criteria for Performance Excellence*. Milwaukee: American Society for Quality, 2003.

Fahey, Liam. *Competitors: Outwitting, Outmaneuvering, and Outperforming*, New York: John Wiley & Sons, 1999.

Fleisher, Craig S., and Babette E. Bensoussan. *Strategic and Competitive Analysis: Methods and Techniques for Analyzing Business Competition*. Upper Saddle River, N.J.: Prentice Hall, 2002.

Gilad, Ben, and Jan P. Herring (eds.). *Advances in Applied Business Strategy, Supplement 2B*. Greenwich, Conn.: JAI Press, 1996.

McGonagle, John J., and Carolyn M. Vella. *Outsmarting the Competition: Practical Approaches to Finding and Using Competitive Information.* Naperville, Ill.: Sourcebooks, 1990.

McGonagle, John J., and Carolyn M. Vella. *A New Archetype of Competitive Intelligence.* Westport, Conn.: Quorum Books, 1996.

McGonagle, John J., and Carolyn M. Vella. *Protecting Your Company against Competitive Intelligence.* Westport, Conn.: Quorum Books, 1998.

McGonagle, John J., and Carolyn M. Vella. *The Internet Age of Competitive Intelligence.* Westport, Conn: Quorum Books, 1999.

McGonagle, John J., and Carolyn M. Vella. *How to Use a Consultant in Your Company: A Managers' and Executives' Guide.* New York: John Wiley & Sons, 2001.

McGonagle, John J. and Carolyn M. Vella. *Bottom Line Competitive Intelligence.* Westport, Conn.: Quorum Books, 2002.

Vibert, Conor. *Web-Based Analysis for Competitive Intelligence.* Westport, Conn.: Quorum Books, 2000.

Index

ABOUT THE AUTHOR

JOHN J. MCGONAGLE is Managing Partner of The Helicon Group. A regular contributor to *Competitive Intelligence Magazine*, he is the author of numerous articles in the areas of competitive intelligence, law, economics, and business, and has co-written six other books on competitive intelligence with Carolyn M. Vella. He is the recipient of the 1998 Fellows Award from the Society of Competitive Intelligence Professionals.

CAROLYN M. VELLA is the Founding Partner of The Helicon Group. The author of numerous articles on competitive intelligence, she is the recipient of the 2003 Meritorious Award from the Society of Competitive Intelligence Professionals.